Making
Disciples

MAKING DISCIPLES

FAITH FORMATION
IN THE WESLEYAN TRADITION

Sondra Higgins Matthaei

Abingdon Press
Nashville

MAKING DISCIPLES
Faith Formation in the Wesleyan Tradition

Copyright © 2000 by Abingdon Press

This book is printed on recycled, acid-free, elemental-chlorine–free paper.

Library of Congress Cataloging-in-Publication Data

Matthaei, Sondra Higgins.
   Making disciples: faith formation in the Wesleyan tradition / Sondra Higgins Matthaei.
      p.   cm.
   Includes bibliographical references (p.) and index.
   ISBN 0-687-02475-7 (alk. paper)
      1. Methodist Church—Doctrines.   2. Discipling (Christianity)   3. Spiritual formation.
   4. Wesley, John 1703–1791.   I. Title

BX8331.2 .M27 2000
287—dc21   00-038578

Scripture quotations, unless otherwise indicated, are from the King James Version of the Bible.

00 01 02 03 04 05 06 07 08 09—10 9 8 7 6 5 4 3 2 1

MANUFACTURED IN THE UNITED STATES OF AMERICA

For all those faithful disciples
who have nurtured our faith:

Time encircles us—
      past, present, future—
ever-present and indestructible.
          Through the window of time
              we travel together;
          in this moment
      our paths coincide.

Looking backward
      we see our footsteps,
    the record of who we are
        and where we have been
            a trail of living and dying
                learning and teaching
                    giving and receiving.
Our lives frozen in a minute
      microsecond of time.

      Looking forward
          far into the horizon,
              we see the long walk
    of those who traveled this way before.
          People of faith
              following a winding way
                    through time
          leading us into the future.

      And now, we have
          only this moment
              to discern with clarity
                  to live with integrity
                      to love with passion.
Our lives embraced by God
      in the fullness of time.

CONTENTS

ACKNOWLEDGMENTS

It is with much gratitude that I recognize those persons who were instrumental in the design and completion of this book. My conversations with Stephen Gunter furthered the conceptualization of the project. Encouragement from members of the Wesleyan Studies guild, especially Dick Heitzenrater, Randy Maddox, and Rex Matthews, was supplied as needed to provide clarity and direction.

I also want to thank my friends and colleagues in Christian religious education. Mary Elizabeth Mullino Moore worked with me in the days that my interest and research began and has continued to provide support and encouragement along with Linda Vogel and Jack Seymour.

It is only within a community of teaching and learning that such a project is accomplished. Colleagues at Saint Paul School of Theology, particularly team-teaching partners Kris Kvam and Grant White, provided opportunities for sharing my developing research. Additional gratitude is due Hal Knight and the students of Saint Paul School of Theology, who were always eager to talk about our Wesleyan heritage. And I want to thank my friend and colleague Warren Carter, who provided wise words for the journey at the times I most needed to hear them.

Finally, I want to thank my family for the time together they forfeited so I could visit the Wesleys and their world. And it is to those disciples whose faithful witness has preceded us that I owe my deepest gratitude.

INTRODUCTION

My first serious exposure to our Wesleyan heritage came in 1985 through a Claremont School of Theology travel and study seminar on the "Shapes and Shapers of Methodism" in England, the Netherlands, and Switzerland. As a young person I had heard of John Wesley as the founder of our denomination, but I knew little about this rich inheritance from our faith tradition. Then, at forty-three years of age, this middle-class, Anglo-European, Christian woman traveled through a window of time into the eighteenth century and was amazed at what she found. The question that emerged out of this study trip and my beginning research in the Wesleyan tradition was "How did I get to be so Methodist?" I had participated in the life of the Methodist Church, and then The United Methodist Church, all my life but did not have many positive feelings about my Christian education experiences. In fact, that was exactly why I was working on a Ph.D.—I wanted to help prepare church leaders to do effective Christian religious education. So how did I get to be so Methodist? The first question quickly generated a second that has been the focus of my scholarly work for fifteen years and of my ministry for thirty years: "How do people become Christian?" I turned to Wesleyan research to find some answers.

The focus of my historical research was on how the early Methodist movement shaped persons' lives so that they came to know themselves as Christian and Methodist. The method used for this research was based on Richard Heitzenrater's rigorous standards for "levels of study" discussed in *Mirror and Memory*, beginning with "primary studies."[1] I read primary documents such as John Wesley's

11

sermons, diaries, journals, letters, and publications and Charles Wesley's journals and hymns to see what clues to faith formation emerged. As I read these documents, I coded the formative activities and sorted them into categories as they emerged: "John Wesley's aims and struggle," "structures and relationships," "content and method," "resources and disciplines." This interpretation of educational categories generated in the research is what Heitzenrater calls "specialist studies."[2] Also included in this second level of historical research is the context and background of the Methodist movement as well as examination of the connections between the educational categories and John Wesley's theology. This research, along with reading what others wrote about the Wesleys' educational enterprise, led to later modifications of my own categories: resources became part of "content," spiritual disciplines part of "practices," and the category "processes" was added.

The result of this research was a proposal for a Wesleyan ecology of faith formation composed of relationships, structures, practices, and processes grounded in John Wesley's understanding of the Trinity, the church, and salvation. Examples, anecdotes, and case studies from the Wesleys' experience are used throughout this book for illustration. I often use the words of the Wesley family in the text because I think their voices should be heard. However, John Wesley's language will be changed to be more inclusive if it does not alter his meaning. As Randy Maddox observed, John Wesley remained a "man of his time," but he did demonstrate a beginning awareness of exclusive language when he changed "Christian men" to "Christian" in an edited work.[3] Susanna Wesley's language will also be changed because of her pioneer spirit in believing the Wesley daughters should learn how to read and write before they were expected to do household chores. In Susanna's words, "the putting children to learn sewing before they can read perfectly, is the very reason why so few women can read fit to be heard, and never to be well understood."[4]

The final step in my method was to begin to draw insights and implications from the research. Heitzenrater calls this "comprehensive studies" as the researcher tries to "summarize and synthesize"[5] what has been done. As part of this level of historical research, I have given a brief review of current literature on Wesley and education in chapter 1 and have made limited connections to contemporary edu-

cational theory and practice at appropriate points in the text. In the final chapter, I draw out implications for faith formation in the Wesleyan tradition and discuss what is needed in a ministry of Christian faith formation for the new century.

While others had explored particular aspects of the Wesleys' educational enterprise, my goal was to explore as many of the activities of the early Methodist movement as possible to see how faith formation happened. The exercise of examining the totality of the Wesley's educational enterprise has not been attempted before, and it probably takes some degree of questionable sanity and a great amount of determination to do so now. Years of reading primary sources in search of the components of an educational ecology has led me to the conclusion that there will always be more to do. It is time to record what I have learned thus far.

Part 1 of this text addresses "Foundations for Making Disciples." In chapter 1, "Making Disciples: Formation for Holiness of Heart and Life," I define and discuss the meaning of faith formation in terms of Christian identity and vocation, faith formation in the Wesley household, and some contemporary interpretations. Finally, examination of some foundational convictions leads to a proposal for a Wesleyan ecology of faith formation.

In chapter 2, "What It Means to Be Christian: The Aim of Formation for Holiness of Heart and Life," the discussion focuses on John Wesley's own search for a mature faith. We will explore Wesley's personal struggle with the relationship between faith and good works through ongoing discussions with Susanna Wesley, William Law, and Peter Böhler. Out of these experiences came John Wesley's conviction that we respond to God's grace by loving God through loving our neighbor.

The focus of chapter 3, "Community and Communion: Vision and Context of Formation for Holiness of Heart and Life," addresses John Wesley's conviction that a life of holiness is formed and nurtured through growing communion with the Triune God in Christian community. In this chapter, I begin to construct a Wesleyan ecology of faith formation based on my proposal that faith formation in the Wesleyan tradition has three phases: "invitation to communion," "deepening communion," and "full communion" with God.

The second part of this book explores "Formation in Communion:

Three Critical Questions." Chapter 4 addresses a question from the first Methodist Conference in 1744: "What to Teach?" The interrelationship of belief and practice is explored using the Fetter Lane Society as a case study. A process of gaining, clarifying, and extending shared Christian belief and practice included both instruction and nuture in the Methodist movement.

Chapter 5 addresses the question of "Who Shall Teach?" through an examination of the importance of formative relationships in the Methodist movement. The discussion reveals that the Wesleys believed that teachers were to be "life patterns" of a holy life, teaching what it meant to love God and neighbor by their own example. The Wesleys' emphasis on face-to-face teaching relationships is highlighted by their use of "Christian family" as a metaphor for the church.

Chapter 6 is the first of two chapters that address another question from the 1744 conference, "How to Teach?" In this chapter, structures for teaching are addressed beginning with the debate between Samuel and Susanna Wesley over critical learning and practical divinity and then moving to an examination of some of the structures for holy living and critical learning in the whole economy of the people called Methodists.

Chapter 7, " 'How to Teach?': Practices and Discipline," turns to formative practices of the Christian faith first learned in the Wesley household, made evident in the ministry of members of the Holy Club en route to Georgia, and finally formulated in John Wesley's theology of the means of grace. These works of piety and works of mercy served to deepen love of God and love of neighbor through the guiding and perfecting work of the Holy Spirit.

The final part of this book addresses the implications of my reflection for faith formation for a new communion. In chapter 8, "Making Disciples for a New Day," I construct a total picture of a Wesleyan ecology of faith formation. I also reflect on renewing the Wesleyan tradition in our work as church leaders and educators in a new day and dream of Christian formation for making disciples in the new century.

The question of how persons become Christian and my passion for sharing the story of our Wesleyan tradition provided my primary motivation for writing this book for churches in the Wesleyan tradi-

tion. My thesis has been that studying formation for holiness of heart and life in the early Methodist movement does provide insight for Christian faith formation in our churches today. I offer this research and these insights to Christian educators and teachers; students of polity, Christian education, and Wesleyan studies in seminaries; as well as judicatory leaders, pastors, and scholars. It is my hope that this book will serve as a resource in study groups for church professionals, for seminary students, and for ecumenical discussions. For it is on these church leaders that formation for holiness of heart and life depends in the new century.

Part I

FOUNDATIONS FOR MAKING DISCIPLES

Making disciples is an important ministry of any Christian community. In part I of this text we return to our Wesleyan roots to explore the biblical, historical, and theological foundations that contributed to faith formation in the early Methodist movement, and then we examine the nature of the Christian community as the context for faith formation.

Chapter 1	addresses the question of how we define the task of making disciples and proposes that we recover a Wesleyan ecology of faith formation for holiness of heart and life.
For Your Reflection:	How did you come to know yourself as Christian?
Chapter 2	explores the question of what it means to be Christian and to have a living faith by exploring John Wesley's own growth in faith.
For Your Reflection:	What does "faith" mean to you?

Chapter 3   examines the question of what it means to be the church and proposes that the Wesleyan understanding of the nature of the church is communion in community.

For Your Reflection: How has the church supported or hindered your growth in faith?

MAKING DISCIPLES

Formation for Holiness of Heart and Life

How do we come to know ourselves as Christian? What must we do to be saved? How do we pass on a living faith? These age-old questions of the Christian tradition are also crucial questions for those who are involved today in Christian ministries of proclaiming, inviting, teaching, caring, and serving. Those who are passionate about sharing the good news, inviting others into the fellowship of the church, nurturing and caring for those who are growing in faith, and joining with others to do God's work in the world are concerned with how persons become disciples of Jesus Christ.

This book explores the process of faith formation for holiness of heart and life in the Wesleyan tradition and is based on the assumption that God's grace is already at work in each person prior to our efforts in faith formation. God's prevenient grace invites a response

of **"faith,"** here defined as "actively seeking and discerning meaning in relationship to God, then intentionally responding to God's action in our lives" through Christian discipleship.[1] The word **"formation"** connotes "to shape," or "to form,"[2] a process that occurs over time. The term "faith formation" will be used here rather than "spiritual formation" to emphasize that we are exploring how persons become Christians within a particular historical tradition. In contrast, spiritual formation is a term that is often used to signal development of a person's relationship to the totality of life, sometimes outside of the Christian tradition. As Robert O'Gorman, Professor of Pastoral Studies at Loyola University, has written, "Spirituality is more concerned with helping persons adapt to the demands of everyday life than providing a sense of transcendence."[3]

Christian faith formation occurs through the partnership of God's action and human action. God's grace works within persons to deepen their relationship with Jesus Christ through the instruction, nurture, and care of the faith community leading them to respond to the enabling work of the Holy Spirit in faithful Christian discipleship. So *faith formation* will be used here to signify our participation in God's work of inviting persons to relationship to God, self, others, and creation. The church's role in faith formation is to create an intentional process of developing Christian identity and Christian vocation within a particular denominational tradition. In this case, our understanding of faith formation is shaped by our inheritance from the Wesley family and their passion for instructing and nurturing persons for faithful Christian discipleship.

So how do we come to know ourselves as Christian? Some of us cannot remember a time when we were not part of a church community. Participation in church was at the heart of our family life and never questioned. We were raised on potluck dinners, Christmas Eve candlelight services, Sunday school classes, church camps, and a variety of worship experiences. We attended youth group meetings and took our first steps toward leadership in the church through a youth group. When we left home, we might have taken a short "vacation" from the church, but we were soon back with our new families. Over the years, we continued to participate and to take increasing leadership in the life of the church. Participating in the life of the church throughout a lifetime formed our lives of Christian discipleship.

Others of us have come more recently to the church for a variety of reasons. We may have been drawn to the church because we were searching for something that would give meaning to our lives. Or we have decided that we want our children to grow up with values that will guide their lives. If we have not had previous church experience, we learn about Christian discipleship through the worshiping, teaching, caring, and serving ministries of the church. Our Christian identity matures in adulthood as we learn what it means to be Christian in our faith, relationships, and actions.

DEVELOPING CHRISTIAN IDENTITY AND VOCATION

Both of these examples highlight the assumption that we grow in faith by participating in Christian community. Therefore it is imperative for each local church, especially churches in the Wesleyan tradition, to consider how we contribute to faith formation for holiness of heart and life. The formative task of passing on the Christian faith tradition is especially critical for a local church in light of Thomas Frank's contention that "most people experience a denomination only at their own particular point of entry—in a local congregation of a certain community."[4] In other words, persons are going to learn the beliefs, values, and identity of their denominational tradition through participation in the life and witness of a particular congregation. This growth in faith occurs not just through religious instruction or religious experience, but through a combination of influences such as worship, witness, study, prayer, service, and fellowship that shape our faith through participation in the life of the church. Yet although this text recognizes that faith formation occurs primarily in a local congregation, it also offers the hope of a shared vision for formation of Christian identity and vocation across the Wesleyan connection.

One benefit of focusing on faith formation is that it causes us to assess what it is that constitutes the Christian life. Faith formation instills Christian values and beliefs and guides the development of a Christian lifestyle so that each person might respond in faith to God's prevenient grace. The process of faith formation nurtures Christian identity and vocation in disciples who are called to do God's work in the world. Formation in Christian identity and vocation occurs through participating in the life of the church and sharing responsi-

bilities for teaching, leading, caring, and serving as we learn more about what it means to be Christian.

Developing Christian identity and Christian vocation is a lifelong process of responding to God's grace through growth in discipleship. *Christian identity* means coming to know oneself as a Christian, having assimilated the values, beliefs, and lifestyle of one who professes to be a follower of Jesus Christ. John Wesley expressed this "knowing" as receiving assurance of a new relationship with God through Jesus Christ and increasing in holiness—love of God and neighbor—through the perfecting work of the Holy Spirit. Stated in the contemporary words of Charles Foster, a Christian educator at Candler School of Theology, "The purpose of church education . . . is to 'build up' or construct communities of faith to praise God and serve neighbors for the sake of the 'emancipatory transformation of the world.' "[5] At the heart of Christian identity is commitment to Christian vocation—love of God and love of neighbor.

Christian vocation is the response a person makes to God's free, but "resistible,"[6] grace through Jesus Christ. God invites us into new relationship and we may respond with either "yes" or "no." If the answer is "no," God's grace continues to be available to us as we seek meaning for our lives. A "yes" leads us into Christian vocation, defined by John Wesley as loving God by loving our neighbor. To be Christian is to commit ourselves to a vocation of discipleship, "doing all to the glory of God." As Samuel Wesley wrote, "the principle spring and motive, to which all the former [human motives] should be only secondary, must certainly be the glory of God, and the service of his church, in the edification and salvation of our neighbour."[7] And Susanna Wesley echoed a similar theme in one of her morning meditations: "We must let our good works be seen to the praise and glory of that God which gives us grace to perform those good works, but never that we may be seen or taken notice of or esteemed of [humanity]."[8] The Wesleys believed that God has given us all that we have and that these gifts should be used to further God's work on earth. We are stewards of our talents and our resources so that they may be used to the glory of God. In other words, Christian vocation is our response to God's grace by doing God's will rather than following our own desires for glory.

Christian identity and vocation are shaped not only by God's work in us and participation in our faith community but also by our culture and the events in the world in which we live. We are Christian in a particular place and in a particular time. The way we see ourselves as Christian is affected by our cultural inheritance, including family of origin, the region or country of our birth, racial or ethnic identity, gender, class, and age. We are affected by the events of the world in which we live, especially those events that raise questions about what it means to be faithful disciples. Our Christian faith helps us find meaning for our lives in the midst of the opportunities and challenges of our lives.

Nurturing Christian identity and Christian vocation has been the educational task of the church across the centuries as the church explored ways to pass on the faith to new generations. In recent years, the call for more emphasis on spiritual formation has grown as Christian churches have recognized the need for greater intentionality in what I am calling "faith formation." The search for meaning in a complex global society is bringing some people into the church for the first time. Other persons are coming back to church in a denomination they do not know. As a result, we can no longer assume that our church members have grown up in the faith with a lifelong identity in one denominational tradition.

The task of Christian faith formation is to help persons recognize the working of God's prevenient grace and their need for repentance. God's work of trasformation begins with baptism and initiates the Christian life, while faith formation cultivates human response to God's grace. The aim is for persons to claim an "owned faith," defined by noted Christian educator John Westerhoff as a conversion experience that "involve[s] a major change in a person's thinking, feeling, and willing."[9] In other words, owned faith is lived faith—a witnessing and serving faith. Conversion, whether instantaneous or gradual, is a transformative experience through which we come to know God's forgiveness and salvation in Jesus Christ. The intent of Christian faith formation is to share the good news of God's grace in Jesus Christ and to help people recognize their need for that grace while learning what it means to be faithful in everyday life. But faith formation can fall prey to abuse by putting rigid expectations and limits on the ways a person grows in faith. Wesley's questions of "what to teach" and "who shall teach," as well as "how to teach,"

23

become relevant questions for critical reflection on the shape of faith formation today.[10]

One of the Wesleys' strongest convictions was that God transforms our lives through the work of the Holy Spirit, but theologian Randy Maddox indicated that John Wesley sometimes avoided using the word "conversion" because it was often understood to mean that the transformation was complete in justification, implying no further growth in holiness was needed.[11] It is noteworthy that Susanna Wesley, in a discussion with her son Charles about justifying faith, wrote in 1738:

> I do not judge it necessary for us to know the precise time of our conversion. 'Tis sufficient if we have a reasonable hope that we are passed from death to life by the fruits of the Holy Spirit wrought in our hearts. . . . Our Lord acts in various ways and by various means on different tempers, nor is the work of regeneration begun and perfected at once. Some (though rarely) are converted by irresistible grace. . . . We can draw no general rules, nor ought we too curiously to search after the knowledge of the operations of God's Holy Spirit. [God's] ways are past finding out![12]

Given the influence of Susanna Wesley's teaching on her sons, it should not come as a surprise that John Wesley came to believe that salvation indeed begins with an experience of God's transforming grace but continues through the work of the Holy Spirit to bring persons into a new relationship with God. A new or restored relationship with God would be seen in the fruits of peace, hope, and love of God and neighbor.[13] Through this new relationship with God, lives are transformed, and this change is evident in Christlike living. Not only are individual lives changed by faith, but Christians are also called to join together to transform all that is destructive or unloving in the world as they respond to God's love for them.

In the Wesleyan tradition, faith formation and transformation are both acts of God's grace and an invitation for human response. Faith formation is necessary preparation for transformation, although even a church's most thorough plan of formation cannot guarantee transformation. As John Wesley observed in a letter to Philothea Briggs in 1773, "All our wisdom will not even make [the children] *understand*, much less *feel* the things of God." They need to be "awakened" by

God.[14] Our role as educators and leaders in the church is to create an environment for growth in faith, for sharing our own faith, for offering challenges, and for providing support, but the result of a transformed life comes from God's initiative of grace and an individual's response.

It is at this juncture that the relationship between Christian education and faith formation becomes critical. The ministry of Christian education addresses the tasks of shaping Christian identity and vocation *through* faith formation by helping us develop our relationship with God so that we may witness to our love for God by loving our neighbor. As Christians, we believe that all we have is a gift from God and that God calls us to use what we have been given in faithful discipleship. As we grow in faith, we become partners with God in doing God's work in the world. And God's work is the work of love—loving God and loving our neighbor, what John Wesley called "holiness of heart and life."

CHRISTIAN DISCIPLESHIP: HOLINESS OF HEART AND LIFE

For John Wesley, Christian vocation is a life of holiness, "faith working in love," that first embodies the commandment to love God through an inward or personal holiness—**"holiness of heart."** In Wesley's sermon "The Almost Christian," he described the first commandment:

> For thus saith [God's] Word: "Thou shalt love the Lord thy God with all thy heart, and with all thy soul, and with all thy mind, and with all thy strength." Such a love of God is this as engrosses the whole heart, as takes up all the affections, as fills the entire capacity of the soul, and employs the utmost extent of all its faculties.[15]

Holiness of heart is loving God with our whole being. In more contemporary language, church historian Charles Yrigoyen Jr. described holiness of heart: "Inward holiness involves total commitment to God, singleness of intention, centering one's life completely on God. It includes believing in, trusting, loving, worshiping, and obeying God. It consists of constant reliance on God's grace and using the gifts God gives to become what God intends us to be."[16] Holiness of heart focuses on deepening our relationship with God through acts of piety. What Wesley called "works of piety" are expressions of this

inward holiness and include spiritual practices such as corporate worship, private and public prayer, studying Scripture, and participating in the sacrament of Holy Communion. Wesley believed that God meets us in these spiritual practices to deepen our love of God and neighbor.

Faith working in love also means outward evidence of a new relationship with God as expressed through love of neighbor or social holiness—**"holiness of life."** As the second commandment teaches us, we are to love our neighbor; John Wesley's instruction was, "If any [person] ask, 'Who is my neighbour?' we reply, 'Every [person] in the world; every child of [God]. . . .' "[17] No one is excluded from this understanding of neighbor. As Yrigoyen wrote, "Outward holiness entails the manner in which we show our love for God in our love for our neighbors, remembering that the neighbor is **anyone** and **everyone** else."[18] John Wesley expected Methodists to participate in "works of mercy," such as visiting prisoners, caring for the sick, feeding the poor, and teaching orphans, expressing love of neighbor through outward holiness or holiness of life.

Those who follow in the Wesleyan tradition are known for holiness of heart through works of piety and holiness of life through works of mercy. In 1742, John Wesley described the mark of a Methodist: "a Methodist is one who has 'the love of God shed abroad in his [her] heart by the Holy Ghost given unto him [her]'; one who 'loves the Lord his [her] God with all his [her] heart, and with all his [her] soul, and with all his [her] mind, and with all his [her] strength.' "[19] According to Wesley, there are several gifts or "fruits" of loving God and neighbor: happiness in God, contentment with one's state, prayer without ceasing, purity of heart, desire to please God in all things, keeping God's commandments, doing all to the glory of God, and doing good to all persons.[20] Faith formation in the Wesleyan tradition nurtures lives of faith so that Christians might know the gifts of God's grace.

Faith Formation in the Wesley Household

For John and Charles Wesley, a primary aim of Christian faith formation was to prepare persons to repent of their sin and to receive God's redemptive grace so that they might surrender their wills to God and be transformed for a holy life. John Wesley first expressed

this goal in personal terms: "My *great* desire is to have 'Christ formed in my heart by faith.' "[21] Later in life he summed up his ministry, "What end, but to save sinners?"[22] Wesley's emerging understanding of how this happens was reminiscent of his own experience in the Wesley household.

Susanna Wesley, as the primary teacher of Christian education for her family, wrote that her purpose was to "take a more than ordinary care of the souls of my children and servants."[23] Inspired by accounts of Danish missionaries, she wrote in a letter to her husband:

> I thought I might live in a more exemplary manner in some things; I might pray more for the people and speak with more warmth to those with whom I have an opportunity of conversing. However, I resolved to begin with my own children, and accordingly I proposed and observed the following method: I take such a proportion of time as I can best spare every night to discourse with each child by itself on something that relates to its principal concerns. On Monday I talk with Molly, on Tuesday with Hetty, Wednesday with Nancy, Thursday with Jacky, Friday with Patty, Saturday with Charles, and with Emily and Sukey together on Sunday.[24]

Susanna Wesley's dedication to faith formation for members of her household, as well as for members of Samuel Wesley's parish, is evident in her commitment to regular religious conversation. It takes time and effort to prepare persons to repent of their sin and to receive God's grace.

With the Wesley household turned into "a small private boarding school,"[25] faith formation began with Susanna Wesley teaching her young children proper behavior for a holy life, particularly observing the Lord's day, not only by going to church but also with "other acts of piety and devotion."[26] When the children reached the age of understanding, Susanna then taught them the meaning of the Christian life. Susanna Wesley's intent was to form the wills of her children. "In order to form the minds of children, the first thing to be done is to conquer their will, and bring them to an obedient temper. To inform the understanding is a work of time, and must with children proceed by slow degrees as they are able to bear it."[27] If one of the marks of a Christian life is surrendering our wills to God, then the training of what we call the affections or emotions needs to start in

childhood. Susanna believed "that religion is nothing else than the doing the will of God, and not our own; that the one grand impediment to our temporal and eternal happiness being this self-will."[28] And Susanna Wesley knew that learning to do God's will proceeds by "slow degrees."

The Wesleys' ministry reflected adherence to this pattern of learning a lifestyle of obedience to God and then acquiring understanding both prior to and following justification. John Wesley believed that formation for holiness of heart and life begins with holy living in love of God and neighbor. Both John and Charles Wesley invested their time and energy exhorting the early Methodists to practice a holy life because they knew from their own upbringing and experience that faith formation required time and practice. And faith understanding would only come in time.

A second aim of faith formation for John Wesley was the church's role in nurturing and supporting human efforts to respond to the prompting of the Holy Spirit for ongoing growth in faith, including holding a person accountable for faith and life. The means of instructing, exhorting, and supporting needed to be appropriate to age, level of knowledge, and readiness for learning. Ultimately, preaching and participation in small groups provided the basic means for growth in faith and understanding in the Methodist movement. And the Wesleys "collected scores of letters noting spiritual victory," according to Stephen Gunter, author of *The Limits of "Love Divine."* [29] The Wesleys repeatedly lifted up examples of faithful Methodists who had been transformed through justification, assurance, and the perfecting work of the Holy Spirit, such as Mrs. Witham, the leader of a London band. John Wesley wrote, "She was an eminent pattern of calm boldness for the truth; of simplicity and godly sincerity; of unwearied constancy in attending all the ordinances of God; of zeal for God and for all good works; and of self-denial in every kind."[30] These models of a holy life led John Wesley to emphasize that sustained growth in holiness—making disciples—was only possible within the context of the life of the faith community.

Contemporary Voices

As we explore faith formation for holiness of heart and life in the Wesleyan tradition, we already have some substantive Wesleyan

scholarship on which to build a proposal for making disciples today. Some particular elements of faith formation in the early Methodist movement have already been explored by other scholars and are briefly surveyed here as contributions for thinking about Christian faith formation in our time.

Charles Wallace spent thirteen years editing *Susanna Wesley: The Complete Writings*, a volume of the extant writings of Susanna Wesley with thoughtful introductory material contributing fresh insight for each section as well as thorough notes.[31] The book provides access to an important body of literature and a rich source for those who are interested in faith formation in the Wesley household in the eighteenth century. These writings illustrate the importance of parents as teachers in faith formation. Echoes of Susanna Wesley's ability in theological discourse and insight, as well as educational philosophy, can be found throughout the early Methodist movement, especially in the work of John and Charles Wesley. Susanna Wesley's dedication to the faith formation of her children throughout her lifetime stands as testimony to a remarkable woman who was a living witness to the abundance of God's grace.

David Watson's contribution to Wesleyan scholarship has been the retrieval of the intent and structure of the early Methodist class meetings and a revival of the small-group structure for spiritual growth in his books *Accountable Discipleship* and *The Early Methodist Class Meeting*.[32] Watson provided carefully researched history on the development of the small-group structure for adults in the Methodist movement. He proposed a contemporary "Covenant Discipleship" model for adults to provide support and accountability for growth in faith. While the shared leadership of the mutually accountable Covenant Discipleship Groups differs from the system of tightly supervised leaders of the original small groups for adults in the Methodist movement, Covenant Discipleship Groups are found throughout Methodism today and illustrate one element of faith formation.

Two authors have written adult study books on holiness of heart and life that contribute to discipleship education. **Charles Yrigoyen** wrote *John Wesley: Holiness of Heart and Life* as an adult study book for The United Methodist Church, particularly designed for the School of Christian Missions.[33] This resource demonstrated that well-

29

informed, accessible resources could be made available for adults in the church—an example of Wesley's "plain truth for plain people."[34] Yrigoyen's discussion of formation for holiness of heart and life in the Wesleyan tradition and the study guide by Ruth A. Daugherty add to our knowledge of formation for adults in the Wesleyan tradition. **Stephen Seamands** also expressed the hope that congregations would recover a passion for holiness of heart and life in his book *Holiness of Heart and Life*.[35] This study book addressed the doctrine of God and challenged the reader to consider the implications of John Wesley's teaching about holiness of heart and life.

Gayle Felton and Mariellen Sawada provide two examples of United Methodist resources concerning the needs of children and youth. Christian educator and historian **Gayle Carlton Felton** has been working in the area of Wesleyan heritage and ministries with children. In "John Wesley and the Teaching Ministry: Ramifications for Education in the Church Today"[36] Felton described Wesley's "hymns for children," "instructions for children," and "lessons for children," analyzing each in terms of its purpose in the Methodist movement. In other recent work, Felton addressed the connection between baptism and the education of children.[37] **Mariellen Sawada** has provided a much-needed contemporary example of formation for holiness of heart and life in a study for youth. *John Wesley: Holiness of Heart and Life*[38] contains creative learning activities based on solid grounding in the Wesleyan tradition. Sawada demonstrated how a creative pedagogy brings new awareness to the study of our Wesleyan tradition in discipleship education.

D. Michael Henderson's dissertation on *John Wesley's Instructional Groups*,[39] written in 1980, assessed principles of instruction and provided background for the Wesleys' small adult groups by examining each type of group (society, class, band, select society, and penitent band) from an educational perspective. Henderson's contribution to Wesleyan scholarship is his discussion of the interrelationships between the various groups and the way each group marks progress in growth in faith. His assessment of the effectiveness of this group structure in terms of "mode," "methods," and "leadership" provides helpful input into this element of faith formation for adults.

Each of these authors has made a contribution to the growing literature on faith formation in the Wesleyan tradition. Some of these

works were completed prior to recent discoveries in Wesleyan research, so their contributions need to be assessed in light of those findings. However, the authors' discussions contribute to our understanding of specific elements of faith formation in the Wesleyan tradition and point to the need for more intentionality in cultivating discipleship through faith formation.

A PROPOSAL FOR MAKING DISCIPLES

The purpose of this book is to return to our Methodist roots to examine the interrelationship of elements that shaped Christian identity and vocation within the eighteenth-century Methodist renewal movement. Questions from the first Methodist conference in 1744 of "what to teach" and "how to teach"[40] point to the necessity for a shared commitment about doctrine and practice—the content and method of formation for holiness of heart and life.

The thesis of this book is that by studying the way formation for holiness of heart and life took shape in the early Wesleyan tradition, we might gain insights for Christian faith formation in our churches today. My intent is not to transpose what John and Charles Wesley did into our time and place but to see what we are able to learn from our Wesleyan heritage that helps us look anew at faith formation. By examining the context, intent, and function of formative relationships, structures, and practices of the early Methodist movement, we may be able to discern some clues about recapturing the meaning and recreating the wholeness of faith formation in the Wesleyan tradition.

Some foundational convictions are operative in the preparation and construction of this work. First, members of the Wesleyan connection at the beginning of the twenty-first century need to rethink how best to nurture faith for our time. We have an opportunity to respond with creativity and celebrate the multicultural and theological diversity of our churches, developing shared interests and commitments across the connection.[41] In addition, the connectional world church provides an opportunity for active witness to love and justice in a world that has great need of such a witness. A discussion about the meaning of formation for holiness of heart and life in a global church would provide a fruitful beginning as we rethink what it means for us to love God and neighbor in a new century.

31

Second, John Wesley's own experience of working toward an "economy" of formation for holiness of heart and life provides affirmation and insight for making disciples in our time. Wesley addressed this idea as he began "A Plain Account of the People Called Methodists," saying, "Some time since you desired an account of the *whole economy* of the people commonly called Methodists. . . . I sent you this account, that you may know not only their *practice* on every head, but likewise the *reasons* whereon it is grounded, the *occasion* of every step they have taken, and the *advantages* reaped thereby."[42] Accounts of ministry from both John and his brother Charles provide a context for our study of their developing thought and practice of ministry, although we should realize that the Wesleys' accounts must be read with a critical eye toward discerning what is viable in our situation.

A third conviction is that formative processes are closely tied to theological assertions about doctrines such as the nature of God, sin and salvation, the church's mission and ministry, and eschatology. The focus in this work will be on what John Wesley called the "Three-One God," designating that "God is Three and One,"[43] as well as the church's mission and ministry, recognizing that discussion of these theological themes will necessarily hold consequences for interpretation of other theological doctrines.

Fourth, the author's conviction that the Way of Salvation may be described as growing in communion with the "Three-One God" provides an accessible means of identifying and naming how God acts in a process of growing in faith through "invitation to communion," "deepening communion," and "full communion with God and neighbor."[44] This interpretation, to be discussed in chapter 3, is consistent with John Wesley's understanding and leads us to think about the community's role in cultivating individual growth in faith.

And finally, this opportunity to explore connections between the past and the present challenges us to rethink and reinterpret our heritage in light of present needs in a way that faithfully leads us into the future. In his work on theology and evangelism in the Wesleyan tradition, Professor of Evangelism James Logan wrote that his goal was "recovery of the trajectory of wholeness, both of grace and mission,"[45] from eighteenth-century Methodism into the present and beyond. It is this trajectory of our Wesleyan heritage in unfolding,

developing, ever-new witness to the Christian faith that this enterprise and other contemporary voices address.

A Wesleyan Ecology of Faith Formation

In light of these convictions, I am proposing that we need to create a Wesleyan ecology of faith formation for our churches. The word "ecology" is used here to indicate the interconnection of all these formative elements.[46] In common usage, "ecology" addresses the relationships between human beings and the natural world, but the word provides a helpful metaphor for a new understanding of the ministry and mission of the church. In 1971, noted process theologian John Cobb wrote of our relationship with all of creation that

> we must learn to view the aspects of reality as parts of an interconnected system in which each depends, directly or indirectly, on every other. . . . **Equally important is that we perceive ourselves as part of this interconnected, [inter]dependent, and interacting complex of events and things**. . . . Stewardship and co-creaturehood must replace conquest and dominance as the basic image of our relation to the rest of nature.[47]

In a world that has been fragmented in many ways, this image of interconnection and interdependence raises the hope of finding wholeness in our life together as we seek to make disciples through formation of heart and life. In 1992, researchers Coalter, Mulder, and Weeks reviewed the interrelationship of Presbyterian institutions and practices and concluded, "It is painfully evident that the ecology of Presbyterian nurture has been critically disrupted."[48] They called for a renewal of the ecology for nurturing faith. My proposal for a Wesleyan ecology of faith formation also attempts to renew this same kind of "interconnected, interdependent, and interacting complex" of relationships, structures, and practices to nurture faith for churches in the Wesleyan tradition.

The Wesleys discovered the importance of an interconnected system of instruction and nurture through their own ministry. They knew that it was important to preach the good news so that God might work through this witness to bring people to faith, but they soon learned that more was needed. When the rapidly expanding need for preaching outpaced the available time and energy it took to

form and nurture societies, the Wesleys experimented with Methodist preaching missions that were not accompanied by the usual pattern of establishing societies for nurturing and sustaining faith formation. In the context of early Methodism, invitation through preaching without the continuing nurture of a society left dismal results, according to Richard Heitzenrater, who writes, "The preacher had little opportunity for instructions, the awakened souls could not 'watch over one another in love,' and the believers could not 'build up one another and bear one another's burdens.' "[49] When the Wesleys visited these parishes months later, little was left of the fruits of the preaching mission. As the Wesleys discovered, preaching the good news alone is not enough to sustain human response to God's transforming grace. The practice of a holy life nurtured through a combination of worship, sacrament, Scripture, and Christian conference is needed for forming Christian disciples.

The church in our time needs to create a Wesleyan ecology of formation for holiness of heart and life that includes **preaching and witness** to the good news of God's grace, ongoing **instruction and nurture** in the faith, **pastoral care** to support persons on their journeys of faith, opportunities for **service** in behalf of our neighbors, and **fellowship** with other Christians on the journey. Specialization and narrowed areas of expertise in professional ministry have pulled apart these once interrelated aspects of the church's ministry. A case in point is the division in the academy of invitation, initiation, and nurture into separate scholarly disciplines of evangelism and Christian education —often with little communication between the two. Likewise they are often divided into separate areas of work in the local church. By the end of this study, we may find that the challenge of faith formation in the Wesleyan tradition is not so much a problem of missing elements as of missing interconnections. Creating a Wesleyan ecology of formation for holiness of heart and life for our time may call us to work together in new ways.

I am proposing that we need to create a Wesleyan ecology of faith formation in order to nurture persons and churches in their growing relationship with God through God's grace in Jesus Christ so that we may all become more Christlike in our daily living. One contribution of constructing this ecology is that it will begin to recover the wholeness of the formational enterprise that the Wesleys and the early

Methodists envisioned. The challenge is in finding some way to carefully distinguish the individual parts of this ecology without breaking them apart from each other or blurring the distinctions to the point that the richness of the interconnections are lost. The goal of formation for holiness of heart and life is captured in the words of Thomas Frank: "What we are looking for here are the practices that enable people to grow in the knowledge and love of God and to become communities of witness and service."[50] In other words, we need to refocus our educational endeavors in the church on Christian discipleship through formation for holiness of heart and life. My intent is to examine the elements of the Wesleys' theology and ministry that contributed to a Wesleyan ecology of faith formation, an interconnecting network of relationships, structures, and practices that constituted an environment for nurturing and sustaining a holy life in communion with God and others. It is my hope that insights gained from research into John Wesley's total educational enterprise will provide the impetus for faithful and imaginative approaches to Christian faith formation today.

Chapter 2

WHAT IT MEANS TO BE CHRISTIAN

The Aim of Formation for Holiness of Heart and Life

If the aim of Christian faith formation is to share in the work of making disciples, then we must know what it means to be Christian. We begin by assuming that Christians grow in faith and discipleship through the work of the Holy Spirit and participation in the community of faith. As Randy Maddox observed, this growth is consistent with the Wesleyan tradition: "Not only did Wesley view growth in the Christian life as a continual possibility, it was his normative expectation."[1] But what does it mean to be Christian?

In "The Character of a Methodist," John Wesley clearly stated the aim of faith formation for holiness of heart and life:

[A Methodist] is a Christian, not in *name* only, but in *heart* and in *life*. [A Methodist] is inwardly and outwardly conformed to the will of God, as revealed in the written Word. *He [she] thinks, speaks, and lives*

37

according to the "method" *laid down in the revelation of Jesus Christ.* His
[or her] soul is "renewed after the image of God," "in righteousness
and in all true holiness." And "having the mind that was in Christ" he
[or she] "so walks as" Christ "also walked."[2]

To be Christian in the language of the Wesleyan tradition means having a "living faith" made evident through love of God and neighbor,
a living faith that continues to grow across a lifetime. In the words of
Susanna Wesley: "Love to God, and love to our neighbour, which
often in Scripture is called charity, is, or ought to be, the principle and
rule of all our thoughts, words, and actions, with respect to either.
And whatever we do for God or [humanity] that flows not from this
principle, and is not squared by this rule, is wrong, as wanting a good
foundation, and a right conduct."[3] While Susanna's son John readily
understood the meaning of charity, he did not come to a clear view
of the nature of faith as easily. This chapter explores how John Wesley
came to understand and articulate a theology that grace for all and a
response of living faith were prerequisite to, as well as the result of,
salvation.

As John Wesley's theology developed, he was often criticized for
being inconsistent. And in some ways, the criticism was accurate.
While the theological themes at the heart of Wesley's understanding
of faith remained the same, his interpretations took on new perspectives and new depth as his Christian identity and sense of Christian
vocation grew. This growth was not particularly orderly or systematic. Wesley's theology grew out of the interaction of study, worship,
and experience, and he was not afraid to change his mind about his
theological stance. An astute observer of himself and others, what
Wesley learned from experience significantly shaped his theology.
And Wesley's considerable knowledge, as well as his experiences
and interactions with others, contributed to his growing understanding of the nature of faith itself, which in turn affected the shape of his
ministry and mission.

THE SEARCH FOR A LIVING FAITH

John Wesley's search for a living faith is important for our consideration because it addresses the aim of faith formation for holiness of
heart and life. What do we need to be saved from? What are we saved

for? How are we saved? John Wesley's exploration of the nature of faith was closely tied to the primary question of his spiritual search: "What must I do to be saved?" In his young adult years, John Wesley was preoccupied with the question of saving souls, particularly his own. In a narrative of his faith journey written in May 1738, John Wesley reported that he had "been strictly educated and carefully taught that I could only be saved *by universal obedience, by keeping all the commandments of God,* in the meaning of which I was diligently instructed."[4] But in reflecting on his years at Charterhouse school (ages eleven to seventeen), Wesley wrote: "And what I now hoped to be saved by, was, (1) *not being so bad as other people;* (2) *having still a kindness for religion;* and (3) *reading the Bible, going to church, and saying my prayers.*"[5] During his university years, Wesley was even less clear, "I cannot well tell what I hoped to be saved by now."[6] The answer to this question took John Wesley years to find and articulate.

John Wesley's struggles with faith give us insight into our own faith journeys and help us see how the church can best participate in the faith formation of those under its care. A review of the development of John Wesley's understanding of faith illustrates the kind of growth that may occur across time in a person's theological thinking. Coming to understand and articulate that God alone provides for salvation and that humans can do nothing to merit salvation was John Wesley's lifelong work. In his dissertation at Harvard Divinity School, Rex Matthews identified three distinct periods of development in John Wesley's use of faith language that reflects an underlying theological understanding. The first period of development occurred prior to 1738 and John Wesley's Aldersgate experience, during the time he understood faith as assent to rational propositions. Matthews described the language of faith at this early stage in Wesley's theological growth as *"fides,* assent to propositional truth."[7] John Wesley's journey in faith becomes a case study in faith formation for us as we track his thinking and experience during this time through correspondence and written reflections.

Early Discussions of Faith

An indication of John Wesley's interest in articulating the nature of faith came during his college days in Oxford. In a letter in July 1725, John advanced his understanding of faith during an ongoing

39

theological discussion with his mother, Susanna: "Faith is a species of belief, and belief is defined, an assent to a proposition upon rational grounds. Without rational grounds there is therefore no belief, and consequently no faith."[8] John also indicated that it would take a strong argument to change his mind about this claim. However, Susanna did not accept this notion of faith and responded within a month, "You are somewhat mistaken in your notion of faith. All faith is an assent, but all assent is not faith."[9] She argued that there are two ways to know the truth—through reason and revelation, but reason is the tool of science while revelation discloses the "proper objects of faith."[10] Susanna observed that the nature of the revealer gives authority to the revelation: "The true measure of faith is the authority of the revealer, the weight of which always holds proportion with our conviction of his ability and integrity. Divine faith is an assent to whatever God has revealed to us, because [God] has revealed it."[11] Susanna knew that John was relying on reason more than revelation; he needed to trust God more.

Another letter from Susanna in November indicated that she was still not happy with John's understanding of faith. She repeated her argument: "Yet I insist upon it that the virtue of faith, by which through the merits of our Redeemer we must be saved, is an assent to the truth of whatever God hath been pleased to reveal, because [God] hath revealed it, and not because we understand it."[12] By the end of November, John had studied the readings his mother had suggested, and wrote "I am therefore at length come over entirely to your opinion, that saving faith (including practice) is an assent to what God has revealed, because [God] has revealed it, and not because the truth of it may be evinced by reason."[13] But this agreement was not the end of the discussion.

Over the next several years, John Wesley continued to raise the matter of faith with his mother in their correspondence, and one letter indicated that they discussed the matter at Epworth as well.[14] Susanna Wesley believed that a living faith influenced practice, including words and actions, and she wanted John to share that faith. Nine years later, she again wrote, "By faith I do not mean an assent only to the truths of the gospel concerning him, but such an assent as influences our practice, as makes us heartily and thankfully accept him for our God and Saviour, upon his own conditions."[15] Even with

his stated acquiescence to his mother's point of view, John still held to his predominantly rational idea of faith and had not yet come to experience what he later would know—growing in faith and understanding is an ongoing process of formation and transformation.

During these early years, John Wesley's efforts were primarily directed toward what **he needed to do** in order to merit salvation, with the assumption that this was what others needed to do as well. As a college undergraduate in Oxford, John Wesley fashioned a disciplined life of Scripture reading, prayer, fasting, Holy Communion, and doing good works for others with members of a small group of pious young men, including Charles Wesley, who formed a group known as the Holy Club. Later, in a letter to Richard Morgan Sr., John Wesley recounted the beginning of the group: "In November, 1729, at which time I came to reside at Oxford, your son [William Morgan], my brother, and myself, and one more [Robert Kirkham], agreed to spend three or four evenings in a week together. Our design was to read over the classics, which we had before read in private, on common nights, and on Sunday some book in divinity."[16] Development of a deeper piety and ministry came later.

During this time, John Wesley was greatly influenced by the model of piety and ethical living proposed by William Law in *Christian Perfection* and *A Serious Call to a Devout and Holy Life*. These writings spoke to John Wesley's interest in faith and spiritual discipline. In an 1890 biography of John Wesley, Luke Tyerman reported that John Wesley visited Rev. Law in 1732 and "commenced a friendship which lasted for several years."[17] And J. Brazier Green commented from his research on Wesley and Law that both "John and Charles Wesley visited Law at Putney on several occasions."[18] Prior to the mission trip to Georgia, John Wesley evidently met with Law and did not understand all that they discussed. He wrote about this in a letter on December 19, 1733, to Susanna Wesley. The letter has not been found, but Wesley's diary noted, "with Mr. Law, not understood all he said."[19] Susanna Wesley's reply came in January 1734: "Mr. Law is a good and valuable man; yet he is a man, and therefore no marvel that he could not be so explicit as you could have wished in speaking of the presence of God."[20] In spite of this perceived shortcoming, John Wesley became a diligent disciple of Law's teachings. Not only did he read Law's works. Wesley's diary reflects the use of Law's writ-

41

ings for his own edification, as well as for the spiritual guidance of others during his trip to Georgia.[21]

Various accounts about John Wesley's life and work during this time convey the impression that Wesley was trying harder and harder to work out his own salvation through obedience to the will of an authoritarian God with little assurance that he was succeeding. This led to Wesley's crisis in faith when he discovered he could not attain that kind of faithfulness on his own. Life events and significant relationships served to push him to further develop his understanding of the nature of faith. A "failed" mission trip to Georgia, the termination of his relationship with William Law, and a subsequent relationship with Moravian Peter Böhler led to a turning point in Wesley's understanding of faith. He began to move from understanding faith as *fides* or *"assent* to truth claims" to faith as *fiducia* or *"trust* in God's love," the second period of development in Wesley's faith language, according to Matthews.[22]

A Turning Point

John Wesley's mission to Georgia has been well documented elsewhere,[23] but it is important to note Wesley's stated intention for this trip, "My chief motive, to which all the rest are subordinate, is *the hope of saving my own soul.* I hope to learn the true sense of the gospel of Christ by preaching it to the heathens."[24] Embarking on a mission to save his soul, the trip to Georgia challenged John Wesley's faith, raised questions about his judgment, and taught him much about ministry with diverse groups of people. But he did not find the answer to the question of how to save his own soul. On the trip home, Wesley wrote,

> I went to America to convert the Indians; but Oh! who shall convert me? . . . I asked long ago, What must I do to be saved? The Scripture answered, "Keep the commandments. Believe, hope, love; follow these tempers till thou hast fully attained, that is, till death, by all those outward works and means.[25]

John Wesley returned to England in a crisis of faith. He had practiced Christian discipline better than most, but even Wesley's diligent obedience to God's law had not led him to salvation. In a terrible storm at sea, Wesley witnessed the calm faith in God's deliverance of a

group of Moravians. To Wesley's dismay, he found he did not share such a faith and feared death before he attained a holy life. Wesley knew he had not experienced justification and he feared for his eternal life. He had come to realize the frailty of his faith:

> In my return to England, January 1738, being in imminent danger of death, and very uneasy on that account, I was strongly convinced that the cause of that uneasiness was unbelief, and that the gaining a true, living faith, was the "one thing needful" for me. But still I fixed not this faith on its right object: I meant only faith in God, not faith in or through Christ. Again, I knew not that I was *wholly void of this faith,* but only thought *I had not enough* of it.[26]

Wesley knew that his diligent practice of spiritual discipline based in Scripture and supported by Law's teachings had not produced a saving faith, but he did not yet have an answer to his quest.

The End of a Relationship. When John Wesley returned from Georgia, a series of four letters between Wesley and William Law terminated the personal relationship between them. Wesley had used Law's treatises as a model of piety for several years, but now wrote that Law's model of Christian discipline was unworkable for ordinary mortals, that "it was too high for [humans], and that by doing the works of this law should no flesh living be justified."[27] Wesley's own experience had taught him that humans were not capable of earning salvation by obeying God's law alone. Without ever seeing William Law, Wesley concluded in a letter of May 14, 1738, that his teacher's inadequacies of faith had led to his own failures. Wesley further expressed doubt that Law had ever experienced a living faith in Christ.

In a response written on May 19, 1738, Law refused to take responsibility for John Wesley's crisis in faith. He answered each of Wesley's criticisms carefully and suggested that guidance could be found in his writings or in the other books he had recommended.[28] Wesley replied on May 20, 1738, leveling four charges against Law for failing his responsibility as a teacher to point out that Wesley did not have a living faith:

> "But how are you chargeable with my not having had this faith"? If, as you intimate, you discerned my spirit, thus:

(1). You did not tell me plainly I had it not. (2). You never once advised me to seek or pray for it. (3). You gave me advices proper only for one who had it already, and (4) advices which led me farther from it the closer I adhered to them.[29]

In other words, John Wesley blamed his teacher, William Law, for everything that had gone wrong to cause this crisis of faith. Finally, on or about May 22, 1738, Law responded more vehemently asking, "Who made me your teacher? Or can make me answerable for any defects in your knowledge? You sought my acquaintance, you came to me as you pleased, and on what occasion you pleased, and to say to me what you pleased."[30] Law questioned why the church that had trained Wesley and the bishop who had ordained him were not equally responsible for Wesley's apparent lack of faith.

About the same time as Law's final letter, John Wesley wrote the account of his pilgrimage of faith leading to his "warmed heart" at Aldersgate. In this account, Wesley stated, "But meeting now with Mr. Law's *Christian Perfection* and *Serious Call* (although I was much offended at many parts of both, yet) they convinced me more than ever of the exceeding height and breadth and depth of the law of God."[31] Wesley had just accused Law of failing in his teaching and in his faith, yet included Law as one of two people named in his spiritual pilgrimage account!

John Wesley's relationship with William Law was an important element in his faith formation because William Law provided an important model for piety that Wesley continued to use and publish over the years. Perhaps Law did understand Wesley's spiritual crisis better than Wesley thought at the time. On January 9, 1789, Wesley quoted Law's advice in a letter of counsel to Miss Bolton: " 'Sir, you are troubled,' said Mr. Law to me, 'because you do not understand how God is dealing with you. Perhaps if you did, it would not so well answer his design. He is teaching you to trust Him farther than you can see Him.' "[32]

A Transforming Relationship. In February 1738, before the final exchange of letters with William Law, John Wesley met Peter Böhler, nine years his junior, who was about to embark on a mission to Carolina as a representative of the Moravians. The two immediately became friends and they spent time conversing, walking, and traveling together. Wesley's relationship with Peter Böhler developed

quickly and was very intense from February to May of 1738, when Böhler left for Carolina. Ten references in Wesley's 1738 diary depict Wesley spending time with Böhler, usually "at home," or "conversing," walking and traveling together. The primary topic of their discussions was "living faith." John Wesley's *Journal* recorded his struggle to understand and to accept Böhler's ideas about living faith and religious experience. "So that when Peter Böhler, whom God prepared for me as soon as I came to London, affirmed of true faith in Christ (which is but one) that it had those two fruits inseparably attending it, 'dominion over sin, and constant peace from a sense of forgiveness,' I was quite amazed, and looked upon it as a new gospel."[33]

Peter Böhler was a living witness to the kind of inner faith that John Wesley sought. Böhler understood Wesley's crisis of faith, and Wesley's needs of the moment were met through Böhler's enthusiasm in sharing his faith. Since Böhler had experienced a saving faith, he guided Wesley's formation in faith. As Martin Schmidt, author of a theological biography of Wesley, observed, "He helped Wesley in an important way to rid himself of placing too great an emphasis upon a Christian ethic, and so from a certain restrictive factor which had been present in his striving after holiness. He made him realize that a simple personal relationship to Jesus the Saviour is the heart of the relationship with God."[34] Just before Peter Böhler left for Carolina, he urged Wesley "not to stop short of the grace of God."[35] And in a letter on May 10, Böhler counseled Wesley to trust in God and to give up his unbelief.[36] Two weeks later John Wesley attended a society meeting in Aldersgate Street and felt his heart "strangely warmed." He wrote, "I felt I did trust in Christ, Christ alone for salvation, and an assurance was given me that he had taken away *my* sins, even *mine*, and saved *me* from the law of sin and death."[37]

Peter Böhler brought John Wesley what William Law could not. Both William Law and Peter Böhler were significant influences on John Wesley's faith formation. William Law provided a **model for piety** through his teachings. Law prescribed a model for a "devout and holy life" in obedience to God's law, a model John Wesley respected and used throughout his life. The conflict over the inadequacies of Law's teachings even pushed Wesley toward a turning point in his understanding of faith. In Wesley's spiritual crisis, he

learned that total obedience to God's law alone is not the way to salvation. This realization led Wesley to Peter Böhler, whose life provided a *model of piety*. Böhler, as a living example of a holy life, guided John Wesley to a conversion of the heart. Now Wesley's focus in faith would turn to **what God does for us**.

At Aldersgate, Wesley *felt* God's assurance, and his image of God changed. In a discussion of Wesley and authority, Robert Moore concluded that John Wesley changed his image of an authoritarian God through the experience of unconditional acceptance in his relationship with Peter Böhler, who refused to give up on him. The old image of God was an authority figure to be obeyed; the new image was a God who reached out to human beings, even imperfect human beings, in love. Faith as obedience to God's law was transformed into obedience as a faithful response to God's love.[38] After Aldersgate, Wesley's emphasis was on *what God does* for us, and "faith mean[t] *fiducia*, trusting confidence in God as Saviour."[39] Now Wesley enthusiastically went to the other extreme and preached justification by faith alone, to such an extent that he was criticized for leaving good works and human responsibility out of it altogether.[40] But within a short time, Wesley was seeking to articulate a more balanced view between faith and works, and that search continued for several years.

The final period of John Wesley's development of faith language began in the 1760s, according to Matthews. The mature Wesley's interpretation of faith incorporated **both *fides* and *fiducia* grounded in spiritual experience**. Maddox observed that Matthews "argues persuasively that the understanding of faith as spiritual experience became *foundational* for the mature Wesley, with faith as trust and faith as assent being grounded in this 'objective' experience."[41] Wesley's emphasis was now on **what God does and what we do**, recognizing that any response on our part is totally dependent on God's grace. Wesley proclaimed that God's grace is at work in all persons who then, through God's grace, have a choice about their response to that grace. Out of this more balanced understanding of faith and salvation came one of Wesley's major theological contributions—his interpretation of prevenient grace, God's grace indwelling persons free for all:

How freely does God love the world! While we were yet sinners, "Christ died for the ungodly." While we were "dead in sin," God

"spared not his own Son, but delivered him up for us all." And how "freely with him" does he "give us all things"! Verily, free grace is all in all!

The grace of love of God, whence cometh our salvation, is free in all, and free for all.[42]

Prevenient, or preventing, grace is offered to everyone through the Christ event. Even though humanity has fallen into sin, the power to live a faithful life is within each person through the work of the Holy Spirit. Because of prevenient grace, God working in us, we are able to respond to God in faith through loving our neighbor.

GRACE FREE FOR ALL

Through observations of his own experience and that of others, John Wesley learned that growth in faith toward salvation is a process initiated and nurtured by God's grace.[43] Wesley eventually came to believe that salvation is both instantaneous and gradual,[44] but as Maddox stated, "human salvation—viewed in Wesley's terms—would be fundamentally *gradual* in process."[45] In a landmark sermon, "Working Out Our Own Salvation," John Wesley articulated his understanding of the relationship between God and humanity and the way that relationship grows through the Way of Salvation. The sermon was based on the text from Philippians 2:12-13: "Work out your own salvation with fear and trembling; for it is God that worketh in you, both to will and to do of [God's] good pleasure."[46] In this sermon, Wesley emphasized that humans can never do enough to earn salvation, but we must have faith that salvation comes through Jesus Christ. Salvation is a gift of God's mercy and grace through God's act of love in Jesus Christ. Later, Wesley succinctly stated his understanding of justification by faith in "Principles of a Methodist":

> I believe three things must go together in our justification: upon God's part, [God's] great mercy and grace; upon Christ's part, the satisfaction of God's justice by the offering his body and shedding his blood, "and fulfilling the law of God perfectly"; and upon our part, true and living faith in the merits of Jesus Christ.[47]

Through justification, we are redeemed and called as faithful disciples to "do all the good we can" in love for God who has given us

47

new life. But God has not yet finished with us. We continue to grow in faith through the working of the Holy Spirit. And this whole pilgrimage from Creation to Redemption to Sanctification is called the Way of Salvation.

John Wesley believed God provides the Way of Salvation for us. Maddox argued convincingly that for Wesley, "God's *grace* works powerfully, but not irresistibly, in matters of human life and salvation; thereby empowering our *response-ability*, without overriding our *responsibility*."[48] As Wesley's theological understanding developed, he incorporated the idea of ongoing growth in faith. The result is what is known as *via salutis* or the Way of Salvation, summarized by this formula: "(1) all [persons] need to be saved; (2) all [persons] can be saved; (3) all [persons] can know they are saved; (4) all [persons] can be saved to the uttermost."[49] This formula represents the steps on the Way of Salvation and provides theological grounding for formation for holiness of heart and life.

All Persons Need to Be Saved

For John Wesley, the salvation story begins with a traditional Christian view of God's creation and the fallen state of humanity through original sin. Wesley differed from others who were part of the Evangelical Revival in his view that humans could be moved by God's prevenient grace to do good rather than evil. Even though Wesley believed in the depravity of humanity, he had a generally hopeful view that humans would turn away from sinfulness with God's help. In his sermon, Wesley wrote,

> First, we are to observe that great and important truth which ought never to be out of our remembrance, "It is God that worketh in us both to will and to do of [God's] good pleasure." The meaning of these words may be made more plain by a small transposition of them: "It is God that of [God's] good pleasure worketh in you both to will and to do."[50]

Wesley knew from his own experience that religious community and spiritual discipline are needed to promote willing and doing. Idleness is the greatest danger. Philip Watson, a Reformation scholar, asserted that Wesley's main goal was to aid persons in experiencing a living faith in Christ evidenced in the fruits of the Spirit: love,

peace, and joy.[51] But recognition of sinfulness and the need for forgiveness must be the first step.

All Persons Can Be Saved

When people recognize their sinfulness with the help of God's prevenient grace, the hope is that all will be saved through God's action for us in Jesus Christ. **God** working **in us** through the Holy Spirit provides the prevenient **grace** that brings us to the moment when we are convinced of our **need** for forgiveness and encourages us to repent. In Wesley's words, "salvation begins with what is usually termed . . . 'preventing grace'; including the first wish to please God, the first dawn of light concerning [God's] will, and the first slight, transient conviction of having sinned against [God]."[52] This grace is called prevenient or preventing because it is present even before we are aware of it. Through prevenient grace, persons are able to grow and to change, to make positive decisions, to love God and love their neighbor—all with God's help.

Once we have repented, John Wesley believed that we continue to work out our own salvation until we receive God's assurance of our justification made evident in a holy life. Wesley used a phrase from Isaiah to direct us in holy living: "Cease to do evil; learn to do well" (Isaiah 1:16-17). And to provide further guidance, Wesley gave very specific examples about how we can respond to that grace "already given":

> And "learn to do well"; be zealous of good works, of works of piety, as well as works of mercy. Use family prayer, and cry to God in secret. Fast in secret, and "your Father which seeth in secret, he will reward you openly." "Search the Scriptures"; hear them in public, read them in private, and meditate therein. At every opportunity be a partaker of the Lord's Supper. "Do this in remembrance of him," and he will meet you at his own table. Let your conversation be with the children of God, and see that it "be in grace, seasoned with salt." As ye have time, do good unto all [humanity], to their souls and to their bodies. And herein "be ye steadfast, unmovable, always abounding in the work of the Lord."[53]

This process of living faithful lives until we have faith is reminiscent of an incident in Wesley's own life when he was in total despair and

about to stop preaching because he felt such a lack of faith. Peter Böhler counseled, "Preach faith *till* you have it, and then, *because* you have it, you *will* preach faith."[54] Like Wesley, we begin to work out our own salvation by living in personal and social holiness, loving God and neighbor, *until* we have experienced assurance of our salvation. After justification, we continue to live in holiness *because* we have received God's grace.

All Persons Can Know They Are Saved

With repentance of sin and acceptance of God's grace comes justification and assurance, another important theme of John Wesley's theology. Wesley believed that through the witness of the Spirit we know and feel God's forgiveness and know and feel that we are saved.

> Salvation is carried on by "convincing grace," usually in Scripture termed "repentance," which brings a larger measure of self-knowledge, and a farther deliverance from the heart of stone. Afterwards we experience the proper Christian salvation, whereby "through grace" we "are saved by faith," consisting of those two grand branches, justification and sanctification. By justification we are saved from the guilt of sin, and restored to the favour of God.[55]

Justification brings a fundamental change in our lives as we are adopted as God's children and born anew. Now salvation is evident through the way we live our lives.

Normally, assurance comes with being "restored to the favour of God," and the journey of faith continues. The justified leave a life of sinfulness behind and are reborn into a life of righteousness. However, John Wesley was realistic enough to know that humans would falter in this journey. English scholar Rupert Davies described Wesley's view: "The justified person does not commit outward voluntary sin, but inward sin continues, and sanctification refers to its gradual conquest; the seeds of anger, lust, and pride are as powerful as those of any weed, though they do not involve guilt in themselves."[56] A perfecting process by the Holy Spirit is all that saves us from this ongoing encounter with sin.

The idea of Christian perfection was probably the most troubling for John Wesley's contemporaries. What is meant by this doctrine is

that it is possible for us to continue growing toward Christlikeness in our living and in our relationships with the Holy Spirit's help. Christian perfection, or perfect love, means that "one who has reached perfection loves God with the whole self, and the neighbor as self."[57] But even one who has reached perfection continues to grow in grace and will never be as perfect as Christ was. In response to a criticism of this doctrine, Wesley replied, "We willingly allow, and continually declare, there is no *such* perfection in this life as implies either a dispensation from doing good and attending all the ordinances of God; or a freedom from ignorance, mistake, temptation, and a thousand infirmities necessarily connected with flesh and blood."[58] While we can never escape our humanity, our love of God and neighbor will continue to be perfected by the Holy Spirit on the way of salvation.

All Persons Can Be Saved to the Uttermost

What John Wesley meant by being saved to the uttermost is that we grow into holiness by the refining work of the Holy Spirit in us. This process of sanctification begins at justification:

> By sanctification we are saved from the power and root of sin, and restored to the image of God. All experience, as well as Scripture, shows this salvation to be both instantaneous and gradual. It begins the moment we are justified, in the holy, humble, gentle, patient love of God and [humanity]. It gradually increases from that moment, as a "grain of mustard seed, which at first is the least of all seeds, but" gradually "puts forth large branches," and becomes a great tree; till in another instant the heart is cleansed from all sin, and filled with pure love to God and [humanity]. But even that love increases more and more, till we "grow up in all things into him that is our head," till we attain the measure of the stature of the fullness of Christ.[59]

Sanctification is the result of the Holy Spirit's refining fire or perfecting grace that is available to those who embark on the journey of loving God and loving neighbor.

WESLEY'S THEOLOGY AND FAITH FORMATION

The aim of Christian faith formation is to cultivate a living faith that comes from an experience of God's grace through the atoning

work of Jesus Christ and the perfecting work of the Holy Spirit—justification and sanctification. In exploring the contours of John Wesley's faith journey, we see thematic emphases emerging. The themes of Wesley's theology reflected in the Way of Salvation are particularly illuminating for those who are concerned with formation for holiness of heart and life. First Wesley proclaimed that our salvation comes from God. The idea that all persons have access to God's grace directly through Jesus Christ means that all persons are offered the Way of Salvation. Davies stated it most powerfully: "Salvation is due entirely to God's gracious, unbounded, undiscriminating, and undeserved love, which is absolutely free to all, without exception."[60] To exclude *anyone* from the opportunity to experience God's grace within the life of the faith community is not consistent with Wesleyan theology. Therefore, a Wesleyan ecology of faith formation must take all of the God-given diversity in our midst into account.

Second, the Way of Salvation calls us to a holy life. John Wesley's understanding of God's grace indwelling all persons and his conviction that each Christian is called to personal and social holiness provides a theological foundation for formation of holiness of heart and life. John Wesley believed that salvation was the result of what God has done **for us** in Jesus Christ and **in us** through the work of the Holy Spirit. Prevenient grace is God acting in us through the Holy Spirit so that we may respond to the love of God by loving our neighbor. The choices we make about our response to what God has done form our part in our own salvation. And whatever transformation happens in our faith must be evident in practice. Loving God and loving neighbor is our call to Christian discipleship. This combination of personal holiness through works of piety and social holiness through works of mercy provides a basic framework for faith formation in the faith community.

Finally, John Wesley believed that salvation is grounded in God's transforming grace. It is this grace that provides a way of salvation so that persons may come to a new relationship wih God. Much is to be learned about faith formation through the examples of others. John Wesley's own journey in faith is critically important to understanding formation for holiness of heart and life because it provides some clues about the elements of faith formation, including relationships, structures, and practices.

But John Wesley's theology also raises a question for us as we consider what is needed for Christian faith formation in our time: If we agree with Wesley's belief that God provides the Way of Salvation, then what is the church's role in this process? With Wesley's strong emphasis on God's action on our behalf, how do we define our role in faith formation and transformation for holiness of heart and life? What is it that God does? What can we do as educators and leaders in the church to nurture this process of growing in faith? We begin to find clues to answer these questions as we turn to consider the context for a Wesleyan ecology of faith formation—the community of faith.

Chapter 3

COMMUNITY AND COMMUNION

Vision and Context of Formation for Holiness of Heart and Life[1]

In the Wesleyan tradition, a living faith is a gift from God and requires cultivation and nurture in a community of faith. In this chapter, we explore communion with God and each other as the vision and the faith community as the context of formation for holiness of heart and life. Christian educators have long recognized the importance of the church as the context for Christian faith formation. However, I will argue that the Wesleys' notion of "communion in community" brings important biblical, theological, and educational vision to the enterprise. John Wesley's emphasis on communion with God through a relational and repentant faith provides a needed counterbalance to contemporary preoccupation with individualism and autonomy. Three sermons on the "Sermon on the Mount" and Wesley's *Explanatory Notes Upon the New Testament* reveal a vision of

life in communion, as well as expectations of growth in communion, on the Way of Salvation. Charles Wesley's hymns are used for illumination in this discussion because they were instrumental for teaching Wesleyan theology in the Methodist movement and contributed to the development of communion, particularly since they were to be sung in community. As Geoffrey Wainwright from Duke University wrote, "The blending of voices may express and strengthen the bonds of affection within the 'community of love.'"[2] We begin by examining the Wesleys' understanding of communion in the words of Charles Wesley.

COMMUNION

1 Father, Son, and Spirit, hear
Faith's effectual, fervent prayer!
Hear, and our petitions seal;
Let us now the answer feel.

2 Still our fellowship increase,
Knit us in the bond of peace,
Join our new-born spirits, join
Each to each, and all to thine!

3 Build us in one body up,
Called in one high calling's hope:
One the Spirit whom we claim
One the pure, baptismal flame;

4 One the faith and common
Lord,
One the Father lives adored,
Over, through, and in us all,
God incomprehensible.

5 **One with God**, the source of bliss,
Ground of our communion this;
Life of all that live below,
Let thine emanations flow![3]

This Charles Wesley hymn conveys the meaning of faith in God in Three Persons and the hope that through this faith we will become "one with God" as the "ground of our communion." The use of the words "person" and "communion" are critically important here. As John Zizioulas, a Greek Orthodox scholar, claimed: "The significance of the person rests in the fact that [a person] represents two things simultaneously which are at first sight in contradiction: particularity and communion. . . . A person cannot be imagined in [herself or] himself but only within [her or] his relationships."[4]

John Wesley used the term "Persons" for the Trinity precisely

because it reflected this understanding. The Persons of the Trinity are known through their relationships with each other and with us. According to Randy Maddox, "Wesley's major reason for emphasizing the distinct 'personhood' of each [Person] of the Godhead would appear to be preservation of the *relational* character of our experience of Divine grace in all its dimensions."[5] However, John Wesley repeatedly affirmed that the three Divine "Persons" are also one. "It remains, that *these three are one*. They are one in essence, in knowledge, in will, and in their testimony."[6]

The word "communion," in Latin *communio,* means a fellowship of one with another; further definitions include "mutual participation," "interchange of ideas and feelings," and "sympathetic companionship."[7] In other words, communion is a deep mutual sharing in the life of another, or as Zizioulas described it, "a fundamental interdependence."[8] And Robert O'Gorman described communion as the "bonding of separate identities into a web."[9] Through the bonding and mutual sharing of communion, we experience the fullness of community with God, with each other, and with creation.

The Wesleys' understanding of our relationship with the Three-One God unites the meanings of "person" and "communion." To be in relationship with God and each other as a condition of personhood raises the possibility of communion. God in Godself is communion. Zizioulas illustrated this point from the church's tradition: "Instead of speaking of the unity of God in terms of His [sic] one nature, [Basil] prefers to speak of it in terms of the *communion of persons*: communion is for Basil an ontological category. The *nature* of God is communion."[10] Indeed, John Wesley believed that nothing in creation is separate from God: "all that is therein as contained by God in the hollow of [God's] hand, who by [God's] intimate presence holds them all in being, who pervades and actuates the whole created frame, and is in a true sense the soul of the universe."[11] In other words, God seeks communion with humanity and calls humans to live in communion with each other and the world.

COMMUNION *OF* THE TRINITY: SOURCE OF GRACE

The communion of God in Three Persons is clearly central to John Wesley's theology: the Trinity "enters into the very heart of Christianity; it lies at the root of all vital religion."[12] John Wesley's

57

belief in the unity of the Trinity is captured in Charles Wesley's hymn paraphrasing part of the Athanasian Creed:

7 The Father is both God and Lord;
   Both God and Lord is Christ
     the Son;
   The Holy Ghost, the glorious
     Third,
   Both God and Lord his people
     own.

8 Both God and Lord, who
    him believe,
   Each Person by himself we
    name:
   Yet not three Gods or Lords
    receive,
   But One essentially the same.[13]

These words emphasize what the Wesleys believed—God is One. In a letter to Mary Bishop, John Wesley wrote, "With regard to the Trinity, . . . what am I required to believe? Not the *manner* wherein the mystery lies. This is not the object of my faith; but the plain *matter of fact*, 'These Three are One.' "[14] Wesley was not as concerned with how the Persons of the Trinity are related. He was more concerned with the fact of the Trinity and the communion of the three Persons as the source of grace. Commenting on "The Lord our God is one Lord" (Mark 12:29), Wesley wrote, "This is the foundation of the first commandment. . . . The Lord our God, the Lord, the God of all . . . is one God, essentially, though three persons. From this unity of God it follows, that we owe all our love to [God] alone."[15] For Wesley, the emphasis is always on God's action and our dependence on God's grace.

While recognizing the oneness of the Godhead, John Wesley did distinguish each of the Persons of the Trinity by what Maddox called "their most defining work: creation/providence, redemption, and sanctification."[16] Each Person in the communion of the Trinity participates in our salvation. As Geoffrey Wainwright stated, "Our salvation is for Wesley the differentiated but united work of Three Persons of the Godhead; it sets us into an appropriate relation to each Person, and **it gives us a share in their divine communion.**"[17]

The Creator-God's distinctive work is "Creator/Sustainer" of creation, "Provider" of care for humanity and all of creation, "Governor/Judge" as ruler of creation, and "Physician" in healing and restoring creation.[18] According to Maddox, John Wesley valued Physician and Provider most;[19] God is personal—a loving "Father,"[20] the giver of grace. This loving Creator-God is the source of prevenient grace, the Person who cares for creation and offers salvation to

58

us. Wesley deeply believed in this relational interaction between the gift of grace that is available to all and human responsibility to respond to that gift.

While Creator-God is the source of grace, **Christ's distinctive work** in the communion of the Trinity is what Maddox called the "pardoning Initiative of God's *responsible grace*."[21] In justification, Christ overcomes our sin and provides the way for renewed relationship with God. John Wesley wrote that justification is "what God *does for us* through his Son."[22] The life, death, and resurrection of Jesus Christ provide evidence of God's love for humanity, and it is only through Christ's work of love that our sinfulness is overcome and we are restored to communion with God.

In the communion of the Trinity, the **distinctive work of the Holy Spirit** is to sustain and perfect our growth in holiness as "empowering Presence" and "inspiring Physician."[23] God is at work in human life through the empowering presence of the Holy Spirit to raise awareness of our sinfulness and need for repentance, and the Holy Spirit effects our sanctification—growing in holiness, in love of God and neighbor. According to Wesley, sanctification is what God *"works in us* by his Spirit."[24] But John Wesley was clear that God would not force humans to respond: "the God of love is willing to save all the souls that [God] has made. . . . But [God] will not force them to accept of it. . . . Choose holiness by my grace, which is the way, the only way, to everlasting life."[25] We grow in holiness through the power of the Holy Spirit as Inspiring Physician working in us. With the enabling work of the Holy Spirit, we respond to God's grace by loving God and our neighbor.

Each and every one of us is invited to participate in the communion of the Three Persons of the Godhead through the prevenient grace of Creator-God, the mediation of Jesus Christ, and the empowering presence of the Holy Spirit. Through the interaction of God's grace-full action and our faithful response, God transforms us for a holy life in communion with God and our neighbor. Not only will we experience new life and communion with the Three-One God through salvation, but we are also called to be "Transcripts of the Trinity"[26]—an embodiment or living representative of this communion in our relationship with others. In the words of Charles Wesley:

You, whom he ordained to be
Transcripts of the Trinity;
You, whom he in life doth hold,
You, for whom himself was sold,
You, on whom he still doth wait,
Whom he would again create;
Made by him, and purchased, why,
Why will you for ever die?[27]

COMMUNION *WITH* THE TRINITY: SALVATION

John Wesley believed that salvation is possible for any and every person. The work of the three Persons of the Trinity provides the grace needed for salvation through the providence of Creator-God, the mediation of Jesus Christ, and the active presence of the Holy Spirit. In the words of Charles Wesley:

3 Soon as our pardoned hearts
     believe
  That thou art pure, essential love,
The proof we in ourselves receive
  Of the Three Witnesses above;
Sure as the saints around thy
  throne
That Father, Word, and Spirit are
  one

4 O that we now, in love
     renewed,
  Might blameless in thy
    sight appear;
Wake we in thy similitude,
  **Stamped with the Triune
    character;**
Flesh, spirit, soul, to thee resign,
And live and die entirely
    thine![28]

Salvation and growing in communion with God involve a gradual, but "not automatic,"[29] process of building relationship and participating in the divine character. In April 1777, John Wesley wrote to a Miss March, who evidently was concerned that her primary relationship was with the Holy Spirit rather than with the Trinity. Wesley indicated that he had a description of an experience similar to hers from Charles Perronet. "He too was led at first to Jesus the Mediator, and seemed in a manner to have no concern with the Father and the Holy Ghost. Afterwards he had communion with the Father, next with the Spirit, and then with the whole Trinity. You therefore are afraid where no fear is. Our Lord is not displeased at your following [God's] Spirit."[30] From this example, we can see that growing in com-

munion with the Trinity is a process that happens over time, and it may be experienced differently by each person. Maddox creatively described this process of salvation as "a *dance* in which God always takes the first step but we must participate responsively, lest the dance stumble or end."[31]

In the previous chapter, we learned that the Way of Salvation begins with the Creator-God's work of preventing grace, which raises awareness of our sinfulness and calls us to repent, and justifying grace, which brings forgiveness of sin and redemption through the mediation of Jesus Christ. Faith continues to grow through sanctifying grace and a transformation of heart and life by the perfecting work of the Holy Spirit. Finally, faith is fulfilled in the consummation of grace. John Wesley described this movement as a series of stages or steps: pardon or forgiveness, holiness or grace, and heaven or glory.[32] According to Henry Rack, author of *Reasonable Enthusiast*, "Wesley thought psychologically: there are degrees of faith in progression from justification to the indwelling of the Holy Spirit."[33] Ultimately, faithful human response to God's salvific activity in the interaction of the "dance" is necessary for the Way of Salvation to continue.

Drawing on John Wesley's understanding that salvation involves transforming religious experience and a progression of growth in relation to God, I contend that, for Wesley, **communion is both a means and an end of the Way of Salvation**. In other words, the Way of Salvation may be described from the perspective of growing communion with the Three-One God and with our neighbor. I am proposing that it is consistent with Wesley's theology to talk of Christian faith formation in terms of three phases: "invitation to communion," "deepening communion," and "full communion."[34] The danger in this proposal is that the reader will assume these formational phases are three fixed stages, rather than a paradigm for an unfolding relationship with the Three-One God and our neighbor that develops in "fits and starts" over time. But I am convinced that this interpretation of the Way of Salvation provides a framework for creating a Wesleyan ecology of formation for holiness of heart and life. Growth in faith begins with an **invitation to communion** through the Creator-God's prevenient grace. Repentance and pardon through the justifying grace of Jesus Christ initiates a **deepening communion** with the Three-One God through the perfecting work of the Holy Spirit, until **full communion** with God is

reached in glory. So let us turn to the Way of Salvation once more to look for John Wesley's language of communion as he describes God's work in our growth in faith.

Invitation to Communion

According to John Wesley, the Beatitudes provide the scriptural grounding for the Way of Salvation and also give evidence of growing communion with God. "The Son of God, who came from heaven, is here **showing us the way to heaven,** to the place which he hath prepared for us, the glory he had before the world began. He is teaching us the true way to life everlasting, the royal way which leads to the kingdom."[35] The Beatitudes show us the Way of Salvation step by step. In Wesley's words, "And accordingly he here pronounces eight blessings together, annexing them to so many **steps in Christianity.**"[36] For us, a blessing usually indicates approval or favor.[37] But in the biblical tradition, a blessing is a statement that changes the life of the hearer. In his book *Genesis,* Walter Brueggemann described a blessing from God as the power of the spoken word to shape human lives. A blessing from God is a bestowal of divine favor initiating a special vocation.[38] The recipient of a blessing is a person or a community called by God. But a biblical blessing is never private. It shapes the vocation of a people. Once a blessing is given, it is passed on to future generations and thus binds families or communities together across the centuries. The blessings of the Beatitudes bind us together as Christians and guide our growing communion with God.

In John Wesley's interpretation, the first three Beatitudes (Matt. 5:3-5) describe a Creator-God who removes barriers to faith during the early portion of the Christian faith journey. The Creator-God's **invitation to communion** leads to a renewed relationship with God. In the second part of his sermon "Upon Our Lord's Sermon on the Mount," Wesley wrote:

> Our Lord has hitherto been more immediately employed in removing the hindrances of true religion: such is pride, the first, grand hindrance of all religion, which is taken away by "poverty of spirit"; levity and thoughtlessness, which prevent any religion from taking root in the soul till they are removed by holy *mourning*; such are anger, impatience, discontent, which are all healed by Christian *meekness.*[39]

In the Way of Salvation, according to Wesley, "real Christianity always begins in poverty of spirit, and goes on in the order here set down till the 'man [or woman] of God' is made 'perfect.' "[40] Poverty of the spirit (Matt. 5:3) is a "disposition of heart"[41] of those who have been convinced of their sin by the work of the Holy Spirit. God's promise for those who live under God's rule in poverty of spirit is the communion of the kingdom of heaven—God **within** us. "And what is righteousness but the life of God in the soul, the mind which was in Christ Jesus, the image of God stamped upon the heart, now renewed after the likeness of [the One] that created it?"[42]

John Wesley was aware that even those who are convinced of their sin and grow in grace through God's prevenient grace continue to need God's grace. Mourners (Matt. 5:4) have repented, but now mourn for their own sins and the sins of others[43] because they increasingly "see temptation and sin—which they fondly supposed were gone never to return—arising again."[44] God's promise for those who mourn is that Christ the King and the Holy Spirit as Physician will bring comfort and healing "in this world, and eternally in heaven."[45] So Wesley proclaimed, "This 'full assurance of faith' swallows up all doubt, as well as all tormenting fear, God now giving them a sure hope of an enduring substance and 'strong consolation through grace.' "[46]

John Wesley's understanding of meekness (Matt. 5:5) is also consistent with a relational and experiential faith. In relation to God, meekness is "a calm acquiescence in whatever is [God's] will concerning us"; in relation to neighbor, it is "mildness to the good and gentleness to the evil."[47] The meek seek to live in love of God and neighbor. God's promise is that the meek will inherit the earth, being content with all that God has given them: "It pleases them because it pleases God; so that while their heart, their desire, their joy is in heaven, they may truly be said to 'inherit the earth.' "[48] Those who are content in this life "shall hereafter *possess* the new earth."[49] In other words, the heart of Jesus' message for beginning the faith journey is that humans must know themselves to be totally dependent on God's grace to break down barriers to communion with God and to forgive their sin.[50]

Deepening Communion

The next phase of the Christian journey described in the Beatitudes addresses the Holy Spirit's perfecting work in those who have been

63

justified and are growing in **deepening communion** with God. John Wesley believed that **hunger and thirst for righteousness** (Matt. 5:6) "is the strongest of all our spiritual appetites."[51] In other words, we long for communion with God: "The being 'joined unto the Lord in one Spirit'; the **having 'fellowship** with the Father and the Son' . . . this is the religion, the righteousness [a person] thirsts after. Nor can he [or she] rest till he [or she] thus rests in God."[52] God promises to satisfy this hunger and thirst with the gift of righteousness and holiness. But John Wesley also noted that the righteous continue to thirst "for more and more of the water of life. This thirst shall endure for ever."[53] Wesley also emphasized that even those who have reached true holiness are still being perfected by the Spirit: "It plainly follows, that though a [person] were pure, even as Christ was pure, still [that person] would have room to increase in holiness, and in consequence thereof to increase in the favour, as well as in the love of God."[54]

Once those who hunger and thirst for righteousness are filled, their attention turns toward others—to loving their neighbors (Matt. 5:7). "And the more they are filled with the life of God, the more tenderly will they be concerned for those who are still without God in the world. . . . 'The **merciful**,' in the full sense of the term, are they who 'love their neighbours as themselves.' "[55] Those who have God's assurance of their salvation are able to trust God and care for others in love receiving not only "the blessing of God upon all their ways . . . but likewise . . . an 'exceeding and eternal weight of glory' in the 'kingdom prepared for them from the beginning of the world.' "[56]

Full Communion

The final group of Beatitudes addresses how those who are sanctified continue to grow toward full communion with God and their neighbor. John Wesley's introduction to his third sermon on the Sermon on the Mount illustrates the need for ongoing self-assessment: "But it is that love of our neighbour which springs from the love of God; otherwise itself is nothing worth. It behoves us therefore to examine well upon what foundation our love of our neighbour stands: whether it is really built upon the love of God; whether 'we' do 'love [God] because [God] first loved us'; whether we are 'pure in heart.' "[57] John Wesley then summarized the Way of Salvation as he described the **pure in heart** (Matt. 5:8) who have been sanctified and

"purified from pride by the deepest poverty of spirit . . . so that now they love the Lord their God with all their heart, and with all their soul, and mind, and strength."[58] The power of God's grace has removed hindrances to the faith; a change of heart is evident in the willingness to give oneself totally to God. Now the promise of communion with the Three-One God is given to those who love God wholeheartedly. God "will bless them with the clearest communications of [God's] Spirit, the **most intimate 'fellowship** with the Father and with the Son.' . . . They see [God], as it were, face to face, and 'talk with [God] as a [person] talking with [a] friend.' "[59]

For John Wesley the **peacemakers** (Matt. 5:9) love God and neighbor and "utterly detest and abhor all strife and debate . . . forbearing one another in love; endeavouring to keep the unity of the Spirit in the bond of peace."[60] God's promise for the peacemakers is that they will know an even deeper degree of communion, as they are adopted as children of God: "God shall continue unto them the Spirit of adoption, yea, shall pour it more abundantly into their hearts. [God] shall bless them with all the blessings of [God's] children."[61]

The Way of Salvation will not always be easy, as seen in the final two Beatitudes (Matt. 5:10-11) that address those who are persecuted for their faith. Wesley indicated that the faithful are to avoid bringing persecution on themselves, but in the face of persecution, he counseled, " 'Love your enemies.' . . . 'Bless them that curse you.' . . . 'Do good to them that hate you.' . . . If you can do nothing more, at least 'pray for them that despitefully use you and persecute you.' "[62] But the promise of full communion sustains the journey. John Wesley described **full communion** with God in the conclusion of his sermon on "The New Creation": "And to crown all, there will be a deep, an intimate, an **uninterrupted union** with God; a **constant communion** with the Father and his Son Jesus Christ, through the Spirit; a continual enjoyment of the Three-One God, and of all the creatures in [God]!"[63]

The Beatitudes teach us that our Christian vocation is to love God and our neighbor. John Wesley concluded "The Character of a Methodist" with a powerful call to this vocation:

> Let us "strive together for the faith of the gospel"; "walking worthy of the vocation wherewith we are called, with all lowliness and meekness, with long-suffering, forbearing one another in love, endeavouring to keep the unity of the Spirit in the bond of peace"; remembering,

"there is one body and one Spirit, even as we are called with one hope of our calling; one Lord, one faith, one baptism; one God and Father of all, who is above all, and through all, and in you all!"[64]

This statement rehearses the message of the Beatitudes as they depict growing communion with the Three-One God and with our neighbors, providing a scriptural guide for faith formation on the Way of Salvation. As John Wesley stated in the closing of his sermon, "This is the *spirit* of religion; the quintessence of it. These are indeed the *fundamentals* of Christianity. O that we may not be hearers of it only! . . . Let us not rest until every line thereof is **transcribed into our own hearts.**"[65]

FORMATION IN COMMUNION: THE CHURCH

We have learned that God intends for us to live in communion with God and our neighbors, and the Three-One God provides the means for this deepening communion through the Way of Salvation. The implications of John Wesley's theological position for the church as a community of formation are central to our consideration of a Wesleyan ecology of faith formation. How does the church participate in the process of salvation and growing communion with the Three-One God? One answer comes in the words of Charles Wesley:

1 How good and pleasant
    'tis to see
When brethren cordially agree,
    And kindly think and speak
    the same!
A family of faith and love,
Combined to seek the things above
    And spread the common
    Saviour's fame!
The God of Grace, who all invites,
Who in our unity delights
    Vouchsafes our intercourse
    to bless,
Revives us with refreshing showers,
The fullness of his blessing pours,
And keeps our minds in perfect
    peace.

2 Jesu, thou precious
    corner-stone,
Preserve inseparably one
    Whom thou dost by the
    Spirit join;
Still let us in thy Spirit live,
And to thy Church the
    pattern give
Of unanimity divine.
Still let us to each other cleave
And from thy plenitude
    receive
    Constant supplies of
    hallowing grace;
Till to a perfect man we rise,
O'ertake our kindred in the
skies,
    And find prepared our
    heavenly place.[66]

In this hymn, Charles Wesley described the perfecting work of the Holy Spirit as members of the community grow in communion with the Three-One God. The phrases in bold demonstrate the Way of Salvation as God's invitation to **communion, deepening communion** through a holy life, and **full communion** with God.

John Wesley also indicated in his work that the church as a community must be involved in the whole process of salvation when he commented on Matthew 4:17, "Repent, for the kingdom of heaven is at hand." In Wesley's words, "That phrase is not only used with regard to individuals in whom it is to be established, but also with regard to the Christian Church, the whole body of believers."[67] In other words, the church community grows in holiness as its members grow in holiness through God's invitation to communion—repentance and pardon; deepening communion—growth in love of God and neighbor; and full communion—adoption as children of God. In his discussion of the church, Howard Snyder cites noted Wesleyan scholar Albert Outler: "The holiness of the church is grounded in the discipline of grace which guides and matures the Christian life from its threshold in justifying faith to its [fullness] in sanctification."[68] And in his sermon "Of the Church," John Wesley addressed the community's growth in the holy life by calling up images from the Beatitudes such as walking " 'with all lowliness' . . . 'clothed with humility,' . . . 'with all meekness,' . . . with all long-suffering, [and] 'forbearing one another in love.' "[69] These images reveal Wesley's belief that the church as a community is growing in communion with God at the same time it is nurturing growth in communion with God in individuals. As teacher and writer Howard Snyder asserted, the "dialectic between the fallenness of the church and the renewing work of the Spirit was basic to Wesley's outlook."[70] It is only with the renewing work of the Spirit that the church itself is able to participate in the faith formation of its members.

Seeing growth in holiness as increase in loving God and neighbor, John Wesley "insisted that the church must be holy in the fuller sense of nurturing—and expecting—the progressive holiness of each of its members."[71] The church anticipates full communion with God and lives in communion to nurture and sustain its members' growth in love of God and neighbor. In this way, the church participates in the inauguration of God's kingdom on earth. Snyder noted that Wesley worked toward a church that was a "more authentically visible

manifestation of the church as the community of God's people, the eschatological community which was to be the agent *now* of the coming Kingdom of God."[72] In John Wesley's understanding, the Way of Salvation begins on earth and is completed in heaven.[73]

As an agent of the coming reign of God, the church must pattern its life after the communion of the Trinity through relationships, structures, and practices[74] for instruction and nurture in the faith, while the Holy Spirit empowers the perfecting and renewing work of character formation and moral transformation.[75] The outcome of this process was described by John Wesley in "The Character of a Methodist": "And 'having the mind that was in Christ' he [or she] 'so walks as' Christ 'also walked.' "[76] Transformation of heart and life radically alters a person's self-understanding in light of a deepening relationship with God *(Christian identity)* and growth in holiness as a way of life *(Christian vocation)*.

Figure 1 begins to construct a Wesleyan ecology of faith formation for holiness of heart and life. It depicts a linear representation of growing in communion with God reflecting both scriptural and theological foundations. Any attempt to diagram these dynamic relationships is limited, since reality is never as neat or precise as a diagram, so this linear model only begins to give us a way to think about the grounding for a Wesleyan ecology of faith formation. However, in spite of the risk of misunderstanding, I offer this diagram of the process of faith formation discussed in this chapter to help us "see" and understand the Wesleys' view of the Way of Salvation and some of the foundational elements of a Wesleyan ecology of faith formation.

This figure also represents my proposal that a Wesleyan ecology of faith formation can be built on the Wesleys' understanding of the Way of Salvation as growing in communion with God and neighbor through three phases: invitation to communion, deepening communion, and full communion with God. The biblical and theological grounding in the Beatitudes about the Way of Salvation and the work of God's preventing, justifying, and sanctifying grace is summarized. The church community itself, as the context for faith formation, is moving through these same phases as the community grows in communion with God, according to Wesley. While nurturing the faith journeys of its members, the church is to pattern its life after the communion of the Trinity and continue to grow in communion with God and neighbor.

FIGURE 1
A WESLEYAN ECOLOGY OF FAITH FORMATION
VISION AND CONTEXT

INVITATION TO COMMUNION	DEEPENING COMMUNION	FULL COMMUNION
Preventing and Justifying Grace "The God of grace, who all invites."[77]	Sanctifying Grace "Still let us in thy Spirit live."	Glorification "Till to a perfect man we rise."
Vision: **Scriptural Foundation:** Matt. 5:3-5. Poverty of spirit, mourning, and meekness are evidence that God has removed barriers to faith so that humans might know themselves as totally dependent on God's grace and "become as little children." Love God and neighbor.	*Vision:* **Scriptural Foundation:** Matt. 5:6-7. Hunger and thirst for righteousness is filled by God so that we might love God and neighbor more fully. The merciful love their neighbors as themselves. Increase in love of God and neighbor.	*Vision:* **Scriptural Foundation:** Matt. 5:8-9. The pure in heart and the peace-makers love God with all their hearts and souls and minds and strength. God will adopt them as God's children. Fully love God and neighbor.
Theological Foundation: God as loving Parent is the giver of prevenient grace and invites us to repent of our sin. God's justifying grace overcomes barriers to communion through Christ's work in the atonement, and communion with God is restored.	**Theological Foundation:** The sanctifying grace of the perfecting work of the Holy Spirit empowers us to grow in love of God and neighbor.	**Theological Foundation:** Sanctification is participating in the Divine character and constant communion with the Three-One God.
Context: The Church Repentance of sin and anticipation of full communion with God. Life patterned after communion of the Trinity. Life together as curriculum for formation.	*Context: The Church* Renewing work of the Spirit to build community of faith. Life patterned after communion of the Trinity. Nurturing progressive growth in holiness.	*Context: The Church* Life in communion with God and neighbor. Life patterned after communion of the Trinity. Agent now of the coming Kingdom of God.
Christian / Christian **Identity Vocation**	**Christian - Christian** **Identity Vocation**	**Christian \ Christian** **Identity Vocation**

Some additional observations about this figure may be helpful. First, persons move through these phases in growing communion with God in a much less predictable manner than can be depicted here. John Wesley was quick to state that faith wavers and people fall away. But the direction of growth in faith is clear and the small groups in the Methodist movement supported growth in Christian identity and vocation. Growth in Christian identity is weighted in the beginning phase (signified by /), while more weight is placed on Christian vocation in the final phase (signified by \). Second, members of a faith community will represent all of these phases at any given time. As John Wesley observed, there are various degrees of faith and people grow in their own time as they are awakened by and respond to God's grace. And finally, each of the three persons of the Trinity is at work in each phase. For example, a redeeming relationship with Jesus Christ is available to us in the first phase, as is the work of the Holy Spirit, who brings awareness of our need to repent.

To say that Christian faith formation occurs through the process of living and growing in communion with God and practicing a holy life within Christian community is consistent with John Wesley's understanding of the Three-One Godhead and the Way of Salvation. As a result, our life together becomes the "curriculum"[78] of formation for holiness of heart and life. To paraphrase Peter Böhler's admonition to John Wesley, "You practice a holy life *till* you have it; and then, *because* you have it, you *will* practice a holy life."[79] What John Wesley called "practical divinity," instruction in knowledge requisite to salvation, becomes the church's task and focuses on love of God and neighbor.[80] Selected verses from a Charles Wesley hymn offer a glimpse of the church's calling:

> 1 Christ from whom all blessings flow,
>   Perfecting the saints below,
>   Hear us, who thy nature share,
>   Who thy mystic body are.

2 Join us, in one spirit join,
   Let us still receive of thine;
   Still for more on thee we call,
   Thee who fillest all in all!

3 Closer knit to thee our Head,
   Nourish us, O Christ, and feed!
   Let us daily growth receive,
   More and more in Jesus live.

5 Move, and actuate, and guide,
  Divers gifts to each divide;
  Placed according to thy will,
  Let us all our work fulfil.

7 Sweetly may we all agree,
  Touched with softest sympathy;
  Kindly for each other care,
  Every member feel its share.

8 Wounded by the grief of one,
  Now let all the members groan;
  Honoured if one member is,
  All partake the common bliss.

9 Many are we now, and one,
  We who Jesus have put on;
  There is neither bond nor free,
  Male nor female, Lord, in thee![81]

This description of life in communion is consistent with what Maddox identified as John Wesley's "characteristic informal definition of the church: the spiritual community of God's people."[82] Life in communion includes sharing sympathy, kindness, and grief with each other, as well as celebrating diverse gifts and freedom in God together.

As a result, the church is called to instruct persons in the faith and cultivate the "holy tempers" of "love, joy and peace" that motivate holy lives[83] to the end that each person grows in a deepening relationship with God and others. Practicing a holy life requires that a community of faith embody that same holy life in love of God and neighbor and provides relationships, structures, and practices through which others might be formed and transformed through the empowering work of the Holy Spirit.

As we continue to explore questions raised in this discussion and address the challenges to faith in our time, we share the Wesleys' vision of communion with God and others. Together we affirm that God is the source of grace, Jesus Christ is the initiator of God's pardoning grace, and the Holy Spirit is the empowering presence of God's perfecting grace. God's saving grace is available to all persons so that they might grow in communion with God as both a means and the end of the Way of Salvation. And formation for holiness of heart and life occurs in the process of growing in communion with God and other persons.

In light of this vision the church is called to pattern her life after the communion of the Trinity. We recognize that the community of faith is growing in communion with God and others at the same time it is called to nurture and sustain the growth of its members. The church participates in God's work of formation for holiness of heart and life

71

by living in communion with God and by providing relationships, structures, and practices for instruction and nurture in the faith. These affirmations lead us to turn now to consider the question of "what to teach" in a Wesleyan ecology of formation for holiness of heart and life—growing in communion with God and neighbor. And as we grow in communion with the Three-One God on our own journey of faith, we pray with Charles Wesley,

> 1 Into thy gracious hands I fall,
>   And with the arms of faith embrace!
> O King of glory, hear my call!
>   O raise me, heal me, by thy grace!
> Now righteous through thy wounds I am;
>   No condemnation now I dread;
> I taste salvation in thy name,
>   Alive in thee, my living head!

> 2 Still let thy wisdom be my guide,
>   Nor take thy light from me away;
> Still with me let thy grace abide,
>   That I from thee may never stray;
> Let thy word richly in me dwell;
>   Thy peace and love my portion be
> My joy t'endure and do thy will,
>   Till perfect I am found in thee.

> 3 Arm me with thy whole armour, Lord!
>   Support my weakness with they might;
> Gird on my thigh thy conqu'ring sword,
>   And shield me in the threatening fight:
> From faith to faith, from grace to grace,
>   So in thy strength shall I go on;
> Till heaven and earth flee from thy face,
>   And glory end what grace begun.[84]

Part II

FORMATION IN COMMUNION: THREE CRITICAL QUESTIONS

Faith formation was a critical issue for the early Methodists. It was so important that the first Methodist Conference in 1744 discussed "what to teach" and "how to teach" in order to shape the Methodists' life together. A third question addressed by the Wesleys was "who shall teach?" In Part 2, we explore these questions in light of the proposal that growing in faith means growing in communion with God and our neighbor and use them to help us build a Wesleyan ecology of faith formation.

Chapter 4	"What to Teach?" addresses the relationship of instruction in faith and nurturing a holy life as characteristic of living in communion with God and neighbor.
For Your Reflection:	How did you learn about beliefs and practices of faith in your church?

Chapter 5   "Who Shall Teach?" examines the question of teaching relationships, particularly qualities expected by the Wesleys and the settings for teaching.

For Your Reflection: Think of a teacher who significantly influenced your growth in faith. What qualities made this teacher special?

Chapter 6   "How to Teach?" explores the question of how structures for Christian faith formation were developed in the early Methodist movement.

For Your Reflection: How did your experiences at home, school, and church shape your growth in faith?

Chapter 7   "How to Teach?" discusses the question of the types of practices or methods of teaching used for faith formation in the early Methodist movement.

For Your Reflection: What Christian disciplines are most important for your growth in faith?

Chapter 4

"WHAT TO
TEACH?"

We have begun to construct a Wesleyan ecology of faith formation by establishing the Wesleys' biblical and theological understanding of the Way of Salvation, and I have proposed that salvation for the Wesleys means growing in communion with the Three-One God. As we examined the role of the church in light of this understanding, I argued that the church must tend to its own life in communion with God as a means of nurturing individual lives of faith. In the context of communion with God and each other, the Church's task is to nurture human response to God's initiative of grace through Jesus Christ—to make disciples.

In this chapter, we examine the question of "what to teach," particularly the interrelationship between theological exploration and practicing a holy life in faith formation through Christian instruction

and nurture. In the words of Gayle Felton, teaching for the Wesleys "was to be both a cognitive process of didactic learning and a formative process of spiritual nurturing."[1] Formation in faith involves **"instruction,"** teaching beliefs and practices of the faith. In the words of Presbyterian educator Sara Little, "Beliefs which engage the thinking powers of the person as they emerge out of and inform faith, sustained, reformed, and embodied by the faith community, can be an important factor in bringing integration and integrity to life."[2] The shared belief of the faith community shapes the way we live our individual lives and guides the way we do faith formation in community. On the other hand, our individual experiences of growing in faith impact the shared belief of the community and the way we do faith formation. In other words, practice mirrors belief and belief is shaped by practice.

Formation in faith also involves affective growth and requires **nurture** of a lifestyle as well as instruction. In examining "the organic character of family life" at the end of the nineteenth century, Horace Bushnell, a Congregational pastor, came to the conclusion that Christian nurture means "that the child is to grow up a Christian and never know himself [sic] as being otherwise."[3] Bushnell believed that it took the larger community, particularly parents and the church, to create an environment in which to form Christians—to pass on the beliefs, values, and practices of the Christian faith and life. This premise is true for all who would be disciples, regardless of age. Christian faith formation occurs in a faith community that helps us find meaning in our lives as we grow in communion with God, the created world, and our neighbor.

Theological questions generated in the intersections of our lives fuel the process of faith formation. Just as John Wesley searched for what he must do to be saved, we too search for answers to questions about the meaning of our lives. Theologian and educator Mary Elizabeth Mullino Moore has offered the metaphor of "intersection" to describe the way God meets us as we encounter others and ourselves in the midst of life experience in the world.[4] God at work in the intersections of life through the ongoing work of the Holy Spirit is a central theme in Wesleyan theology, so an image of God meeting humans in the intersections is an appropriate metaphor for our discussion of instruction in faith and nurturing a Christian life. Shared

Christian belief and spiritual practices are characteristic of living in communion.

We have already explored the Wesleys' assumptions about community and communion as the vision and context for faith formation. Now we will address the question of **what to teach**. As contemporary communities of faith seek ways to make disciples, the question of what to teach continues to be a topic of ongoing dialogue. If we are invited into communion with God and each other through God's prevenient grace, a Wesleyan ecology of faith formation must include instruction in the faith and nurture of a holy life. The intent of this discussion is to illustrate the interrelationship of belief and practice through a case study of conflict over doctrine and practice in the Fetter Lane Society. I do not intend to diminish the importance of nurturing a Christian lifestyle in formation for holiness of heart and life by focusing on a doctrinal dispute. In fact, arguments about belief were important for the Christian life. Methodists were to be thinking Christians because theological reflection contributes to a deeper life in faith. Guidance in theological reflection is one form of spiritual nurturing.

John Wesley noted in his *Journal* that for five days beginning Monday, June 25, 1744, the Methodists gathered in their first conference in London.[5] Henry Rack reported that "the matters to be discussed were said to be 'what to teach, how to teach and what to do, i.e. how to regulate our doctrine, discipline and practice.' "[6] The discussion began with doctrine, particularly "faith, justification, assurance, [and] sanctification."[7] Methodist studies scholar Thomas Langford defined doctrine as "the declaration of the collective understanding of the Church expressed in agreed-upon formulations such as creeds."[8] Coming to a shared understanding of belief involves interpretation of Scripture, knowledge of the historical tradition of the church, and reflection on God's work in the world through our own life experience. The commitment that the Methodists would continue as part of the Church of England informed discussions of doctrine in 1744.[9] The early Methodists clarified and affirmed shared beliefs that guided discussion about discipline, organization, group structure, and the role of leaders.

While people involved in the early Methodist movement participated in theological reflection that led to clarification of the

distinctive nature of Wesleyan theology, the Methodist movement was already deeply grounded in Scripture and traditional Christian formulations of doctrine, such as the creeds. John Wesley himself was formed in the Anglican tradition with tempering by a family heritage in the Puritan tradition, and these influences are reflected in what he taught. Martin Schmidt creatively summarized Wesley's inheritance:

> It brought together the heritage of Puritanism, Anglican churchmanship, and that concern for the care of souls, social activity and missionary zeal, derived from the revival of the Religious Societies. At the same time it drew its sustenance from Puritan culture of family life and from the nurture of individual souls found in Romanic mysticism. To this was joined the influence of the Halle type of pietism. Finally a place was given to liberal scholarship, and the harmonious, mystical piety of a Henry Scougal was held in high esteem. To all this was added Susanna Wesley's personal gift as a teacher. Although this was charismatic in the deepest sense of the word, it was nevertheless most methodically cultivated and practised. Through this rich polyphony one leading theme resounds like a *cantus firmus*: it is that of the love of God which empowers man [sic] towards perfection. It might almost be said that here, in the cradle, the main content of John Wesley's thought was already being proclaimed.[10]

Out of this background, John Wesley taught that Methodists shared much in common with all Christians, particularly the primacy of love of God and love of neighbor.[11] For Wesley, love of God and neighbor was both belief and practice. Yet, as Stephen Gunter observed, Wesley's reinterpretation of "common" doctrine was seen by many as "different doctrine."[12] In Wesley's thinking, the "givens" for developing theological discussion were, first, that Scripture is authoritative in the interpretation of Christian faith and life through tradition, experience, and reason. Second, the truth of Scripture is confirmed by human experience: "Experience is sufficient to *confirm* a doctrine which is grounded on Scripture."[13]

In order to understand the importance of the relationship between belief and practice for formation in communion, we will look at a particular example of faith formation in the early Methodist movement between 1739 and 1743. I will argue that when members of Methodist societies were exploring their faith and participating in the

theological disputes of their time along with their preachers and leaders, they contributed to the development of a shared understanding of Methodist belief. Yet the reverse is also true: the practice of a holy life was shaped by the Methodists' participation in the development of shared doctrinal understanding.

CONFLICT IN THE INTERSECTION

The Wesleys knew that doctrine is critically important for Christian faith formation because it is an interpretation of faith. The thesis of this chapter is that a process of gaining, clarifying, and extending Christian belief and practice included both instruction and nurture in eighteenth-century Methodism. In other words, shared belief and theological exploration are significant in shaping Christian practice from a Methodist perspective. While Christian formation is guided by doctrine, it is also influenced by culture, so we turn first to the formative elements of the eighteenth century that shaped the life and work of the Wesleys and the Methodist movement. In the interaction between Methodism and its particular social and historical context, shared belief and practice were formed. Recognizing that the variety and complexity of ingredients shaping the Methodist movement have been discussed in greater depth elsewhere,[14] a brief summary here notes some significant issues raised by events in the eighteenth century that impact the question of what to teach through instruction and nurture in faith formation.

Evangelical Renewal

The seventeenth and eighteenth centuries were marked by a worldwide evangelical revival in the church that preceded the Methodist movement in England. Richard Heitzenrater stated that these movements "were variously marked by strong preaching, evangelical conversions, and assorted manifestations of spiritual vitality, ranging from increased individual piety to enthusiastic group frenzy."[15] In the rationalistic environment of eighteenth-century England, it is not surprising that these spontaneous expressions of religious fervor would create frequent charges of "enthusiasm."

Methodists were part of this evangelical renewal. The Wesleyan emphasis that God's grace provides every person with a Way of Salvation through an invitation to communion with God and neigh-

79

bor generated interest and excitement about attending to the work of the Spirit. Methodist converts talked openly about their faith experiences and the practice of a Christian life, an uncommon and uncomfortable practice for their time.[16] Their claims of special inspiration and vocation given directly by God created both theological and ecclesiastical conflicts. Such spontaneous response to claiming God's direction for one's life sometimes led to excesses of presumption and behavior, in contrast to the careful spiritual propriety of the established church. As Stephen Gunter observed, "these people were considered clearly irrational."[17]

The evangelical revival also challenged commonly accepted structures for faith formation. Formational issues about how to teach converts the heritage and lifestyle of Christians needed to be addressed because spontaneous, emotional conversions prompted by revival preaching may not have been preceded by long preparation through catechetical study of faith, as would have been the case in the established church. In effect, the institution of the church was bypassed as the way to salvation. Gunter suggested that the evangelical revival challenged the idea that "salvation was very much in and through the church,"[18] raising the questions "What should the church teach under these circumstances?" and "How should the church teach under these circumstances?"

Theological Disputes

Theological disputes with the Church of England, the Calvinists, the Moravians, and those within the Methodist movement who were influenced by these positions led to increasing clarity about what to teach. The Wesleys' response to theological questions was foundational for instruction and nurture in the Methodist movement.

From the beginning, the Wesleys were committed to the Anglican tradition and saw the Methodist movement as renewal of the church. One critical theological discussion developed about the relationship between justification by faith and good works. Leaders in the Anglican Church leveled charges against the Wesleys and the Methodists that emphasis on the assurance of one's salvation through justification by faith "alone" tended to neglect good works.[19] John Wesley's response was that humans can do nothing to merit God's

saving grace, but human response to God's grace "must produce good works."[20] This belief was the impetus for the Wesleys' teaching about personal and social holiness—loving God by loving one's neighbor. Because the Wesleys intended for the Methodists to remain in the Anglican Church, they often argued their case with church leaders. Charles Wesley's *Journal* recorded several meetings with church authorities to explain their interpretation of belief and practice.[21]

A second theological dispute developed between the Wesleys and George Whitefield. Charles Wesley's *Journal* records that the Wesleys worked closely with George Whitefield in the early years of the Methodist movement. On December 26, 1739, Charles wrote, "George Whitefield preached. We had the sacrament this and the four following days. On Thursday my brother preached; on Friday, George Whitefield; and on Saturday, Mr. Robson."[22] Earlier in that same year, Whitefield was actively trying to get the Wesleys to develop their ministry in Oxford. Charles wrote that he "gave us so promising account of Oxford, that I found myself strongly inclined to go."[23] And Whitefield also became involved in one of the Fetter Lane conflicts according to Charles Wesley: "At Fetter-lane a dispute arose about lay-preaching. Many, particularly Bray and Fish, were very zealous for it. Mr. Whitefield and I declared against it."[24]

Later, a breach in the relationship resulted from growing theological differences. The Wesleys' dispute with George Whitefield, who represented the Calvinist point of view, centered on the issues of imputed righteousness and predestination. The Wesleys and Whitefield agreed on their view of human sinfulness and the need for God's grace,[25] but Whitefield and the Calvinists believed that "Christ's righteousness alone is imputed to us for our salvation and that we have no righteousness but Christ's."[26] As Richard Heitzenrater observed, John Wesley agreed that God's work **in Christ** is "the *cause* of our salvation," but Wesley was also moving toward the belief that God works **in us** so that we might have faith in Christ, "the required *condition* of our salvation."[27] Through God's work in Christ *and* in us, we are transformed and "*become* righteous (sanctified or holy),"[28] loving God with all our heart, soul, and mind, and our neighbor as ourselves. As a result, John Wesley believed Christian perfection or sanctification is possible in a person's lifetime through the work of the Holy Spirit.[29]

In contrast, George Whitefield believed that persons truly saved are always saved; the justified will persevere in the faith without backsliding.[30] John Wesley was convinced that God's grace is available to all and salvation is offered to all. But from his own experience, Wesley also knew that some that were justified fell from grace, so he concluded "there are degrees of faith in progression from justification to the indwelling of the Holy Spirit."[31] This view echoed Susanna Wesley's belief that, "A [person] must first be born and then pass through the several stages of infancy, childhood, and youth, before he [or she] attain to maturity. So Christians are first born of water and the spirit and then go through many degrees of grace . . . before they become strong Christians."[32]

A third theological conflict developed between John Wesley and the English Moravians, centering on the issue of "stillness," the conviction that Christ is the only means of grace. The English Moravians believed that Christians are to be still before God and refrain from "the means of grace," particularly the Lord's Supper, until they have "true" faith in Christ.[33] Wesley believed that participating in the Lord's Supper, Scripture study, and prayer strengthened one's growth in faith because God works in us through these means of grace. As we will see later in this chapter, conflict over belief and practice erupted in the Fetter Lane Society because of Moravian Philip Henry Molther's teaching about stillness. Gunter summed up the conflict: "Molther instructed his hearers to 'wait' until God made them holy; Wesley preached the 'pursuit of holiness.' "[34]

In contrast to waiting on God's action in passive dependence, the Wesleys believed the means of grace were spiritual practices in which Christ meets humans in their desire to escape from sin. In his response to the Moravians, Charles Wesley wrote, "I described the stillness of the first Christians (Acts ii.42;) who continued *in* the Apostles' doctrine, and *in* fellowship, and *in* breaking bread, and *in* prayers."[35] And John Wesley argued for "scriptural stillness"[36] and enumerated the means of grace:

> The way to attain faith is to *wait* for Christ and be *still*,
> In using "all the means of grace."
> Therefore I believe it right for [one] who knows [one] has not faith (i.e.,
> that conquering faith),
> To go to church;

To communicate;
To fast;
To use as much private prayer as [one] can, and
To read the Scripture;
(Because I believe there are "means of grace," i.e., do ordinarily convey
God's grace to unbelievers; and
That it is possible for [one] to *use* them, without *trusting* in them).[37]

In this point of view, the Lord's Supper becomes both a "confirming" and a "converting" means of grace.[38] Theologically, this led the Wesleys to conclude that faith formation meant Methodists were to practice a holy life in love of God and neighbor through participating in the means of grace while waiting upon God in faith for assurance of their salvation.

These theological discussions held critical importance for teaching belief and nurturing practice in formation for holiness of heart and life in the early Methodist movement. First, John Wesley's view that there are degrees of faith allowed for repeated chances to try again if persons fell from grace. Wesley's teaching about justification, assurance, and sanctification also provided impetus and motivation for further growth in faith, because persons could know they had been saved and others could see that they were growing in faith through their lifestyle. So formation for holiness of heart and life not only included preparation for receiving faith but also continued after justification so that persons might be sustained in their growth in faith through instruction and nurture in the faith community.

Second, John Wesley's teaching that the pursuit of holiness through holy living meant attending to the means of grace led to explicit instructions for a holy life. A person's relationship with God grows through inward holiness, so Wesley emphasized attending worship and participating in holy Eucharist in the Church of England as often as possible. In other words, Methodists heard the word proclaimed through preaching and experienced the word through the Eucharist as means of grace for a holy life. Methodists were to respond to this word of God's grace by participating in social holiness through works of mercy for their neighbors.

Third, practicing the attitudes, spiritual disciplines, and way of life of a Christian was taught and encouraged by the small groups to which Methodists belonged. Classes, in particular, focused on holy

living guided by the general rules: "doing no harm," "doing good," and "attending upon all the ordinances of God."[39] One of the fruits of the class system was weekly class sessions when each member answered questions of self-reflection that ultimately taught Methodists the language of faith—how to talk about their faith and, more important, how to share their religious experiences. So when theological disputes arose, it followed that lay members of the Methodist movement were encouraged to participate.

FAITH FORMATION IN THE INTERSECTION

In our brief examination of the social and historical context in which the Methodist movement developed, we have uncovered several questions related to what to teach in formation for holiness of heart and life. What kind of faith formation is needed for a rapidly increasing number of converts who have not been part of the established church? What kind of preparation is needed for preachers and leaders? What instruction and nurture are needed in a process of faith formation that prepares and sustains spiritual growth? How do we teach the unique biblical and theological understanding of the Wesleyan tradition and draw implications for living a holy life?

Wesley's commitment to the practice of discipline as a way to deepen spiritual life, the necessity of an experience of God's transforming grace, and the pursuit of a holy life shaped faith formation for holiness of heart and life. Gunter asserted that by 1735 these "essential components" of Methodism were in place: "the willingness to submit to discipline to attain spiritual vitality; the importance of an experiential knowledge of salvation; the conviction that the pursuit of holiness in its highest earthly form was indispensable; and the knowledge that all of these together, without the exception of any one, was the correct path."[40] It is clear that Wesley could not have come to such a conclusion or organized such a ministry if he had not first believed that because of God's grace, there is in each person a God-given bit of "inherent holiness" that can grow with nurture or be lost.[41] The emphasis here is clearly on religious experience and the practice of a holy life, but, as we shall see, shared practice is informed by shared belief.

An example of the kind of energy John and Charles Wesley were willing to devote to nurturing formation for holiness and heart and

life can be found in the case of the Fetter Lane Society.[42] The events surrounding Fetter Lane illustrate the claim of this book that theological exploration was significant for shaping belief and lifestyle at the same time it was leading Wesley to clarify his teaching about the distinctive nature of Methodist theology. I will argue that theological dispute and lack of shared belief in the Fetter Lane Society provide a window into the reasons why shared belief and practice of faith are inseparable.

The Case of the Fetter Lane Society

As a young man, John Wesley met the Hutton family through his brothers.[43] Later, Wesley became friends with James Hutton and his sister after John awakened them with his preaching. In January 1738, James wrote that with the help of Charles Wesley he had "opened shop" in his parents' home by inviting a group of Methodists to meet there.[44] When John Wesley was in London, he met with this group to "pray, sing, and read the Scriptures."[45] From correspondence during 1738, it is evident that John Wesley relied on Hutton, a bookseller, to assist him with the business of the Methodist movement, such as delivering important papers,[46] as well as sending hymn books, collections of prayers, and sermons for distribution.[47]

During the spring of 1738, John Wesley complained to Moravian Peter Böhler about the lack of organization in Hutton's group. As a result, Böhler invited a few people, including the Wesleys and Hutton, to join him in a band whose agenda was the "spiritual health" of its members.[48] This group soon became the Fetter Lane Society. In his journal on May 1, 1738, Wesley recorded the first three rules of the society:

> This evening our little society began, which afterwards met in Fetter Lane. Our fundamental rules were as follows:
> In obedience to the command of God by St. James, and by the advice of Peter Böhler, it was agreed by us—
> 1. That we will meet together once a week to "confess our faults one to another, and pray for one another that we may be healed."
> 2. That the persons so meeting be divided into several "bands," or little companies, none of them consisting of fewer than five or more than ten persons.
> 3. That everyone in order speak as freely, plainly, and concisely as

he can, the real state of his heart, with his several temptations and deliverances, since the last time of meeting.[49]

With the society's practices in place, Böhler left England and John Wesley became the primary consultant for James Hutton and the Fetter Lane Society, but the Moravian influence continued.

Regular correspondence between John Wesley and James Hutton during 1738 and 1739 includes descriptions of Wesley's work and a request for prayers, but his letters also reflect advice and counsel offered to Hutton concerning the structure and leadership of the society. Problems of doctrine had already surfaced at Fetter Lane early in 1739. In May, Wesley reminded Hutton: "You seem to forget what I told you: (1), that being unwilling to speak against predestination we appealed to God, and I was by lot commanded to preach and print against it. . . . Yet generally I speak on faith, remission of sins, and the gift of the Holy Ghost."[50]

When Moravian Philip Molther arrived in London in October 1739, the situation was ripe for further conflict around belief and practice. In the Wesleys' absence, Molther was persuasive in convincing members of the society to accept a doctrine of stillness, abstaining from the Lord's Supper until they were assured of faith. John Wesley attempted to counter Molther's view with his own interpretation of scriptural stillness. His description of a society meeting on November 7, 1739, provides a glimpse into the dispute: "At eight our society met at Fetter Lane. We sat an hour without speaking. The rest of the time was spent in dispute; one having proposed a question concerning the Lord's Supper, which many warmly affirmed 'none ought to receive till he [or she] had the full assurance of faith.' "[51]

By December, the level of conflict over what to teach within the society had increased. John Wesley returned to London upon receiving letters indicating that the society was in disarray. On December 19, 1739, he wrote: "I accordingly came to London, though with heavy heart. Here I found every day the dreadful effects of our brethren's reasonings, and disputing with each other. Scarce one in ten retained his first love, and most of the rest were in the utmost confusion, biting and devouring one another. I pray God ye be not consumed one of another!"[52] On the last day of December, John

Wesley "had a long and particular conversation" with Molther in an attempt to understand and to resolve differences about belief and practice. Wesley's *Journal* records his written account of their differences, as he understood them.[53] In the following days, John Wesley once again tried to unite the Society:

> Tuesday, January 1, 1740, I endeavoured to explain to our brethren the true, Christian, scriptural *stillness*, by largely unfolding those solemn words, "Be still, and know that I am God." Wed. 2. I earnestly besought them all to "stand in the old paths" and no longer to subvert one another's souls by idle controversies and strife of words. They all seemed convinced. We then cried to God to heal all our backslidings. And [God] sent forth such a spirit of peace and love as we had not known for many months before.[54]

But the peace was short lived.

In February 1740, John Wesley met with some members of the Fetter Lane Society who shared his concern, and by April a new society was formed with clear distinction from the Fetter Lane Society. The Foundery Society held "regular preaching services" and included a growing number of disaffected participants from the Fetter Lane Society.[55] In March, James Hutton wrote to John Wesley expressing concern for Wesley's spiritual well-being:

> How will you be amazed when you come to experience more than you do at present! I wish you well over the fiery trial. I love you, and I must speak all I have in my heart, and I hope you will not take it amiss.
>
> If you do desire indeed experienced labourers and helpers to assist you, our Saviour will find them for you. **But every soul who may have received some grace is not at once fit to be a labourer.**[56]

John Wesley's letter to James Hutton on April 12, 1740, clearly responds to the primary matter of contention: "I have little time, and much to write tonight. Dear Jemmy, suffer people to use the means of grace. If this caution is needless, I shall rejoice, for I am your loving brother."[57]

On April 25th, both John and Charles Wesley met with Philip Molther for two hours, during which Molther explicitly denied the validity of John Wesley's interpretation of degrees of faith and means

of grace.[58] Following the meeting, Charles Wesley sent his account of the conversation to a friend in Bristol:

> Many here insist that a part of their Christian calling is liberty *from* obeying, not liberty **to** obey. The unjustified, say they, are *to be still*; that is, not to search the Scriptures, not to pray, not to communicate, not to do good, not to endeavour, not to desire; for it is impossible to use means without trusting in them. Their practice is agreeable to their principles. Lazy and proud themselves, bitter and censorious toward others, they trample upon the ordinances, and despise the commands, of Christ. I see no middle point wherein we can meet.[59]

It was clear that the Wesleys had exhausted all of their ideas about reconciling the Fetter Lane Society and that a split was near.

The break with Hutton and the Fetter Lane Society began in May 1740, when a chapel was procured for their worship services and the leaders voted to ban Wesley from preaching in it.[60] John Wesley was close to giving up on June 11, according to comments in his journal: "In the evening I went to Fetter Lane and plainly told our poor, confused, shattered society wherein they had erred from the faith. It was as I feared. They could not receive my saying. However, I am clear from the blood of these men [and women]."[61] On July 20, Wesley went to a love feast at Fetter Lane, not speaking until the end, when he read his ultimatum reflecting his stand on what to teach:

> About nine months ago, certain of you began to speak contrary to the doctrine we had till then received. The sum of what you asserted is this:
> 1. That there is no such thing as *weak faith*; that there is no justifying faith where there is ever any doubt or fear, or where there is not, in the full, proper sense, a new, a clean heart.
> 2. That a [person] ought not to use those *ordinances* of God which our Church terms "means of grace," before he [or she] has such a faith as excludes all doubt and fear, and implies a new, a clean heart.
> 3. You have often affirmed that "to search the Scriptures," *to pray*, or *to communicate*, before we have this faith, is *to seek salvation by works*, and that till these works are laid aside no [one] can receive faith.
> I believe these assertions to be flatly contrary to the Word of God. I have warned you hereof again and again, and besought you to turn back to the law and the testimony. I have borne with you long, hoping you would return. But as I find you more and more confirmed in the

error of your ways, nothing now remains but that I should give you up to God. You that are of the same judgment, follow me.[62]

John Wesley left Fetter Lane that day with about eighteen or nineteen persons who were in sympathy with his point of view.[63] It was some time before Wesley finally gave up hope for reuniting with the Fetter Lane Society. On May 6, 1741, Wesley recorded a meeting for prayer about reunion with the Fetter Lane Society: "But it was clear to all, even those who were before the most eagerly desirous of it, that the time was not come."[64] The Wesleys attempted to hold a uniting conference in August 1743 to address tensions in the revival movement between the Methodists, the Moravians, and the predestinarians, but the attempt failed.[65]

The Case for Shared Christian Belief and Practice
The case of the Fetter Lane Society did not conclude in the way the Wesleys intended, particularly given John Wesley's vision for the church as communion with God and each other. In our discussion of full communion with God, we noted Wesley's emphasis on the peacemakers (Matt. 5:9) who love God and neighbor and "utterly detest and abhor all strife and debate . . . forbearing one another in love; endeavouring to keep the unity of the Spirit in the bond of peace."[66] Guided by this vision, both John and Charles Wesley attempted to bring peace and restore communion by resolving the theological differences at Fetter Lane, but they did not succeed.

However, Fetter Lane does provide a glimpse into what John Wesley envisioned as instruction and nurture for formation of holiness of heart. Promoting shared belief and common practice is essential for living in communion with one another. The question of what to teach divided the leaders and members of the Fetter Lane Society and interrupted the process of faith formation. The split in the society did provide an opportunity for instruction and nurture to continue for each group—the Moravians and the Methodists—in accordance with their own faith tradition. It seems clear from this case that some degree of consensus about what to teach is critical for instruction and nurture in faith formation.

I am proposing that three phases of faith formation involving instruction and nurture for shared belief and practice are evident in

the Fetter Lane Society. This proposal is not meant to establish fixed stages of sequential growth, but points instead to a dynamic process of Christian faith formation through instruction and nurture.[67] The first phase, **gaining Christian belief and practice,** was crucial for shaping Christian identity and vocation within the Methodist movement and emphasized an **instructional** mode. In the instructional mode, persons were taught the beliefs and practices of the Christian life through such means as John Wesley's sermons, writings, letters, face-to-face counsel, and Charles Wesley's hymns.

In the case of the Fetter Lane Society, John Wesley's letters are an illustration of one form of instruction and nurture that contributed to faith formation for leaders and was part of Wesley's plan for gaining shared belief and practice. A letter from John Wesley to James Hutton in November 1738 addressed several organizational matters related to Wesley's understanding of living in communion. The first concerned Wesley's belief that all persons have access to the means of grace, so none should be denied. When Hutton wrote concerning problems that arose in a "general meeting of the bands" about relationships between men and women, he suggested that the women meet by themselves rather than attending the general meeting on Wednesday evenings.[68] Wesley responded, "I do very exceedingly disapprove of the excluding women when we meet to pray, sing, and read the Scriptures. I wish it might not be done before we have talked together, at least unless you *first* fix a night for them to come by themselves, which I firmly believe will give more offence."[69] Two days later Wesley wrote Hutton again, repeating his concern that a separate meeting time be set before excluding women from the general meeting.

Another area of concern for John Wesley was related to the nature of the faith community. Hutton wanted to appoint "monitors" who would report the faults of a proposed "president of the band."[70] Wesley questioned the idea of having a president of a band with nothing to do and indicated there was no need for monitors: "I have thought much (my brother is out of town with Mr. Wells) of the monitors, and am very much afraid that design is not right. And that for several reasons. First, it seems needless. Every man in my band is a monitor, and I his."[71] Wesley's letter reflected his understanding that each person cares for every other in the faith community—a pattern of communion seen in

the Trinity. In the end, Wesley's letters to Hutton did not engender consensus about belief and practice, so differences about the leadership and practices of the society continued.

A second phase, **clarifying Christian belief and practice,** emphasized a **dialogical** mode. The authors of *Common Fire* define dialogue as "the underlying rhythm of a reciprocal exchange with our environment."[72] Dialogue shapes "our sense of self" (in this case, Christian identity) and reflects "the quality of those with whom we converse."[73] In this second phase, the exchange between the Wesleys and the Methodists was critical for clarifying the beliefs and practices of a Christian life.

One example of clarifying Christian belief and practice in the case of Fetter Lane is John Wesley's letter to James Hutton on December 1, 1738, regarding the relationship of the Fetter Lane Society to the Church of England: "Are we members of the Church of England? First then let us observe her laws, and then the by-laws of our own society. First secure the observance of the Friday fast. Then I will fast with you, if you please, every day in the week. Only let us except Sundays and the solemn festivals, to fast on which is contrary (to say no more) to the laws of our own Church."[74] Wesley clearly saw Fetter Lane as a loyal part of the Church of England, while also recognizing the strong Moravian influence in the society.

A second example of clarifying Christian belief and practice comes through one of the formational activities that addressed theological exploration and doctrinal disputes—Christian conferencing. John Wesley's strategy of speaking openly to overcome differences is evident in his accounts of Christian conferencing. In his journal on June 16, 1739, Wesley reported such an attempt at Fetter Lane:

Sat. 16. We met at Fetter Lane to humble ourselves before God and own [God] had justly withdrawn [God's] Spirit from us for our manifold unfaithfulness. We acknowledged our having grieved [God] by our divisions, "one saying, I am of Paul, another, I am of Apollos"; by our leaning again to our own works and trusting in them instead of Christ; by our resting in those little beginnings of sanctification which it had pleased [God] to work in our souls; and above all by blaspheming [God's] work among us, imputing it either to nature, to the force of imagination and animal spirits, or even to the delusion of the devil. In that hour we found God with us at the first. Some fell prostrate upon

the ground. Others burst out, as with one consent, into loud praise and thanksgiving. And many openly testified, there had been no such day as this since January the first preceding.[75]

Another form of conferencing through private conversation with those who were upset, mistaken, or lost also contributed to faith formation. In April of the next year, John Wesley had conversations with individual members of the society:

> Ten or twelve persons spoke to me this day also, and many more the day following, who had been greatly troubled by this new gospel and thrown into the utmost heaviness; and indeed wherever I went I found more and more proofs of the grievous confusion it had occasioned; many coming to me, day by day, who were once full of peace and love, but were now again plunged into doubts and fears and driven even to their wit's end.[76]

This account illustrates the amount of sustained formational work needed to help people understand various interpretations of faith in order to live in communion with one another.

The third phase, **extending Christian belief and practice** through an **embodied** mode, emphasized practice of the means of grace and holy living in communion with God and neighbor. The Wesleys' central teaching about love of God and neighbor through responsible grace comes to life in this phase. This phase can be found in both new Methodists and those who have a mature understanding of Christian belief and practice. Those who were seeking salvation entered the Methodist societies and were immediately instructed to practice a holy life until they received the assurance of salvation. A holy life is also characteristic of mature Christians who live in communion with the Trinity and embody God's grace in their relationships with others.

Because of the nature of the Fetter Lane case, evidence of extending Christian belief and practice is not readily found in the accounts of the Fetter Lane Society. There is no mention in the accounts of caring for the sick or the orphaned, visiting prisoners, or any other act of social holiness. This society had broken down and the bands were in disarray. The members of the Fetter Lane Society could not even agree on the practice of spiritual disciplines as occasions for coming to know God, for developing one's relationship with God, and for

living one's faith through social holiness. Since the Moravian belief in Christ as the only means of grace predominated at Fetter Lane, practicing the spiritual disciplines that Wesley advocated was deemed useless, if not harmful. The process of faith formation for gaining, clarifying, and extending shared Christian belief and practice for holy living that the Wesleys envisioned could not thrive in this fractured environment.

The Wesleys used some additional practices that served the process of gaining, clarifying, and extending Christian belief and practice. **Plain truth** was one formative practice long advocated by John Wesley as a means of instruction. In 1739, a controversy erupted after a preaching event in Bath, and several women followed John Wesley into the home where he was staying. Wesley's anger was evident when he spoke: "For I speak plain truth; a thing *you* hear little of and do not desire to hear."[77] Another example of Wesley's plain truth can be seen in the conflict in the Fetter Lane Society when ideas of the French prophets were beginning to take hold. In June 1739, Wesley noted his response: "At six I warned the women at Fetter Lane (knowing how they had been lately shaken), 'Not to believe every spirit, but to try the spirits whether they were of God.' Our brethren met at eight, when it pleased God to remove many misunderstandings and offences that had crept in among them, and to restore in good measure 'the spirit of love and of a sound mind.' "[78]

A second formative practice was **dialogue**, not only through face-to-face meetings with individuals and groups but also through sending and receiving letters. If letters reflected the spiritual progress Wesley advocated, they would be read at class and band meetings for instruction in the holy life. In the case of the Fetter Lane Society, a letter of December 13, 1739, brought disturbing news:

> Many of our sisters are shaken: J[enn]y C[hamber]s says that she never had faith. Betty and Esther H[opson] are grievously torn by reasonings. . . . Mr. B——n expounds much, and speaks so slightingly of the means of grace that many are much grieved to hear him; but others are greatly delighted with him. Ten or fourteen of them meet at our Brother Clark's with Mr. Molther, and seem to consult about things as if they were the whole body. These make a mere jest of going to church or to the Sacrament. They have much confounded some of our sisters; and many of our brothers are much grieved.[79]

93

Instead of supervisory letters of the kind he sent to James Hutton and the Fetter Lane Society, this letter precipitated Wesley's immediate return to London.

Another formative practice was plain account **writings** that helped Wesley clarify his own theological understanding in contrast to others, such as the Moravians, but they also became "curriculum resources" for Methodists. John Wesley, in an opening preamble to an extended response to the Moravian controversy, wrote "I took occasion to give a plain account both of the work which God had begun among us and of the manner wherein the enemy had sown his tares among the good seed, to this effect."[80] In the following days Wesley expounded on this "basic Christian teaching" to counter the influence of those who advocated stillness.[81]

Worship and expounding on Christian teaching led to another important formative practice—the **sermon**. For example, the Moravian controversy was the impetus for Wesley's sermon on "The Means of Grace," written in the years following the Fetter Lane Conflict to address quietist tendencies that persisted in the Methodist movement.[82] Wesley posed the question to be addressed: "Are there, under the Christian dispensation, any 'means' ordained of God as the usual channels of [God's] grace?"[83] Wesley also addressed charges that practicing the means of grace was intended to merit salvation, "some began to mistake the *means* for the *end*, and to place religion rather in doing those outward works than in a heart renewed after the image of God."[84]

From this case study, we have learned that some agreement about what to teach is critical for faith formation for holiness of heart and life. The three simultaneous phases of developing shared Christian belief and practice are intimately linked with growing in communion with God and neighbor. We were able to glimpse the intent of a Wesleyan ecology of faith formation through the conflict in the Fetter Lane Society. Instruction in Christian belief and nurture of a Christian life are part of the church's role in faith fomation.

GROWING IN COMMUNION THROUGH SHARED BELIEF

Information from our discussion of what to teach in a proposed Wesleyan ecology of faith formation is illustrated in figure 2 and demonstrates the progress of growing in communion through God's grace and the instruction and nurture of the community of faith. The

FIGURE 2
A WESLEYAN ECOLOGY OF FAITH FORMATION
"WHAT TO TEACH?"

INVITATION TO COMMUNION Preventing and Justifying Grace "The God of grace, who all invites."[85]	DEEPENING COMMUNION Sanctifying Grace "Still let us in thy Spirit live."	FULL COMMUNION Glorification "Till to a perfect man we rise."
Vision: **Theological Foundation:** God as loving Parent is the giver of prevenient grace and invites us to repent of our sin. 　　God's justifying grace overcomes barriers to communion through Christ's work in the atonement and communion with God is restored.	**Vision:** **Theological Foundation:** The sanctifying grace of the perfecting work of the Holy Spirit empowers us to grow in love of God and neighbor.	**Vision:** **Theological Foundation:** Sanctification is participating in the Divine character and constant communion with the Three-One God.
What to Teach? **Gaining Christian Belief and Practice:** Emphasizes an **instructional mode** teaching what it means to live in communion.	**What to Teach?** **Clarifying Christian Belief and Practice**: Emphasizes a **dialogical mode** of conversing about the meaning of the communion of faith.	**What to Teach?** **Extending Christian Belief and Practice:*** Emphasizes an **embodied mode** of practicing the means of grace and living in communion with God and neighbor.
Formative Process: Instructing persons in the beliefs and practices of the Christian life. Nurturing the Christian life through the means of grace.	**Formative Process:** Exploring the beliefs and practices of the Christian life. Nurturing the Christian life through the means of grace.	**Formative Process:** Embodying the beliefs and practices of the Christian life. Nurturing the Christian life through the means of grace.

*More evident in the United Society than at Fetter Lane.

process of growing in communion in God and others through gaining, clarifying, and extending Christian belief and practice illuminates the need for ongoing discussions in the Wesleyan tradition about what to teach.

Several insights for what to teach in a Wesleyan ecology of faith formation can be elicited from the case of Fetter Lane Society. First, we have clearly seen the **importance of shared Christian belief and practice.** The Wesleys' commitment to and repetition of the meaning of a holy life—loving God and neighbor in response to God's grace—provided a vision for faith formation. The emerging relationships, structures, and practices of formation for holiness of heart and life were all guided by and accountable to this vision based in Scripture. The basic rules of the United Society—"doing no harm," "doing good," and "attending to the ordinances of God" guided people in holy living while they were being educated in the meaning of faith.

A second insight points to the importance of **the teaching authority of the church.** Issues of "what to teach," "who has authority to teach," and "where to teach" were critical for the early Methodist movement and are the source of much debate today. The Wesleys' work with the Fetter Lane Society illustrates the importance of leadership in the task of teaching. This issue is particularly important for those in search of Christian identity and vocation in the Wesleyan tradition. Richard Robert Osmer has argued that the role of teaching authority in the church is one of "preserving continuity" while reinterpreting the message of faith in new cultural contexts.[86] According to Osmer, leaders teach the "normative beliefs and practices of the church," reinterpreting the meaning of the beliefs and practices of the Christian faith for the contemporary world, and creating educational "institutions, processes, and curricula" for those who would live faithful lives.[87] This means that pastors and leaders need to have some clarity about the shared beliefs and practices of their tradition, their own faith, the life issues faced by those in their care, and the contribution and challenge that cultural and theological diversity brings to our life together.

A third insight comes from the awareness of the theological questions and religious experience of the Fetter Lane Society. The work of the Wesleys points to the fact that we need structure and opportunity for **informed theological exploration.** The word "informed" is

critical here. In the case of Fetter Lane, John Wesley and Philip Molther were both attempting to facilitate informed reflection by sharing the teachings and practices of their faith traditions. The irreconcilable differences in their teachings led to a fractured society. This observation raises the question of how much doctrinal consensus is needed if the church is trying to nurture communion with God and others.

It is not my intent to claim that informed theological exploration means everyone has to agree on every point, because I do believe different points of view enrich theological discussion. But I am asking how we decide what is non-negotiable and what is open to new interpretation. Part of the recovery of teaching authority involves knowing the boundaries of a particular faith tradition while providing times and places for open discussions about the meaning of life through the eyes of faith. Challenges to images of self, relationships with others, care for the environment, and the activity of God in the intersections of life raise questions of meaning. Adults need to develop skills in reflecting theologically on life events—using the foundations of faith as a frame of reference for finding meaning in daily life. The support and accountability of a faith community is needed in this process to counter the strong individualistic tendencies of our culture.

Finally, reflection on the case of the Fetter Lane Society emphasizes once again that for the Wesleys **faith formation begins and ends with holy living** as Creator-God invites us into communion with the Trinity. The thesis of this chapter has been that the process of gaining, clarifying, and extending Christian belief and practice was essential for formation for holiness of heart and life in eighteenth-century Methodism. In the Methodist movement, faith formation included instruction and nurture for persons growing in communion with God and neighbor. Reclaiming the theme of loving God and neighbor as the focal point for faith formation could provide an unclouded vision to those who are unfamiliar with the Christian faith or the Wesleyan tradition and give guidance for living a faithful life. By addressing faithful living in the midst of the dilemmas of life, opportunity is created for gaining, clarifying, and extending shared Christian belief and practice through instruction in the faith, exploring the meaning of faith, and embodying faith in daily life. Practicing

the faith can itself lead to new insight about doctrine and contribute to a shared understanding of the promise of God's grace. Mary Elizabeth Mullino Moore posits that doctrine is the "bearer of the promise" of faith, and the experience of assurance is "the completion of the promise,"[88] and I would add, "the embodied faith of a holy life surely must be a witness to the promise."

Chapter 5

"WHO SHALL TEACH?"

Our discussion of the question of "what to teach" addressed the importance of instruction in Christian belief and nurturing a lifestyle to the end that doctrine or shared belief becomes embodied in love of God and neighbor. Answering the question of "what to teach" now leads to expectations for "who shall teach." With the Wesleys' emphasis on growing in communion with God and neighbor, in addition to John Wesley's vision of peacemaking as the evidence of full communion with God, the importance of teaching relationships cannot be overemphasized. Who models this understanding of communion in their own lives? Who has knowledge of the doctrine behind this vision? Who has the ability to share that faith with others?

Our examination of the early Methodist movement has already

provided some insight into expectations for those who teach. First, the Wesleys understood that **teaching takes place within relationships**. Both John and Charles Wesley spent many hours cultivating relationships by listening, instructing, exhorting, and praying with individuals or with small groups. John Wesley wanted to know not only every Methodist but also the progress of each one's formation in faith. Following several days of meeting with members of the Kingswood Society, John Wesley wrote, "I can't understand how any minister can hope ever to give up his [or her] account with joy unless (as Ignatius advised) he [or she] 'know all his [or her] flock by name, not overlooking the men-servants and maid-servants.' "[1] As a result, John and Charles Wesley worked tirelessly with those who wanted to grow in faith. At one point, when John was meeting daily with the bands in London, he noted, "And the hours from ten to two, on every day but Saturday, I set apart for speaking with any who should desire it."[2] This practice of face-to-face religious conversation as a means of faith formation was undoubtedly influenced by the Wesleys' experience at home, where Susanna Wesley spent so much of her effort on the Christian education of her children. Likewise, John Wesley wanted to be available to any that desired guidance on the Way of Salvation. Even when he was not well, he would meet and pray with those who requested it: "I consented, however, to keep my bed; but on condition that everyone who desired it should have liberty to speak with me."[3] This dedication and willingness to invest oneself in the faith formation of other persons through a teaching relationship is one of the most important qualities needed for those who teach, although we might question the wisdom and health of being constantly available. But in the Wesleys' commitment to faith formation, they knew that a teacher responds to God's grace by instructing others on their journeys of faith.

Second, **teachers instruct persons in the Christian life**. In 1783, John Wesley addressed how those who teach should "train children up in the way they should go." He quoted William Law's view on Christian education and teaching and revealed some expectations for teachers:

> And is it not reasonable to suppose that a Christian education should have no other end but to teach them how to think, and judge, and act according to the strictest rules of Christianity?
> At least one would suppose that in all Christian schools the teaching

them to begin their lives in the spirit of Christianity, in such abstinence, humility, sobriety, and devotion as Christianity requires, should not only be more, but a hundred times more regarded than any or all things else.

For those that educate us should imitate our guardian angels, suggest nothing to our minds but what is wise and holy; help us to discover every false judgment of our minds, and to subdue every wrong passion of our hearts.[4]

In Law's understanding, Christian education teaches persons how to be Christian. His statement reflected his understanding of what to teach and who shall teach in a church that aims to train faithful disciples. John Wesley clearly endorsed this statement in his sermon, but he also recognized that some that have been carefully trained would not live as Christians: "yet before they were old, yea, in the strength of their years, they did utterly depart from it."[5] There are no guaranteed outcomes for those who teach.

Finally, **teachers are mediators of culture**. They have been formed in a particular time and place, and this was certainly true of the early Methodists. Gender, racial/ethnic background, family heritage, social experience, economic status, and historical location shape teachers' identities, particularly their Christian identities. This cultural background is good preparation for teachers to understand their students and the questions that propel their search for faith. Culture enriched the teaching of the Wesleys, as the work of many authors was adapted to use as "curriculum" for faith formation. As Henry Rack, who lectures at the University of Manchester, observed, "In adapting what he [Wesley] had read and approved for himself to tutorial use he was once again acting as a cultural mediator as well as a religious one."[6] But it is important to note that although culture was an important part of the context, it was not the criterion for decisions about who shall teach. The Wesleys' only criterion for all that they and the early Methodists did was love of God and love of neighbor. And that was true for teaching as well. Teachers were to demonstrate love of God and neighbor in their own lives and in their teaching.

THE ROLE OF FORMATIVE RELATIONSHIPS

In this chapter, we address the question of "who shall teach" recognizing that teaching in the Wesleyan tradition occurs within a faith

community and on behalf of a faith community to the end that all might live in communion with God and neighbor. In this discussion, we will find that John Wesley used the image of the "Christian family" as a metaphor for teaching relationships. The image is consistent with Wesley's understanding of salvation—adoption as God's children and full communion with God. Therefore, we come to know ourselves as persons and Christians only through close relationships with God and others, particularly our teachers. So relationships, especially teaching relationships broadly defined, are critical for a Wesleyan ecology of faith formation.

While the question of who shall teach is clearly connected with the question of what to teach, it also raises the question of how people learn. In this chapter, we will find some evidence of John Wesley's understanding about how children learn through his instruction to parents in a sermon, "On Family Religion." We will also examine the Wesleys' expectations of those who taught children in schools and their instructions for preachers to teach in the Methodist movement. Once again, we will see the impact of Samuel and Susanna Wesley, as well as of John Wesley's experience as a tutor at Oxford, on the Wesleys' expectations of those who teach. To be true to the language used by the Wesleys, I will use the term "Christian education" in this section, even though faith formation as I have defined it was clearly the Wesleys' goal for Christian education in the home, in the schools, and in the Methodist movement.

A Christian Education in the Home

Those who teach in the home significantly influence how we come to know ourselves as Christian. Across the centuries, familial relationships and events, whether for good or for ill, have had a profound influence on how persons come to understand the world and their place in it. The role of parents or other primary caregivers as teachers is also critical in a Wesleyan ecology of faith formation. Nazarene scholar Wesley Tracy wrote that John Wesley repeatedly "said to his people that the Methodist revival would dissipate in one generation without a vigorous program of Christian education in the home."[7] And John Wesley's image of Christian education in the home came from his own life experience.

The Wesley Parents. Samuel and Susanna Wesley deeply influ-

enced John Wesley's view of parents as teachers of the Christian faith. Even though the two Wesley parents frequently disagreed, they had deep respect for each other. In September 1706, Samuel wrote to Samuel Jr. who was away at school:

> You know what you owe to one of the best of mothers. . . . Often reflect on the tender and peculiar love which your dear mother has always expressed toward you; the deep affliction of both body and mind which she underwent for you, both before and after your birth; the particular care she took of your education when she struggled with so many pains and infirmities; and, above all, the wholesome and sweet motherly advice and counsel which she has often given you to fear God, to take care of your soul as well as of your learning, and to shun all vicious and bad examples.[8]

We have already seen how the correspondence between Susanna Wesley and her son guided John Wesley's exploration of the nature of faith through many years of searching. But Susanna Wesley also held her husband in high regard and in a letter to her brother in 1722 wrote: "I should think it a thousand pities that a man of his brightness, and rare endowments of learning and useful knowledge, in relation to the church of God, should be confined to an obscure corner of the country, where his talents are buried, and he determined to a way of life for which he is not so well qualified as I could wish."[9] Both of these intelligent and committed parents cared for the souls of their children by providing admonition and guidance even when the children left home. This experience clearly provided the basis for defining the nature of the Christian family later in the Wesleys' ministry.

Susanna Wesley's ongoing guidance for her son's spiritual growth and his emerging ministry with young persons was based on her belief that "you ought therefore to look upon every child as a talent committed to your trust."[10] Her letters to John as a young adult studying at Lincoln College actually served two functions. Guidance for John's work with young persons also became spiritual direction for John himself. In 1725, Susanna wrote:

> I would therefore advise young persons in their beginning of a Christian course to shun the company of profane wits as they would

the plague, or poverty; and let 'em never contract an intimacy with any but such as have a good sense of religion. And if 'tis their hap to live where few of that character can be found, let them learn the art of living alone; and when once they are masters of that rare secret, and know how to converse with God, and themselves, they'll want no other company.[11]

This letter emphasizes the importance of participating in **Christian** community for faith formation. And in the context of Christian community, faith necessary to salvation could not be discussed too frequently with young people. Susanna Wesley urged her son to "speak boldly, without fear; these truths ought to be frequently inculcated, and pressed home upon the consciences of men [and women]."[12] Susanna Wesley's forthright direction and support for her son's ministry continued to shape his Christian identity and vocation throughout his lifetime, and her influence continued even after her death. In Charles Wallace's assessment, "As the letters to her grown sons and the essays prepared particularly with her daughters in mind indicate, she never forsook her pedagogical role, even when her children graduated from her classroom."[13]

Samuel Wesley also took the role of teaching his children seriously. According to Luke Tyerman, Samuel instructed the children in the ancient languages but left the remainder of their education to Susanna.[14] But Samuel Wesley had a significant impact on the developing ministry of his son John, who drew on his father's instruction during a controversy about prison ministry. The Holy Club originally gathered for the purpose of sharing reflections on readings in the classics and later added development of a devotional life. William Morgan, a member of the Holy Club, initiated the group's prison ministry in the summer of 1730. John Wesley reported that Morgan "had called at the gaol to see a man that was condemned for killing his wife, and that from the talk he had with one of the debtors he verily believed that it would do much good if anyone would be at the pains now and then of speaking with them."[15] Morgan insisted that the rest of the group join him in visiting at the prison once or twice a week, and the ministry flourished.

But William Morgan was in frail health, both physically and mentally, and eventually died in 1732. Morgan's father, Richard Sr., blamed the Wesleys for his son's death because he believed that the Holy Club's ministry with the poor and imprisoned, compounded

with the "rigorous fasting" included in the spiritual disciplines of the Holy Club, had led to his son's failing health and death. In a letter to Mr. Morgan, John Wesley stated that William Morgan had not fasted for a year and a half and reported that he himself had consulted with Samuel Wesley about the proper procedure for prison ministry from its beginning in 1730. "I wrote an account to my father of our whole design, withal begging that he who had lived seventy years in the world, and seen as much of it as most private men have ever done, would advise us whether we had yet gone too far, and whether we should now stand still, or go forward."[16]

Samuel Wesley had encouraged his son to continue the prison ministry and shared advice about proper procedure learned from his own experience in prison ministry. "Your first regular step is to consult with him (if any such there be) who has a jurisdiction over the prisoners, and the next is, to obtain the direction and approbation of your bishop."[17] And John Wesley had followed his father's guidance. In spite of William Morgan's death, the Holy Club continued their work of saving the souls of prisoners on death row. Later, Richard Morgan Sr. relented. In addition to helping the ministry financially, he "enter[ed] his second son, Richard, under John Wesley's tutorial care at Lincoln College."[18]

Nowhere was the influence of Samuel and Susanna Wesley more evident than in John Wesley's proposals for the education of children. This influence is reflected as late as 1783 in John Wesley's sermons that addressed the role of parents as teachers in the Christian education of their children. Albert Outler noted the motivation behind these sermons in his introductory notes: "Wesley was aware that the Methodist Revival had already outlasted the normal life span of such movements, and that its future depended quite crucially on 'family religion,' 'the education of children,' 'obedience to parents,' 'obedience to pastors,' etc."[19] To emphasize the importance of Christian education, John Wesley preached a series of four sermons on these topics. We turn now to examine his view of the role of fathers and husbands who teach.

Fathers and Husbands. In his 1783 sermon "On Family Religion," John Wesley addressed what it means to "serve the Lord" and the father's responsibility, as head of the household, for guiding his family in the Christian life. It is curious that this sermon is addressed to men, given the profound influence of Susanna Wesley on her sons'

105

ministry and John Wesley's recognition of the fruits of women's faith in the home, in the schools, and in the Methodist movement. In this case, we could conjecture that women already provided most of the Christian education in the homes, and Wesley wanted to be explicit in his instruction to fathers and husbands as heads of households.

The first instruction to the husbands and fathers was to *"restrain* [their wives, children, and servants] from all outward sin" so that they might serve the Lord.[20] Here, Wesley gave examples of not taking God's name in vain and respecting the Lord's Day. Methods of restraint included "advice, persuasion, and reproof," with the admonition that "whatever is done should be done with mildness; nay, indeed, with kindness too."[21] And Wesley emphasized that prayer for the souls of the members of the household is one of the most important activities for husbands and fathers. In his sermon "The Almost Christian," Wesley had advocated "the constant use of family prayer by those who are masters of families, and the setting times apart for private addresses to God, with a daily seriousness of behaviour" because "he who uniformly practises this outward religion has the form of godliness."[22]

Second, husbands and fathers are to *"instruct"* their households, particularly by attending to the ordinances of God, and to read, meditate, and pray every day: "To take care that every person who is under our roof have all such knowledge as is necessary to salvation."[23] According to Rack, the Wesleys believed the education of children must begin early because "the corruption of human nature should be curbed from the first."[24] Fathers must use words that children will understand, to "speak to them *plainly*," so they will learn to love God.[25] John Wesley had some awareness that language must be adapted to the age of the learner and gave an example of how to talk to a child about the sun and grass and flowers and the God who made them:

> It is God, that made the sun, and you and me, and everything. It is [God] that makes the grass and flowers grow; that makes the trees green, and the fruit to come upon them! Think what [God] can do! [God] can do whatever [God] pleases. [God] can strike me or you dead in a moment. But [God] loves you; [God] loves to do you good. [God] loves to make you happy. Should not you then love [*God*]!"[26]

Wesley indicated that while fathers are teaching their children about God, they should also pray for their children, asking that their hearts

106

be opened to God. In addition, fathers and husbands should teach their children frequently and persevere even if they do not see the immediate fruits of their teaching.[27]

The role of fathers and husbands as teachers does not end when a child leaves home, so John Wesley did not end his instruction about family religion with attention to young children. He also addressed the importance of selecting proper schools for both boys and girls. "At all events, then, send your boys, if you have any concern for their souls, not to any of the large public schools (for they are nurseries of all manner of wickedness) but a private school kept by some **pious man** who endeavours to instruct a small number of children in religion and learning together."[28] For girls, John Wesley recommended "send them to some mistress that truly fears God, **one whose life is a pattern to her scholars**, and who has only so many that she can watch over each as one that must give account to God."[29] The significance of the spiritual life of teachers is clearly indicated here, along with a strong recommendation that teachers work with small groups of children. Christian education through the care of souls requires one-to-one relationships.

Wesley continued his guidance for fathers and husbands by addressing how to help children find proper employment and a "good match" in marriage.[30] In these instructions, John Wesley reflected the ongoing care and support given to him by his parents throughout their lifetimes. Wesley recognized that the fathers' task of teaching would not be easy. "It is undoubtedly true that if you are steadily determined to walk in this path; to endeavour by every possible means that you and your house may thus serve the Lord; that every member of your family may worship him, not only in form, but in spirit, and in truth; you will have need to use all the grace, all the courage, all the wisdom which God has given you."[31] In the end, fathers are to nurture their children's faith through school, young adulthood, marriage, and beyond as long as they live—and trust God to do the rest.

A Christian Education in the Schools

Scholars generally agree that John Wesley did not distinguish himself in the area of Christian education of children. Rack observed that there was "no discernible 'official' policy for founding schools."[32] As we shall see, the Wesleys put considerable effort into establishing

schools at Kingswood and Bristol, but there were problems from the start. Even with the problems, the Wesleys and the Methodists did provide education for many poor children who otherwise would not have gone to school.

The Wesleys and Schools for Children. George Whitefield had an active ministry with the colliers at Kingswood, and introduced John Wesley to field preaching in that area. Whitefield also planned a school for colliers' children (both boys and girls) at Kingswood, but went to America before the school was built. He asked John Wesley to continue his ministry with the miners and their children while he was away, but left the matter of the school unsettled. In April 1739, John Wesley met with the colliers to discuss the school and visited Two-Mile Hill, where Whitefield had placed a stone marking the proposed site for the school. In a report of this meeting, John Wesley wrote, "I wish he [Whitefield] would write to me, positively and decisively."[33] With no specific direction from Whitefield, John Wesley altered the original plan so that Kingswood would be a boarding school rather than a day school. According to Richard Heitzenrater, "he built a school near Two-Mile Hill, with a large hall for preaching, facilities for two schoolmasters, and an invitation to scholars of all ages."[34]

When Whitefield returned, it was clear that he thought that John Wesley had "highjacked" his project.[35] There was also a difference of opinion over who now owned the school building, because Whitefield had been actively raising money for it prior to his departure. Early in 1741, Whitefield made strong public charges against John Wesley about his mismanagement of the Kingswood project. In April 1741, Wesley responded to Whitefield's charges in writing and concluded, "Hitherto then there is no ground for the heavy charge of 'perverting' your 'design for the good colliers.' "[36] Whitefield apologized in October, but the once collegial relationship was now constrained by growing theological differences.[37] The early school continued to serve the miners' children for another sixty years[38] while John Wesley turned his attention to founding the new Kingswood School.

On June 24, 1748, the Wesleys opened the new Kingswood School, also known as "New House," outside of Bristol. This school was designed to educate preachers' sons to provide better education than could be obtained elsewhere, and, hopefully, to provide more preachers for the Methodist movement. The rules and the curriculum of

Kingswood School were approved by the Methodist Conference prior to its opening. At the opening, John Wesley preached on "Train up a child in the way that he should go, and when he is old, he will not depart from it,"[39] and Charles Wesley wrote a hymn for the occasion that addressed the question of leadership.

1 But who sufficient is to lead,
    And execute the vast design?
  How can our arduous toil succeed
    When earth and hell their forces
      join
  The meanest instruments
    t'o'erthrow
  Which thou hast ever used below?

2 Mountains, alas, on mountains
    rise,
  To make our utmost efforts vain;
  The work our feeble strength defies,
    And all the helps and hopes
      of man;
  Our utter impotence we see—
  But nothing is too hard for thee!

3 The things impossible to men
    Thou canst for thy own people
      do:
  Thy strength be in our weakness
    seen,
    Thy wisdom in our folly show;
  Prevent, accompany, and bless,
  And crown the whole with full
      success.

4 Unless the power of heavenly
    grace,
  The wisdom of the Deity,
  Direct and govern all our ways,
    And all our works be wrought
    in thee,
  Our blasted works, we know,
    shall fail,
  And earth and hell at last prevail.

5 But, O Almighty God of love,
    Into thy hands the matter take;
  The mountain-obstacles remove
    For thy own truth and mercy's sake!
  Fulfil in ours thy own design,
  And prove the work entirely thine.[40]

This hymn reflected the Wesleys' view that all human work needs to be transformed by God's work. It also recognized that the design for Kingswood School was ambitious and would only be accomplished with God's help.

With the opening of the new Kingswood School, the educational work with children rapidly developed. Rack reported that "by 1749 there were . . . four Methodist schools in Kingswood: day schools for boys and girls, an orphan one for girls, and the 'New House.' "[41]

Wesley envisioned these schools as Christian families[42] with the masters providing life patterns of holiness. Following the practice of Susanna Wesley, who had met weekly with her children for religious conversation, John Wesley reported in his *Journal* that in the spring of 1749 he set aside an hour a week for the children. "I met the children of our four schools together: namely, the boys boarded in the new house, the girls boarded in the old, the day scholars (boys) taught by James Harding, and the girls taught by Sarah Dimmock. We soon found the effect of it in the children, some of whom were deeply and lastingly affected."[43] In these times of conversing, John Wesley was providing guidance not only for the children in their faith formation but for the masters as well. However, Wesley generally treated the children as little adults, expecting the same discipline and level of devotion he did of adults. No play was allowed in the rigorous daily schedule because "he [or she] that plays as a child will play as [an adult]."[44] The fact that the children did play was cause for great chagrin. "They ought never to play. But they do, every day; yea, in the school."[45]

In addition to the tremendous expense, a major problem with these schools was finding qualified masters to teach, especially since they were unpaid. In Rack's words, "Everything depended on suitable staff, and these were seldom forthcoming."[46] Ideally, a master was to model a holy life in love of God and neighbor, and John Wesley was clear about his expectations of these teachers. "I saw none would answer my intention, but men who were truly devoted to God; who sought nothing on earth, neither pleasure, nor ease, nor profit, nor the praise of men; but simply to glorify God, with their bodies and spirits, in the best manner they were capable of."[47] Wesley did not want the Masters teaching material destructive to religion, particularly by their behavior. But this was often the case, so he was forced to dismiss the masters. In July 1749, Wesley wrote, "I rode over to Kingswood and inquired particularly into the state of our school there. I was concerned to find that several of the rules had been habitually neglected. I judged it necessary therefore to lessen the family, suffering none to remain therein who were not clearly satisfied with them and determined to observe them all."[48] As late as 1786, John Wesley wrote that he was still looking for competent masters.[49]

At least part of the problem seemed to be that John Wesley was not

always a good judge of character in his selection of masters.[50] Whether the cause was a psychological weakness of not being able to make a firm decision, a theological hope that God's grace would eventually bear fruit, or a deep commitment to being a peacemaker,[51] John Wesley was often indecisive about masters (or preachers) whose behavior was problematic. Wesley's own assessment was that "the masters were never right: either they were solemn and earnest and the boys ridiculed them, or they were adequate teachers but lacked piety and management skills."[52] Even with the difficulties, Wesley determined to continue the project. In July 1750, John Wesley wrote, "I walked over to Kingswood and found our family there lessened considerably. I wonder how I am withheld from dropping the whole design, so many difficulties have continually attended it. Yet if this counsel is of God, it shall stand, and all hindrances shall turn into blessings."[53] Some would ask if this were determination to do God's will or poor judgment. Perhaps the fruits of the work witness to the value of the struggle. Kingswood School continues today as a non-denominational and co-educational school with 450 students, maintaining close ties to the Methodist Church.[54]

Women and Education of the Poor. The Christian education of children fared better through the efforts of Methodist women who provided education for the poor. John Wesley was also concerned with the children of the poor, believing they needed to learn "to read, write, and cast accounts; but more especially (by God's assistance), 'to know God, and Jesus Christ whom [God] hath sent.' "[55] So Wesley supported the women's work in this area. It was characteristic of him to incorporate grassroots innovations into the Methodist movement after he saw their fruits. Did they do all to the glory of God? Did they teach what was necessary for salvation? Did they nurture personal holiness and social holiness, love of God and neighbor? Such was the case in the works of the Countess of Huntingdon, Hannah Ball, Sarah Ryan, Mary Bosanquet, and Lady Darcy Maxwell.

The Countess of Huntingdon, Selina Hastings, became involved in religious activity following the birth of her seventh and last child. Margaret Hastings, her sister-in-law, convinced Countess Huntingdon to join the Fetter Lane Society. In late 1741, or early 1742, a spiritual crisis brought the Countess near death, but prayer brought her peace and she began to recover. Mollie C. Davis, a writer of

women's history, described the Countess's activities following her recovery:

> Beginning with her servants, she soon tried to convert everyone she saw. She opened her kitchens, purse strings, and schools for the poor in the area; and then she advanced an attack on the London elite. . . . Working with the Wesleys, she gave them her support freely and worked directly and indirectly to persuade John Wesley of the value of lay and itinerant ministers.[56]

The Countess was able to use her position of influence and her wealth to further the Methodist movement. She opened her home to meetings with sermons by evangelists. Davis reported that the Countess also organized a network of women. She "then initiated an unusual activity for women of her time: She sponsored a missionary group to Wales consisting of select bands of like-minded women and proven evangelists, the first of many excursions she and her friends undertook."[57] The Countess also served as consultant to John Wesley by evaluating the work of preachers and critiquing his publications. After reviewing one section of Wesley's *Journal*, she boldly asked, "Have you done the grace of God justice with respect to your own soul?"[58]

The Countess eventually broke her relationship with the Wesleys when she asked George Whitefield to be her chaplain. As Mollie Davis reported, "She was fast becoming the leader and coordinator of the group of Dissenting ministers who, while still connected, were known as Calvinistic Methodists."[59] Now her theology led her in a different direction, but she continued to be involved in teaching through her evangelical activities, such as holding prayer meetings for women and selling her jewels to build a chapel near her home. She also established a "pension fund for the wives of [itinerant ministers] who died in poverty," and opened a "theological school in Trevecca in South Wales, to train ministers for the Church of England, or for any other Protestant denomination."[60]

Another woman who demonstrated qualities needed in those who teach was Hannah Ball. She had a religious experience in 1773 that led her to write, "I desire to spend the remaining part of my life . . . in labours of love to my fellow-creatures. . . ."[61] Ball devoted her time to visiting the sick and those in jail. She also provided spiritual guid-

ance to friends and neighbors through her letters. But Ball's particular concern for poor children who worked on weekdays led her to organize a Sunday school to teach them basic skills of reading, writing, and arithmetic. Christian piety was fostered through evening prayer or attendance at a society meeting. She also organized small groups of children to meet with tutors. Some of the tutors were volunteers, and some were paid.[62] It should be noted that Hannah Ball's Sunday school began about 1769, several years before that of Robert Raikes, who is publicly credited with starting that institution.[63]

Sarah Ryan and Mary Bosanquet were also concerned for the faith formation of children. They founded a school at Leytonstone in 1763. Earl Kent Brown, who is known for his research on women in the Methodist movement, wrote, "To Mary and Mrs. Ryan it seemed that God was calling them to a special ministry for children. They had been seeking for some time to use their lives better in the service of the poor."[64] When the opportunity presented itself, the two opened a school for destitute orphans, but they also took in adult women who were ill and nursed them to health.[65]

Another woman who made a significant impact on early Methodist education was Lady Darcy Maxwell. In 1770, she founded a nonresident day school to provide Christian instruction for boys who lived at home. She managed this school for forty years, providing an education for eight hundred students, endowing the school to continue after her death.[66] In addition, Lady Maxwell started her first Sunday schools in 1787, one in Edinburgh and another twenty-five miles away. By 1795, she reported that "sixty men and 'many young women' were attending."[67] Maxwell gave a large part of her income to these ministries. She paid the Sunday school teachers herself, contributed more than eight hundred pounds to Wesley's Kingswood School over her lifetime, and hired preachers to work with the country people near Edinburgh.[68]

A Christian Education in the Methodist Movement

Whether these women taught children or adults themselves or sponsored schools for children and adults, they were included in the group of church leaders, both lay and clergy, who shared the evangelical belief that people had direct access to God's grace through the Holy Spirit. It was God who gave them their special vocation to

preach and/or teach, and this sometimes raised questions about their relationship to the Anglican Church.

The Wesleys clearly wanted to avoid separation from the Church of England, but as Methodists were moved to preach and teach, they did so without regard to established parishes.[69] Itinerant Methodist ministers often preached in others' churches,[70] and when church pulpits were not open to them, they would preach in the open air. The advent of "field preaching" yielded such fruit in bringing the gospel to the people that the Wesleys quickly abandoned their concern about the propriety of the method.[71] Yet these practices played havoc with established parishes of the Church of England and the commonly accepted understanding of church order.[72] But John Wesley wholeheartedly believed that God established the boundaries and gave direction for his ministry. "I look upon *all the world* as *my parish*; thus far I mean, that in whatever part of it I am, I judge it meet, right, and my bounden duty, to declare unto all that are willing to hear the glad tidings of salvation. This is the work I know God has called me to. And sure I am that [God's] blessing attends it."[73] And Wesley instructed his preachers accordingly. In contrast to traditional church ministries, this preaching and teaching went to the people—in the fields, on the street corners, in private homes.

The Role of Clergy. Instructions to preachers about the Christian education of members of their parish were somewhat more productive for the Wesleys' work with children and demonstrated the Wesleys' emphasis on Christian family. John Wesley adapted work from other authors into *Instructions for Children* and *Token for Children*. The preacher in each society was instructed to give copy of Wesley's *Instructions for Children* to every Methodist family in the parish and encourage the entire household to learn them by heart.[74] Parents were instructed to meet with their children weekly "to talk to them, pray with them and instruct them."[75] The preachers were to visit the families on a regular basis in order to assess their progress. And, of course, Wesley instructed his preachers in the correct method of discussion, speaking to each person in the household individually. He was to hear what the children had learned as well. All were to be questioned on "some of the weightier points," but answers could be suggested with the questions along with explanations in order to "take the burden off them."[76] Instruction and exhortation were to fol-

low. At the end of the visit, the preacher arranged for the head of household to "call all his family together every Sunday before they go to bed, and hear what they can repeat."[77] Once again the practice of religious conversation is evident here. And Wesley noted the qualities of teachers needed for these tasks. "What patience, what love, what knowledge is requisite for this!"[78]

For the Wesleys, strong preaching was synonymous with strong teaching, providing an opportunity for teaching about God's activity in the lives of individuals or groups. But the preaching was not always from an educated clergy. Formal theological education for pastors was not always appreciated, or even desired, in a cultural climate of anti-intellectualism and anti-clericalism, and excesses in personal behavior led to open hostility to established clergy.[79] It was the need for Christian education for **both laity and clergy**, as well as John Wesley's interest in education, that led to the discussion in the first Methodist Conference in June 1744. Matters of "what to teach, how to teach and what to do, i.e. how to regulate our doctrine, discipline, and practice" were the first priority in this new renewal movement.[80]

The Role of Laypersons. The conviction of God's direction and blessing on a vocation of teaching extended to laypersons as well, raising a second area of contention in relation to church order—the role of lay leadership in the Methodist movement. For Wesley, the function of Christian leadership was to equip others to lead and minister. Nearly every Methodist had a share in ministry through numerous official positions and various ministry projects. However, the expansion of lay-led Methodist societies open to persons from any denomination (including Dissenters),[81] the establishment of separate Methodist meeting houses, and the rapid increase in lay preaching raised questions about whether this was a renewal movement or a separate religious group. The growing number of converts in the Methodist movement created the need for additional leadership in Christian education. Stephen Gunter indicated that the number of participants in the Methodist movement outgrew the Wesleys' oversight and pastoral care, so Wesley "utilized lay preachers, at first very reluctantly, to maintain the momentum and preserve the fruits of his labors."[82] John Wesley encountered this issue directly in a conflict over the preaching of Thomas Maxfield.

In 1739, Susanna Wesley had come to live at the Foundery in London, the central administrative site for the Methodist movement and John Wesley's own residence. When Wesley was away early in 1741,[83] Thomas Maxfield, a layperson, was left in charge of the classes and bands. He was "to read and expound the Scriptures. It was a short and natural step from this to preach to the ready and attentive congregation."[84] When Wesley heard of Maxfield's preaching, he returned quickly from his journey. Maldwyn Edwards, Wesley family biographer, described John Wesley's account with his mother Susanna upon his arrival:

> Even as she asked him what was the matter she must have known. "Thomas Maxfield has turned preacher I find." It was a sentence ominous in its curtness. But Susanna had her effective rejoinder. "John, you know what my sentiments have been. You cannot suspect me of readily favouring anything of this kind. But take care what you do with respect to that young man: for he is as surely called of God to preach as you are. Examine what have been the fruits of his preaching and hear him yourself."[85]

John Wesley took his mother's advice and listened to Maxfield. Wesley's response was "It is the Lord, let Him do what seemeth Him good. What am I that I should withstand God?"[86] Edwards called this advent of lay preaching a "revolutionary move" in the Methodist movement. Lay preaching, along with field preaching that began in 1739, contributed to the impetus of the Methodist movement and to the teaching of Methodist belief and holy living.

Lay leadership also proved to be critically important for teaching relationships in the process of faith formation in the Methodist movement. Tom Albin's research of historical accounts of religious experience of the early Methodists led him to conclude that the role of lay leadership and the support of the community were the most significant influences on transformative religious experience.[87] The fruits of the work of laypersons in faith formation were an even more compelling reason for the Wesleys to encourage lay leadership. And the advent of lay preaching also opened the door for women.

The Role of Women. We have already seen the important role that women had in educating children and adults in the Methodist movement. But the degree of women's leadership is not commonly known.

116

Paul Chilcote, a professor of Wesleyan studies, reported that twice as many women as men participated in the Methodist movement.[88] And Earl Kent Brown observed, "With the exception of his mother, Susanna, [John Wesley's] female associates are almost totally unknown to our generation. This is unfortunate, because women made up a majority of the early Methodists."[89]

The growth in women's leadership in the Methodist movement came with the organization of societies into classes and bands. In these small groups women first found their public voice through prayer and testimony.[90] For some, exhorting and teaching followed. From these leadership roles, it was a short step to women preaching and teaching. In the beginning, John Wesley opposed this move, but the fruits of women in ministry provided abundant evidence to win Wesley's growing support. However, John Wesley's support of the leadership of women led to controversy. Alan L. Hayes argued that protests directed at the Methodist movement were in reaction to Wesley's view of women; the protests were "loaded with outrage against Wesley's affirmation that women are, in things of God, independent of men and equal to them."[91]

The Wesleys never officially left the Anglican Church and so did not ever consent to the ordination of women. At times, John Wesley seemed to be torn between the church's traditional view that women should not preach and the more liberated view that women were making a distinct contribution through their preaching. And his brother Charles clearly opposed the increasing leadership of women. In the end, John Wesley chose to follow the more practical direction as he saw the fruit of women's ministry. In Paul Chilcote's words:

> God was not limited, you see, to the rules of the Church in Wesley's view. While God generally operates through the means—the ordinary channels ordained by Christ—God can never be bound to them alone. When the normal pastoral system fails to bear fruit, God raises up messengers to do what must be done. This, Wesley argued, was the extraordinary situation of his own day. And he used the soundest argument from Scripture, tradition, reason, and experience in order to build his case.[92]

Since Wesley relied heavily on the criteria of fruits of the Spirit, he could not deny the evidence of God's work in women called to preach.

In a sermon, "On Visiting the Sick," preached in May 1786, John Wesley's strongest statement about the status of women reflected a lifetime of growth in understanding and confidence about the role of women in ministry and mission:

"But may not *women* as well as men bear a part in this honourable service?" Undoubtedly they may; nay, they ought—it is meet, right, and their bounden duty. Herein there is no difference: "there is neither male nor female in Christ Jesus." Indeed it has long passed for a maxim with many that "women are only to be seen, not heard." And accordingly many of them are brought up in such a manner as if they were only designed for agreeable playthings! But is this doing honour to the sex? Or is it a real kindness to them? No; it is the deepest unkindness; it is horrid cruelty; it is mere . . . barbarity. And I know not how any woman of sense and spirit can submit to it. Let all you that have it in your power assert the right which the God of nature has given you. Yield not to that vile bondage any longer. You, as well as men, are rational creatures. You, like them, were made in the image of God: you are equally candidates for immortality. You too are called of God, as you have time, to "do good unto all [humanity]." Be "not disobedient to the heavenly calling." Whenever you have opportunity, do all the good you can, particularly to your poor sick neighbour. And every one of *you* likewise "shall receive your own reward according to your labour."[93]

John Wesley gave additional authority to this assertion that women are "called of God" by grounding it in Scripture and indicating that women like Phoebe were leaders in the early church. This point of view proved so divisive that following John Wesley's death, the role of women was once again limited.

WITH PATIENCE, LOVE, AND KNOWLEDGE[94]

If one believes, as the Wesleys did, that God's grace is available to all and that persons are to use their God-given gifts, then the door is open to those who are called to a special vocation of teaching. In the words of John Wesley, "You too are called of God, as you have time, to 'do good unto all [humanity].' "[95] The question of how one evaluates that call then becomes critical. How do we decide who shall teach?

In the examples of parents as teachers, we learned that the care of souls is at the heart of teaching relationships in the Christian family. Parents are to nurture the spiritual lives of children, youth, and adults in their household, instructing them in knowledge necessary for salvation and nurturing their practice of faith. One expectation of teachers is that they participate in the ordinances of God. These Christian practices or means of grace include reading Scripture, meditation, personal and private prayer, and Sunday worship. In other words, teachers are to be "living representatives" of the faith—or in Wesley's words, "a life pattern." The future of the church depends on those who teach others to be Christian, and the care of souls never ends. In a Wesleyan ecology of faith formation, those who teach are instrumental in shaping others' sense of Christian identity and vocation in formation for holiness of heart and life.

From the discussion of schoolteachers, we learned that qualities most needed for those who teach are personal piety and a moral life, the ability to work with children, knowledge of Methodist doctrine, commitment to Christian discipline, and a willingness to make a personal investment of time and effort. These qualities, particularly Christian piety and a moral life, were most visible in the efforts of Methodist women who taught. Rack noted "how effectively these women expressed the special social and spiritual values of domestic, family-centered piety in their environment."[96] They were dedicated, determined, and committed to faith formation of children and adults. They were creative in their ministry of caring for souls. The women's love of God led them to demonstrate love of neighbor through the activities to which they dedicated their lives.

From our examination of church leaders, we discovered the interrelationship between preaching and teaching. Wesley expected preachers in the Methodist movement to continue to grow in faith through disciplined study and conversation. They were to instruct persons in Methodist doctrine, discipline, and practice by visiting each home and conversing with each member of the household. And laypersons whose lives provided patterns of personal and social holiness and whose gifts bore fruit in their work—in the small groups, with the poor, with children or adults—were given authority to preach and teach in order to equip others to love God and neighbor.

Six qualities of those who teach have been lifted out of the discussion in this chapter and recorded in our proposed Wesleyan ecology of faith formation in figure 3. All six qualities are necessary in each phase of growing in communion with God. However, two in particular have been highlighted for each phase, pointing to the fact that different skills may be emphasized in each phase. According to John Wesley, those who teach need to be **totally dedicated to God** with no thought of earthly reward. Teachers were to "glorify God with their bodies and spirits" in the best way they could.[97] Commitment to the **care of souls** requires that teachers provide guidance for the faith journeys of their charges and teach knowledge requisite to salvation. In addition, teachers **represent the Methodist tradition** in doctrine, discipline, and practice. In order to nurture growth in faith in others, teachers must tend to their **own Christian discipline** through participation in the means of grace and attending to the ordinances of God. In Susanna Wesley's words, "Whosoever would successfully attempt the conversion of others must be careful in the first place to reform themselves."[98] Teachers also need the ability to communicate clearly with students in order to develop the **teaching relationship** and must provide a **life pattern** as an example of personal and social holiness. Finally, teachers **continue to grow** in love of God and neighbor. Some comfort was provided in the face of all these expectations when John Wesley recognized that the task would be difficult with no promise of observable results. Teaching would take all the "patience, love, and knowledge"[99] a person could muster. In a Wesleyan ecology of faith formation, these qualities for persons who teach are essential.

Teaching relationships in a Wesleyan ecology of faith formation are also represented in figure 3 and reflect the importance of the movement from more instructional teaching relationships to dialogical relationships to mutually accountable teaching relationships as persons grow in faith. We can also see a shift in authority and power from the parent-child relationship in the instructional mode to the learner claiming more power in the dialogical mode. In the embodied mode, mutual authority and power characterizes the teaching and learning roles in these mutually accountable relationships.

FIGURE 3
A WESLEYAN ECOLOGY OF FAITH FORMATION
"WHO SHALL TEACH?"

INVITATION TO COMMUNION	DEEPENING COMMUNION	FULL COMMUNION
Preventing and Justifying Grace "The God of grace, who all invites."[100]	Sanctifying Grace "Still let us in thy Spirit live."	Glorification "Till to a perfect man we rise."
Who Shall Teach? Qualities: 1. **True dedication to God and to the care of souls.** 2. **Knowledge of Methodist doctrine and practice.** 3. Commitment to Christian disciplines of practicing the means of grace and dedication to teaching others. 4. Ability to work with a diverse group of people. "Plain talk for plain people." 5. Life pattern of personal and social holiness—a model of living faith, seeking nothing on earth, and glorifying God with body and spirit. 6. Evidence of continued growth in love of God and neighbor.	**Who Shall Teach?** Qualities: 1. True dedication to God and to the care of souls. 2. Knowledge of Methodist doctrine and practice. 3. **Commitment to Christian disciplines of practicing the means of grace and dedication to teaching others.** 4. **Ability to work with a diverse group of people. "Plain talk for plain people."** 5. Life pattern of personal and social holiness—a model of living faith, seeking nothing on earth, and glorifying God with body and spirit. 6. Evidence of continued growth in love of God and neighbor.	**Who Shall Teach?** Qualities: 1. True dedication to God and to the care of souls 2. Knowledge of Methodist doctrine and practice. 3. Commitment to Christian disciplines of practicing the means of grace and dedication to teaching others. 4. Ability to work with a diverse group of people. "Plain talk for plain people." 5. **Life pattern of personal and social holiness—a model of living faith, seeking nothing on earth, and glorifying God with body and spirit.** 6. **Evidence of continued growth in love of God and neighbor.**
Teaching Relationships: Instructional relationships. Life pattern. Parent-child. Christian family.	**Teaching Relationships:** Dialogical relationships. Life pattern. Teacher-student. Christian family.	**Teaching Relationships:** Mutually accountable relationships. Life pattern. Mutual participation in teaching and learning. Christian family.

It is important to remember that God is always the focus of and a participant in these teaching relationships. The aim of making disciples is that persons will grow in communion with God and their neighbors through God's prevenient grace. God participates in teaching relationships through the work of the Holy Spirit by giving persons the gifts to teach and to learn and by providing grace necessary for salvation. How do we envision the church's role in creating teaching relationships that contribute to growing in communion with God and neighbor?

Today when many of us hear the word "teaching," we call up an image in our minds of children sitting quietly in rows with a teacher standing in front of them instructing them in the information they are to learn. But the Wesleys have shown us that teaching is much more dynamic and, in the words of Sara Little, "deals with the development of understanding"[101] and lifestyle. While a Wesleyan ecology of faith formation does need to provide instruction grounded in Scripture and the history of the denominational tradition, it also needs to foster individual exploration and creativity for persons of all ages in safe environments for learning. The question is, what kind of teaching relationships cultivate growing in communion with God and neighbor? In 1987 Maria Harris, a contemporary religious educator, wrote that "teaching is the incarnation of the subject matter."[102] In reflecting on her reading of Seneca in 1711, Susanna Wesley wrote, " 'While I teach, I learn,' says Seneca. 'And while I preach to others, I instruct myself.' And again, 'Those are the best instructors that teach by their lives and prove their words by their actions.' "[103] Both of these women discovered that the subject matter comes alive in all that the teacher is and does. Teachers are living representatives of a faith tradition, embodying its beliefs, values, and mission. Teachers embody the promise of faith, and it is through teaching that the church continues.

Chapter 6

"HOW TO TEACH?"

Structures for Teaching

Consensus about what to teach holds implications not only for who shall teach but also for how to teach in a faith community that is to pattern itself after the communion of the Trinity. We will address the question of how to teach in two parts—structures and practices. In this chapter, we turn to the educational structures of the early Methodist movement that provided a framework for Christian formation. Structure has to do with construction, organizing parts into an interrelated whole. And several structures organized together form a system. While we may intentionally create structures, they also emerge through trial and error. And this was certainly true in the early Methodist movement. As we explore structures for teaching in this chapter, we will see the small group structure again, but now the interrelationship of the different groups becomes vital in the faith formation of adults.

In the fourth chapter, I argued that growth in faith means deepening engagement with shared Christian belief and practice from instruction to dialogue to embodiment. In this chapter we begin by addressing a critical issue that impacts how we structure what we teach—the question of "academical studies" versus "practical divinity." This question moves us from a focus on instruction in Christian belief and nurture of a holy life to ask what resources persons need in order to reflect critically on their response to God's grace in faithful discipleship.

A MATTER OF CONFLICTING VISIONS

It probably comes as no surprise that this question was a source of contention between Samuel and Susanna Wesley when they considered the best education for John's preparation for the ministry. Samuel Wesley advocated "academical studies" and believed that faith formation in preparation for ministry required several years of study through a course of critical learning.[1] Susanna Wesley argued for "practical divinity," believing that it was the best preparation for ministry. What she meant by "practical divinity" was clearly explained in a letter to daughter Sukey in 1710. "But, Sukey, it is not learning these things by heart, nor your saying a few prayers morning and night, that will bring you to heaven; you must understand what you say, and you must practice what you know."[2] In other words, practical divinity is having knowledge and understanding necessary for salvation and a living faith—no more and no less.

This apparent conflict over critical learning and practical divinity began innocently enough in September 1724 when Susanna Wesley voiced the hope that John would be his father's curate at Epworth: "I heartily wish you were in Orders, and could come and serve one of his churches. Then I should see you often, and could be more helpful to you than 'tis possible to be at this distance."[3] Two months later, John replied from Oxford, "You said something of it in your last letter which I wish could come to pass, but I am afraid I flattered myself too soon."[4]

In a letter of January 1725, Samuel Wesley expressed his pleasure that John was thinking about Holy Orders and then elaborated on the proper motives for doing so. Even though Samuel discussed reasons to enter Holy Orders, he advised John to wait. "By all this you see I'm

not for your going over hastily into Orders. When I'm for your taking 'em, you shall know it, and 'tis not impossible but I may then be with you, if God so long spare the life and health of your affectionate father."[5] Samuel proposed extensive preparation for ministry through a course of critical learning to provide a strong foundation in classical learning, especially in biblical languages and scholarship. He defined a prolonged assignment for his son growing out of his own effort to create a parallel translation of the Old Testament. John was assigned the Pentateuch and was asked to "read diligently the Hebrew text in the Polyglot, and collate it exactly with the Vulgar Latin, which is in the second column, writing down all (even the least) variations or differences between 'em."[6] In addition, John was to read the Pentateuch twice, add the Samaritan text, and complete the work in a year! This was the assignment for the mornings. Samuel added, "In the afternoon read what you will, and be sure to walk an hour if fair in the fields."[7]

A month later in February 1725, Susanna Wesley once again encouraged her son not to delay, but to prepare for Holy Orders immediately. She recommended a study of practical divinity as the best preparation:

> I approve the disposition of your mind, . . . and I think the sooner you are a deacon the better, because it may be an inducement to greater application in the study of practical divinity, which of all other I humbly conceive is the best study for candidates for Orders. Mr. Wesley differs from me, and would engage you, I believe, in critical learning, . . . which though of use accidentally, and by way of concomitance, is in nowise preferable to the other. Therefore I earnestly pray God to avert that great evil from you, of engaging in trifling studies to the neglect of such as are absolutely necessary.[8]

In the same letter Susanna Wesley recognized that she and Samuel differed on this issue, "But 'tis an unhappiness almost peculiar to our family, that your father and I seldom think alike."[9] Susanna wanted John to go to school immediately rather than delay by working on Samuel's project. So the battle lines were drawn. Samuel Wesley's desire to have his son prepare for orders by working with him came into direct conflict with Susanna Wesley's desire for her son to start his formal preparation for ministry immediately. Within a month,

Samuel Wesley changed his mind about an extended period of study and urged his son to prepare for Holy Orders: "[I] now incline to your going this summer into Orders, and would have you turn your thoughts and studies that way."[10]

After more than two years of ongoing theological discussion through regular correspondence with Susanna Wesley and occasional correspondence with Samuel Wesley, John Wesley was nearing completion of his master's degree. In January 1727, John indicated that he had created a plan to continue his learning following his degree. He wrote to Susanna, "I have drawn up for myself a scheme of studies from which I do not intend, for some years at least, to vary. I am perfectly come over to your opinion, that there are many truths it is not worth while to know."[11] Susanna was pleased with this letter: "There is nothing like a clear method to save both time and labour in anything."[12] By the summer of 1727, Susanna Wesley's dream that John would serve as his father's assistant became a reality. Samuel Wesley, at age sixty-five, accepted a second parish at Wroote and his son, at age twenty-four, served as his curate for two years.

When John Wesley returned to Oxford in November 1729 at the request of Dr. Morley, the rector of Lincoln College,[13] he continued to reflect on the question of a vocation in the academy or the parish. In a letter to Susanna Wesley, John Wesley discussed the knowledge that comes from God and reflected on his previous dilemma: "Shall I quite break off my pursuit of all learning but what immediately tends to practice? I once desired to make a fair show in languages and philosophy. But 'tis past."[14] It appeared that Wesley was torn between the two parental images of biblical scholar and practical theologian, finding value in the first in his studies at Oxford and the second in his ministry at Epworth and Wroote. In reflection, John Wesley wrote, "The strongest impression I had till I was three or four and twenty was, *Inter sylvas Academi quaerere verum* [to seek for truth in the groves of Academe], and afterwards (while I was my father's curate), to save my own soul and those that heard me."[15] Where was the best place to practice his ministry?

Samuel Wesley now had the answer. He wanted one of his sons to continue the ministry at Epworth. As Tyerman observed, "Here [Samuel] had diligently and faithfully laboured as an earnest parish minister for nearly forty successive years. Here most of his nineteen

children had been born. Here he was about to die himself; and here he was anxious that his wife should die."[16] Samuel Wesley, Jr. declined the offer and suggested John. The ailing father, then seventy-two years of age, asked John to take the Epworth ministry in October 1734. Samuel wanted his son to leave the academy for the parish: "Nor am I for a solitary life. God made us for a social life; we are not to bury our talent, we are to let our light shine. . . . And to this academical studies are only preparatory."[17] Now Samuel Wesley wanted John to use his academic studies by tending to the souls at Epworth.

John Wesley shared the same intent of saving souls, but Epworth was not what he had in mind. In November, John wrote that he would not accept the Epworth living. "The question is not whether I could do more good to others *there* or *here*, but whether I could do more good to myself; seeing wherever I can be most holy myself, there, I am assured, I can most promote holiness in others."[18] Five days later, Samuel wrote and rebuffed his son's argument: "It is not dear self, but the glory of God, and the different degrees of promoting it, which should be our main consideration and direction in the choice of any course of life."[19] Within a month, on December 10, 1734, John Wesley made his final argument that "that course of life tends most to the glory of God wherein we can most promote holiness in ourselves and others."[20] His long letter with twenty-six paragraphs defended his refusal in detail and provided the rationale for his contention that Oxford was the best place for his ministry:

> Here are poor families to be relieved; here are children to be educated; here are workhouses wherein both young and old want and gladly receive the word of exhortation; here are prisons to be visited, wherein alone is a complication of all human wants; and lastly, here are the schools of the prophets, here are tender minds to be formed and strengthened, and babes in Christ to be instructed and perfected in all useful learning.[21]

With this letter, the matter of Epworth was seemingly closed, but Tyerman reported that the discussion about John Wesley's responsibilities to his ordination continued between Samuel Wesley Sr., John, and Samuel Jr. On December 12, 1734, Samuel Jr. wrote, "Are you not ordained? Did you not deliberately and openly promise to instruct, to teach, to admonish, to exhort those committed to your charge? . . .

It is not a college, it is not an university; it is the *order of the Church*, according to which you were called."[22]

In this discussion of the Epworth living, Samuel Wesley Sr. seemed to be concerned that the lure of "academical studies" would keep his son in school forever and not in the practice of ministry as his ordination required. Samuel Sr. further clarified his view in a letter to Samuel Jr. concerning John Wesley's refusal to accept the Epworth ministry:

> He seemed to mistake the end of academical studies, which were chiefly preparatory, in order to qualify men to instruct others. . . . As to many sorts of useful knowledge, it may be nearly true; but surely there needs be a knowledge, too, of men and things, (which have not been thought the most attainable in a cloister), as well as of books, or else we shall find ourselves of much less use in the world. . . . Neither can I understand the meaning or drift of being thus ever learning, and never coming to a due proficiency in the knowledge and practice of the truth, so as to be able commendably to instruct others in it.[23]

Samuel Wesley's letter rings of earlier admonitions by Susanna to avoid "trifling studies." The apparent disagreement between the parents about the kind of education needed to prepare their son for ministry had disappeared.

Samuel Wesley died at the age of seventy-two (April 25, 1735) shortly after the controversy over the Epworth living. Frank Baker, an expert in English church history, reported that John and Charles went to be with their dying father on April 4, 1735. "In order to help his father 'end his days in peace' [John] reversed his earlier decision, and very soon after his arrival wrote to his Oxford Methodist colleague, Thomas Broughton, now serving in London, asking him to take the steps which he had already offered to take in order to secure the Epworth living."[24] Broughton tried, but he was not successful. John Wesley stayed on at Epworth as the acting minister for two months after his father's death, and then went to Georgia at the end of August.[25] So Samuel died not knowing the ultimate direction of John's ministry. John himself said in his journal on May 20, 1753, "If those in Paradise know what passes on earth, I doubt not but my father is rejoicing and praising God, who has in [God's] own manner and time accomplished what *he* [Samuel] had so often attempted in vain."[26]

The conflict over the proper preparation for ministry is useful for our consideration of the structures for teaching holiness of heart and life. What knowledge is needed for faithful discipleship in response to God's grace? What structures are needed to form heart and mind so that persons respond to God's grace in faith through holy living and communion with God and neighbor? Critical learning and practical divinity need to be combined for formation in holiness of heart and life. Charles Wesley's hymn "For Children," written for the 1748 opening of the new Kingswood School, reflects this need.

1 Come, Father, Son, and Holy
   Ghost,
   To whom we for our children
   cry!
The good desired and wanted
   most
Out of thy richest grace
   supply!
The sacred discipline be given
To train and bring them up for
   heaven.

2 Answer on them the end of all
   Our cares, and pains, and
   studies here;
On them, recovered from their
   fall,
Stamped with the humble
   character,
Raised by the nurture of the Lord,
To all their paradise restored.

3 Error and ignorance remove,
   Their blindness both of
   heart and mind;
Give them the wisdom from
   above,
   Spotless, and peaceable, and
   kind;
In knowledge pure their minds
   renew,
And store with thoughts divinely
   true.

4 Learning's redundant part
   and vain
   Be here cut off, and cast aside;
But let them, Lord, the
   substance gain,
   In every solid truth abide,
Swiftly acquire, and ne'er forego
The knowledge fit for man to
   know.

5 Unite the pair so long disjoined,
   Knowledge and vital piety:
Learning and holiness combined,
   And truth and love, let all men see
In those whom up to thee we give,
Thine, wholly thine, to die and live.

129

> 6 Father, accept them through thy Son,
>   And ever by thy Spirit guide!
> Thy wisdom in their lives be shown,
>   Thy name confessed and glorified;
> Thy power and love diffused abroad,
> Till all the earth is filled with God.[27]

Charles Wesley's phrases of "knowledge and vital piety," "learning and holiness," and "truth and love" precisely name the issue. Both knowledge and Christian practice serve the aim of growing in communion with God. How to combine these elements to structure the process of faith formation is the question.

THE WHOLE ECONOMY OF THE PEOPLE CALLED METHODISTS

John Wesley learned much about structures for faith formation from the Moravians. Richard Heitzenrater has reported that when ongoing doubts about his own religious experience prompted Wesley to visit the Moravian enclave at Herrnhut, he brought back insights that "furnished practical methods for the structure and function of Christian fellowship in order to provide effective spiritual nurture."[28] The Fetter Lane Society is one example of these structures for spiritual nurture. While the Fetter Lane dispute may have forced John Wesley to clarify his own theological understanding of "the means of grace"[29] as related to the English Moravian doctrine of "stillness," the Fetter Lane Society also provided an illustration of the type of structure needed to sustain faith formation. The small group structures for adults in the Methodist movement were formative in that they created a learning environment for gaining, clarifying, and extending shared Christian belief and practice for growing in communion with God and neighbor.

The design of the Wesleys' small group system for adults is well known, although it was not planned out in advance. As John Wesley observed, the Methodists "had not the least expectation at first of anything like what has since followed, so they had no previous design or plan at all, but everything arose just as the occasion offered."[30] According to David Michael Henderson, the purpose of the small groups was to care for souls, and the groups were "graded

by readiness" in terms of progress in faith formation.[31] Leading members in one group were almost always participants in the next group, for instance, a leader of a class would be in a band, a leader of a band in a select society, and members of the select society were local preachers and members of the circuit. Henderson noted that "the progression which an individual followed through the system was not only an advancement in degree of participation, but also a change of instructional purposes, beginning with behavior."[32] Each group had its own set of rules, including prohibitions, exhortations, and recommended practices such as the means of grace. But, as John Wesley wrote in 1777, "General rules are easily laid down. But it is not possible to apply them accurately in particular cases without the anointing of the Holy One; this alone, abiding with us, can teach us of all things."[33] The Rules for the adult groups in the Methodist movement were intended to provide guidance on the Way of Salvation. They were read frequently in the meetings. And, because of the public nature of the Rules, people knew what was expected of them when they joined the Methodists.

What emerged in the Methodist movement was an organizational structure that provided instruction about God's grace and the Way of Salvation, as well as nurture in the Christian life through acts of piety (personal holiness), and opportunity to practice holy living through acts of mercy (social holiness). Participation in the life of the Methodist community included both critical learning and practical divinity. Each member of a Methodist society received instruction in the faith and nurture for holy living in a system whose purpose was behavioral change, spiritual growth, personal interaction, and community transformation. Henderson's dissertation study of John Wesley's instructional groups concluded: "Part of the genius of the Methodist movement was its concentration on the individual and his [or her] particular needs. Just as Susanna had tailored her spiritual instruction to the needs and interests of each child, so John and his associates individualized the tutoring of every person entrusted to their care."[34] This "tutoring" came through what emerged as an ingenious system of interlocking groups beginning with the Methodist society. But, as Henry Rack declared, "That development . . . was certainly not planned from the start but emerged through a series of accidents and improvisations."[35]

The Society

The "society" was a structure roughly equivalent to what we know as a congregation today, and it was an entry point into the process of faith formation in the Methodism movement. The only requirement for persons joining a Methodist society was "a desire to flee from the wrath to come, and to be saved from their sins."[36] The Wesleys had learned about the value of religious societies from both of their parents and from their Moravian friends. So the emergence of Methodist societies was a natural occurrence. In 1743, John Wesley wrote "The Nature, Design, and General Rules of the United Societies" defining a society: "Such a Society is no other than 'a company of [persons] "having the form, and seeking the power of godliness," united in order to pray together, to receive the word of exhortation, and to watch over one another in love, that they may help each other to work out their salvation.' "[37] The Wesleys used this definition of a society as well as the rules of the societies to recruit and orient new members. As John Wesley reported, "After preaching I desired those who determined to serve God to meet me apart from the great congregation. To these I explained the design, nature, and use of Christian societies."[38] And then, after the explanation, the Wesleys exhorted these persons to further their faith by forming a new society or joining an existing one.

When Peter Böhler gathered together the members of what John Wesley called "our little society"[39] at Fetter Lane, the rules of the society established a structure for membership, including several rules addressing a process by which new persons could be admitted to the society:

5. That any who desire to be admitted into this society be asked, What are your reasons for desiring this? Will you be entirely open, using no kind of reserve? Have you any objection to any of our orders? (which may then be read).
6. That when any new member is proposed everyone present speak clearly and freely whatever objection he has to him.
7. That those against whom no reasonable objection appears be, in order for their trial, formed into one or more distinct bands, and some person agreed on to assist them.
8. That after two months' trial, if no objection then appear, they be admitted into the society.[40]

The formation of strictly Methodist societies later provided an opportunity to learn what it meant to be Methodist—what Methodists believed and how Methodists lived by loving God and loving neighbor. The sermons of John and Charles Wesley, as well as Charles Wesley's hymns, proclaimed God's grace, while members were exhorted to practice a holy life in love of God and neighbor.

The Class Meeting

The class structure developed as an experiment in the Methodist movement when a suggestion was made that the Bristol society be divided into groups of eleven or twelve. The original intent was for class members to be canvassed by leaders for a penny a week to help pay the debt incurred from building the New Room.[41] In the words of John Wesley, "Many met together to consult on a proper method for discharging the public debt. And it was at length agreed (1) that every member of the society who was able should contribute a penny a week; (2) that the whole society should be divided into little companies or classes, about twelve in each class; and (3) that one person in each class should receive the contribution of the rest and bring it in to the stewards weekly."[42] When it became impracticable for leaders to visit each member weekly, the groups began to meet at the leaders' homes or at the meeting house.[43] This class structure soon became the norm for each Methodist society because of the benefits of Christian fellowship. Each person in a society became a member of a class that met weekly to " 'bear one another's burdens,' and 'naturally' to 'care for each other.' "[44] The design of the class was "that we will meet together once a week to 'confess our faults one to another, and pray for one another that we may be healed.' "[45] Classes were coeducational groups, and attendance was required in order to remain a Methodist. Rack observed, "Since the qualification for Methodist membership was not conversion but the desire for conversion, it followed that many were converted after they joined the society and class."[46]

Every member spoke at every meeting, with the process tailored after Susanna Wesley's practice of individual religious conversation with each of her children. Susanna Wesley had admonished John to "enter upon a serious examination of yourself, that you may know whether you have a reasonable hope of salvation by Jesus Christ; that is, whether you are in a state of faith and repentance or not."[47] This

same practice was used to reinforce new behaviors of personal and social holiness as class members assessed their lives each week according to the Rules: "*First,* By doing no harm, by avoiding evil in every kind. . . . *Secondly,* By doing good, by being in every kind merciful after their power, as they have opportunity doing good of every possible sort and as far as is possible to all [people]. . . . *Thirdly,* By attending upon all the ordinances of God."[48] Following these Rules provided evidence that class members continued to desire salvation.

The class leaders, either men or women, were appointed to supervise the progress of class members as they sought to live a holy life, to visit those who missed a meeting, and to report regularly to the Wesleys about the behavior of their members. John Wesley wrote, "I called together all the *Leaders* of the *Classes* . . . and desired that each would make a particular inquiry into the behaviour of those whom he [or she] saw weekly."[49] Members were held accountable for their progress, and a process for dismissal was part of the design: "That no particular member be allowed to act in anything contrary to any order of the society; and that if any persons, after being thrice admonished, do not conform thereto, they be not any longer esteemed as members."[50] Those who strayed were given three chances to amend their ways before being dismissed.

But, as we saw with the Fetter Lane Society, John Wesley tried to bring people back. "I endeavoured all this time, both by explaining in public those Scriptures which had been misunderstood and by private conversation, to bring back those who had been led out of the way."[51] When this failed, Wesley "regulated" the classes and bands, dismissing those who did not follow Methodist doctrine and lifestyle.[52] But Wesley was almost always ready to welcome those who wished to return and try again. "I rode to Berwick and, after preaching, desired all who *had been* of the society to meet me. I spoke to seventeen, who were thoroughly willing to unite again."[53] A relationship with the Christian community was necessary for faith formation, and the Wesleys did all they could to help people stay in relationship with God and their neighbors through the Methodist groups.

The Band

John Wesley borrowed the band structure from the Moravians. Author and ecumenist Rupert Davies reported that Wesley had expe-

rience with bands in Georgia, and then with the Fetter Lane Society.[54] After his visit to Herrnhut, Wesley established bands at Bristol and Kingswood prior to "the formation of the first specifically Methodist society."[55] The bands were for persons who gave evidence of deepening communion with God in their faith journeys and were willing to participate in frank soul-searching. While the societies and classes contained both men and women, married and unmarried, in early stages of growth in faith, bands were more homogeneous, particularly in terms of gender, age, marital status, and level of growth in faith. The rules for the band were very strict, with eleven questions to be answered upon entering the band and five questions addressed at each meeting:

1. What known sins have you committed since our last meeting?
2. What temptations have you met with?
3. How was you delivered?
4. What have you thought, said, or done, of which you doubt whether it be sin or not?
5. Have you nothing you desire to keep secret?[56]

According to Davies, persons who did not adhere to these rules could be "downgraded from band membership to society membership."[57]

The bands met weekly beginning with singing or prayer. According to John Wesley, the members were "to speak, each of us in order, freely and plainly, the true state of our soul, with the faults we have committed in thought, word, or deed, and the temptations we have felt since our last meeting."[58] Wesley also reported that he met with bands of men on Wednesday evening and with women on Sunday, "that they might receive such particular instructions, and such exhortations, as from time to time might appear to be most needful for them."[59] In addition, there were specific days scheduled for "general intercession" and "a general love-feast."[60]

The Select Society and The Penitents

The societies, classes, and bands formed the heart of the structure for faith formation in the early Methodist movement. Two additional groups were less common but important for faith formation as well. Members of the select society were handpicked from those within each society who had reached a deep level of communion

with God through the work of the Holy Spirit in the sanctifying process. This group provided leadership training through deeper exploration of doctrine and total commitment to be life patterns of holy living through Christian service. It was in this group that John Wesley found his own support, accountability, and guidance. "My design was, not only to direct them now to *press after perfection*; to exercise their every grace, and improve every talent they had received; and to incite them to love one another more . . . ; but also to have a *select company* to whom I might unbosom myself on all occasions, without reserve. . . . They had no need of being incumbered with many rules, having the best rule of all in their hearts," but they were bound to observe strict confidentiality, to obey their minister, and to contribute to a charitable fund.[61] Rules of the select society emphasized confidentiality so that each member could speak with candor. Wesley's expectation regarding participation was clear: "Everyone here has an equal liberty of speaking, there being none greater or less than another."[62] In addition, every member of the select society was expected to "bring once a week all he can spare toward a common stock."[63]

Another group, the penitent band, was dedicated to those who had fallen away and needed rehabilitation—persons who did not seem able to conform to the spiritual discipline of the Way of Salvation. Participants needed the desire to overcome their problems, while the Wesleys' goal was to restore them for participation in the class meetings. Henderson indicated that this group operated much as Alcoholics Anonymous does today, meeting on Saturday nights in order to keep the members out of the bars.[64] All of these groups were intended to provide an opportunity to practice a living faith while growing in knowledge of the faith. Davies observed that the difficulty in sustaining this complex system was that "the intricate distinctions between various spiritual states and grades came to be seen as impracticable."[65]

Structures for Holy Living

Holy living involves love of God and love of neighbor through vital piety and social holiness. The emphasis in the Methodist small group structure for adults was clearly on changing behavior for holy living. Preaching, exhortation, and hymn-singing in the society meet-

ings, self-examination and instruction for a holy life in the class meetings, and sharing deeper religious experience and accountability in the bands cultivated the relationship between knowledge and vital piety. In addition, regular participation in worship, particularly in the Lord's Supper, in the Anglican Church was expected.

Two additional structures emerged for nurturing vital piety. First, Wesley's Covenant Service was developed well into John Wesley's ministry. Norman Wallwork, a circuit superintendent, reported that about 1755, "Wesley urged his followers to make an express and solemn Covenant with God."[66] The covenant was to give up oneself in order to serve God: "Thou art become my Covenant-Friend, and I, through thy infinite grace, am become thy Covenant-Servant."[67] In Wallwork's words,

> Wesley clearly believed that it was not enough for the early Methodists to respond to the preaching of the law and the gospel, nor even to be set in the nurture house of the local Methodist band and class meetings. Once each year they were to commit themselves anew to their pilgrim journey. They were to lay hold again on the grace of their covenant God, and this they were summoned to do in the presence of their fellow Methodists.[68]

The Covenant Service, including the Lord's Supper, was held on the first Sunday of the year and was crucial for faith formation.

A second structure that was part of the practice of the bands was the Love Feast, first experienced by Wesley in Georgia through the influence of the Moravians. According to Wallwork, "This service was a common meal, with token food and drink, held for prayer, praise and fellowship, with the emphasis on testimony and thanksgiving."[69] The emphasis on fellowship and Christian family is evident here, once again providing an opportunity to grow in communion with God and each other. As Wallwork observed, "Wesley's intention, both for his preachers in Conference and for his people in the Methodist societies, bands and classes, was to deepen their fellowship and increase their joy. For Wesley, the New Testament knew nothing of solitary religion."[70]

In addition to the structures that enriched vital piety, structures emerged for active involvement in loving one's neighbor. Since many members of the societies were poor, stewards of the societies were

responsible for discovering physical need and seeing that the needs of the poor within the society were met. The responsibility of the stewards was not accidental or incidental, because John Wesley had a deep commitment to the poor. He was one of the first of his time who did not blame the poor for their situation. John Walsh, a noted Oxford scholar, described a change from seeing the poor as those who are "close to God" in the Middle Ages to a distinction between the "good poor" and the "bad poor" in the sixteenth century.[71] John Wesley was unique for his time in that he saw no distinction between good and bad poor. In fact, Walsh claimed Wesley had a "semi-mystical reverence for the poor"[72] that came from his understanding of the nature of the New Testament Church, in which goods were shared as a means of caring for the poor.[73] But Wesley was also convinced that the poor "receive God's revelation more clearly and directly"—that they truly are closer to God.[74] Therefore, loving one's neighbor means meeting the needs of the poor and sick. One plan for doing this was recorded in Wesley's *Journal* on May 7, 1741:

> I reminded the United Society that many of our brethren and sisters had not needful food; many were destitute of convenient clothing; many were out of business, and that without their own fault; and many sick and ready to perish: that I had done what in me lay to feed the hungry, to clothe the naked, to employ the poor, and to visit the sick, but was not alone sufficient for these things; and therefore desired all whose hearts were as my heart,
>
> 1. To bring what clothes each could spare, to be distributed among those that wanted most.
> 2. To give weekly a penny, or what they would afford, for the relief of the poor and sick.
>
> "My design (I told them) is to employ for the present all the women who are out of business, and desire it, in knitting.
>
> "To these we will first give the common price for what work they do, and then add, according as they need.
>
> "Twelve persons are appointed to inspect these, and to visit and provide things needful for the sick.
>
> "Each of these is to visit all the sick within their district, every other day, and to meet on Tuesday evening to given an account of what they have done, and consult what can be done farther."[75]

This plan demonstrates how structures of ministry were created to respond to need within the Methodist movement and to provide opportunity for Methodists to love their neighbors.

In terms of the larger Methodist organization, the Wesleys created a structure in which each member of a society was responsible for someone else. It was assumed that everyone had something to contribute to the care of others. Those who could contributed clothing and money. Some were appointed to visit the sick. Women who were out of work were employed to do knitting for the poor. Rack reported that "Wesley then proposed a regular organization to give employment in knitting at a fair price with supervisors who would also visit the sick."[76] Wesley himself provided a model for others in the Methodist movement through his own regular begging for the poor. Through these activities, Methodists learned that serving each other was doing God's will; the goal was a holy life. Every Methodist was expected to find a way to live in love for her or his neighbor. Henderson observed, "The service involved in mission became the context, not only the result, of serious discipleship."[77] This was practical divinity as Susanna Wesley had envisioned it: "You must understand what you say, and you must practice what you know."[78]

Structures for Critical Learning

Holy living was closely tied to growing in knowledge of faith, so John Wesley did not leave his interest in or his commitment to critical studies behind. He was a voracious learner himself, and it is clear that from his first experience as a tutor in Lincoln College, John Wesley thought of himself as an educator. As Frank Baker noted,

> Another aspect of Wesley's pastoral concern which shows up frequently in his letters is his enthusiasm as an educator. He served as a private correspondence tutor for several young men and women, offering them advice on methods of study, the reading of specific books, and even a five-year course of study, which he urged them to follow faithfully, because, as he told Joseph Benson: "When I recommend to anyone a method or scheme of study, I do not barely consider this or that book separately, but in conjunction with the rest," adding, "And what I recommend, I *know*: I know both the style and the sentiments of each author, and how he will confirm or illustrate what goes before, and prepare for what comes after."[79]

139

If women or men wanted to grow in their knowledge of faith, John Wesley was an eager teacher. Through his correspondence and religious conversations, he was teaching what we would call "directed studies" today—suggesting readings, discussing theological issues, asking questions, and pushing his students to think more deeply.

Because many of the Methodist preachers were uneducated, John Wesley began to create structures to further their education in Methodist doctrine and discipline. In particular, Wesley was concerned for the teaching role of Methodist preachers, since he obviously saw that as a critical task for those in ministry. So John Wesley began to hold retreats for the preachers. These retreats served as a way to regulate doctrine, discipline, and practice, and to educate the uneducated. In March 1747, John Wesley wrote of a Lenten retreat in Kingswood, "This week I read over with some young men a compendium of rhetoric and a system of ethics. I see not why a man of tolerable understanding may not learn in six months' time more of a solid philosophy than is commonly learned at Oxford in four (perhaps seven) years."[80] And during Lent 1749, Wesley held another retreat for assistants. "I had seventeen of them in all. These I divided into two classes, and read to one Bishop Pearson on the Creed, to the other Aldrich's *Logic,* and to both *Rules for Action and Utterance.*"[81]

In addition to the retreats, the Methodist conferences were opportunities for further faith formation through doctrinal discussions and prayer. In 1751, Wesley wrote, "Our conference began, and the more we conversed, the more brotherly love increased. The same spirit we found on Tuesday and Wednesday. I expected to have heard many objections to our first doctrines. But none appeared to have any. We seemed to be all of one mind, as well as one heart."[82] While these conferences gave the Wesleys an opportunity to further the faith formation of their workers, they also served to draw lines in doctrinal disputes and to dismiss those who did not adhere to Wesleyan theology.

CHRISTIAN FELLOWSHIP AND FAITH FORMATION

Teaching relationships and small group structures were so important for the Wesleys because they reflected the nature of Christian fel-

lowship, and Christian fellowship in the shape of a Christian family was the goal of a faith community in the Wesleyan ecology of faith formation. In other words, structures for faith formation in the Methodist movement promoted communion in community. We have already learned that the biblical and theological grounding for this understanding comes from John Wesley's belief that the Way of Salvation leads us to adoption as God's children when we will live in peace and unity with God and each other.

The small-group structures in the early Methodist movement provided opportunities to grow in ever deepening communion with God. While assessing the distinctions between the steps of a person's faith journey became impracticable, we can see how progressing through the group system provided markers of progress in faith growth. Another strength of the small-group system was that expectations were clear for each group. And John Wesley left nothing to chance. When he wrote the "General Rules of the United Societies," he gave specific guidance for each of the three rules. For example, doing no harm meant "avoiding evil in every kind," such as "the taking the name of God in vain."[83] One example of doing good was "by giving food to the hungry, by clothing the naked, by visiting or helping them that are sick, or in prison."[84] And John Wesley defined the ordinances of God as "the public worship of God; the ministry of the Word, either read or expounded; the Supper of the Lord; family and private prayer; searching the Scriptures; fasting, or abstinence."[85] God works through these disciplines for our growth in faith within the fellowship of faith. In his comparison of Wesley's views with those of other Reformers, Colin Williams observed that the societies' "rules for 'attending upon all the ordinances of God' enabled them to supplement the worship of the great congregation in such a way as to enable them to become priests to each other by mutual counsel and encouragement in the fellowship of the Spirit, and by their rules for 'doing no harm' and 'doing good' they sought to relate their common life of obedience to Christ to their contemporary social situation."[86] With the Rules came accountability, primarily through self-examination in the faith within the Christian fellowship of the small group.

The structures that we have discussed are represented in figure 4 as we continue to build a Wesleyan ecology of faith formation. This is a representative list, not an exhaustive list of structures. It is also

important to remember that Christian faith formation is more dynamic than this figure is able to represent, but once again we see the process of growth from God's first invitation to communion to full communion with God through the structures for teaching in the Methodist movement.

FIGURE 4
A WESLEYAN ECOLOGY OF FAITH FORMATION
"HOW TO TEACH?"
(STRUCTURES FOR TEACHING)

INVITATION TO COMMUNION Preventing and Justifying Grace "The God of grace, who all invites."[87]	DEEPENING COMMUNION Sanctifying Grace "Still let us in thy Spirit live."	FULL COMMUNION Glorification "Till to a perfect man we rise."
How to Teach? **Structures:** Society: instruction in the Christian life Class: behavioral change Penitents: rehabilitation Rules for these three groups: Do no harm Do all the good you can Attend to God's ordinance Accountability: Mandatory attendance Examination in faith	**How to Teach?** **Structures:** Society: Reflection on the Christian life Class: behavioral change Rules: Do no harm Do all the good you can Attend to God's ordinances Accountability: Mandatory attendance Examination in fait Band: deeper faith experience Rules: Answer five questions Accountability: Speak freely about state of one's sould and one's faults Examination in faith	**How to Teach?** **Structures:** Society: Exhortation to the Christian life Band: deeper faith experience Rules: Answer five questions each week Accountability: Speak freely about state of one's soul Select Society leaders sharing Rules: Confidentiality Obey minister Contribute to charitable fund Accountability: Mutual examination in faith
Structures for vital piety Structures for holy living	Structures for vital piety Structures for holy living	Structures for vital piety Structures for holy living
Critical / Practical **Learning Divinity**	**Critical - Practical** **Learning Divinity**	**Critical \ Practical** **Learning Divinity**

As we examine the summary of structures in the early Methodist movement in figure 4, we see that critical learning and practical divinity were essential to each phase of growing in communion with God, but the emphasis changed as persons grew in faith. For those who were new to the faith, the emphasis was weighted toward critical learning in the instructional mode (signified by /), since knowledge is necessary for those who practice a living faith. Growing knowledge provides the resources for reflecting on faith in the dialogical mode of deepening communion with God, so critical learning and practical divinity are more evenly weighted. And for mature Christians, the emphasis was weighted toward practical divinity in the embodied mode (signified by \), as Methodists practiced what they knew through personal and social holiness while growth in knowledge continued. This observation does not intend to diminish the Wesleys' sensitivity to the needs of the early Methodists. At any given time, the Wesleys would focus on knowledge or practice of the faith as needed. If persons needed clarification in their understanding of the faith or guidance for holy living, the Wesleys provided it.

The educational question of the relationship between critical learning and practical divinity—learning and holiness—was clearly tied to Christian fellowship and life in communion with God and one's neighbors. What did an early Methodist need to know in order to live a holy life in communion with God and others? What knowledge came through interaction with members of the community? What knowledge was shared through explicit means of instruction? Through preaching, singing, and exhortation in the society meetings, the fellowship of retreats for Methodist leaders, and "courses of study" administered through John Wesley's correspondence, learning became integral to a holy life.

Structures for nurturing a holy life in response to God's grace provided opportunities for critical reflection, as well as spiritual growth in the company of other Methodists. Life patterns were readily available both in face-to-face relationships and through letters shared by the Wesleys. Sharing these accounts of Christian lives and the explicit rules for participation in the Methodist movement provided guidance for holy living.

Structures for critical learning and practical divinity were based on the image of a Christian family, usually with a leader and a small

group—just as Susanna Wesley taught and cared for her small group. Leaders were charged with the care of souls and providing a life pattern of holiness. Teaching through written correspondence to one member of the Methodist family was as important as a class leader tending to several members of the class. In the Methodist system, knowledge and vital piety were united in structures that cultivated a Christian life. These structures contributed to the development of Christian identity and vocation through an emphasis on behavioral change as early Methodists learned to be participants in and responsible for Christian community through love of God and neighbor.

The educational question debated by Samuel and Susanna continues to be a challenge for educators today. If both critical learning and practical divinity are needed, how do we structure faith formation within the fellowship of a faith community so that knowledge informs practice and practice informs knowledge? And what is the role and shape of the Christian family in faith formation in a time when family structures are changing in our society? The Wesleys answered these questions within their own context. The challenge for us is to examine the context within which we live and to create structures for faith formation that provide grounding in knowledge of the faith as well as support for the practice of faith.

Chapter 7

"HOW TO TEACH?"

Practices and Discipline

The question of how to teach is closely connected with how persons learn. The practices of faith advocated by the Wesleys were borrowed and amended or developed through trial and error to meet the learning needs of those who wanted to be saved from their sin. As John Wesley wrote, "We are always open to instruction, willing to be wiser every day than we were before, and to change whatever we can change for the better."[1] We have already seen a number of these practices in the preceding chapters. While we cannot begin to construct an exhaustive list here, we will examine some of the most important practices in more depth.

This chapter addresses the question of method. In the words of Mary Elizabeth Mullino Moore, "Method is a systematic approach for reaching a goal or doing inquiry into an area of study."[2] The Wesleys' goal was saving souls through formation of holiness of heart and life, so the

interaction of critical learning and practical divinity that emerged in the Methodist movement was their method. What we are calling "practices" are what Moore called "techniques" or "particular practices that people use to carry out a method."[3] When the Wesleys assembled a system of practices (the Rules) intended to deepen persons' relationship with God and with each other, they created a Christian "discipline."

Just the fact that the name "Methodist" was applied to the Wesleys' group of young men at Oxford points to the focus on method that this chapter examines. In 1745 John Wesley explained his understanding of the term "Methodists." "By Methodists I mean a people who profess to pursue (in whatsoever measure they have attained) holiness of heart and life, inward and outward conformity in all things to the revealed will of God; who place religion in an uniform resemblance of the great Object of it; in a steady imitation of him they worship in all his imitable perfections; more particularly in justice, mercy, and truth, or universal love filling the heart and governing the life."[4] The Methodists were known for their disciplined life and the practices that enriched their physical and spiritual lives. From a disciplined diet and exercise to acts of piety such as prayer and searching the Scripture to works of mercy such as visiting prisoners, the Methodists practiced a holy life with the help of God's grace. These practices were essential for faith formation in the Methodist renewal movement.

In the beginning of this chapter, we will once again look at the practices of Susanna Wesley as Christian educator in the faith formation of her children and neighbors. Her infectious faith in God's "remarkable providence"[5] was sustained by practices that were passed on to her children. In the second part of this chapter, we will examine the Oxford discipline practiced by the members of the Holy Club in Oxford who went to Georgia. And finally, we will explore John Wesley's understanding of the means of grace as practices of faith and resources for teaching. Each of these topics provides numerous illustrations of the practices of faith that were so important to teaching the faith because they provided for the intertwining of knowledge and vital piety.

PRACTICES OF AN INFECTIOUS FAITH

The Wesleys believed that God has given us all we have and these gifts must be used for the glory of God. This faith provided courage

in the face of disaster, particularly for Susanna Wesley during the second Epworth fire. Usually the focus of the story is on John's narrow escape as the "brand plucked out of the burning,"[6] but Susanna Wesley's story is an equally powerful expression of faith.

On February 9, 1709, Susanna was about forty-one years of age and in the final month of pregnancy with her last child (the seventeenth or the nineteenth).[7] Samuel Wesley heard his daughter, Hetty, cry out when sparks fell from the roof onto her feet and roused the rest of the household. The children escaped through windows and the garden door, but Susanna was trapped when a wall of fire blocked the street door. Susanna sent this account of her experience to a neighboring clergyman in August of the same year.

> I was not in a condition to climb up to the windows; neither could I get to the garden-door. I endeavoured three times to force my passage through the street-door, but was as often beat back by the fury of the flames. In this distress, **I besought our blessed Saviour for help,** and then waded through the fire, naked as I was, which did me no farther harm than a little scorching my hands and my face.[8]

This is a striking example of Susanna Wesley's reliance on the providence of God and evidence that her confidence in God's benevolent care provided the foundation for her faith in a traumatic situation.

Susanna Wesley was never able to contain her infectious faith. From her well-informed decision to leave the Dissenting tradition of her parents before she was thirteen years of age[9] until her death, Susanna Wesley was a faithful witness to God's providential care. She expressed this calling by sharing her faith first with her children and then with her neighbors. Susanna knew the importance of developing the practices of faith in order to grow in faith, so she began to spend Sunday afternoons "reading to and instructing my family" because, as she wrote, "our religion requires a strict observation of the Lord's day."[10] When Samuel Wesley was away in 1712 and his parishioners heard of Susanna Wesley's sessions, they began to join in. The group would sing psalms, hear Susanna read one of Samuel's sermons, and have discussions about faith issues. In effect, Susanna Wesley had formed a religious society, and she knew it: "We banish all temporal concerns from our society. None is suffered to mingle any discourse about them with our reading or singing."[11]

Susanna Wesley had already written of her activities to Samuel when a letter from Samuel Wesley's curate complained that "Mrs. Wesley was having more people at her services than came to the parish church in the morning."[12] Susanna wrote to explain that her primary concern was that she could not ignore the parishioners' souls left under her care.

> As I am a woman, so I am also mistress of a large family. And though the superior charge of the souls contained in it lies upon you, . . . yet in your absence I cannot but look upon every soul you leave under my care as a talent committed to me under a trust by the great Lord of all the families, both of heaven and earth. And if I am unfaithful to him or you, in neglecting to improve these talents, how shall I answer unto him when he shall command me to render an account of my stewardship?[13]

In response, Samuel Wesley suggested that Susanna should have a man read his sermons, but Susanna replied that none of the men could read well enough.[14] But an even greater impropriety occurred when parishioners began attending prayers following the society's meeting.

Susanna Wesley's practice was to read the Order of Evening Prayer with her family after the parishioners had gone. When the parishioners begged to stay for prayers, Susanna acquiesced although she expressed appropriate distress at the obvious impropriety of conducting a complete service of worship. She did not doubt the need of the parishioners for prayer, "but because of my sex I doubt if it is proper for *me* to present the prayers of the people to God."[15] But Susanna Wesley did continue, and Samuel Wesley could not deny her success. In Susanna's words, "Since this our company has increased every night, for I dare deny none that ask admittance. Last Sunday I believe we had above two hundred. And yet many went away for want of room to stand."[16] In addition, Maldwyn Edwards, biographer of the Wesley family, claimed that Samuel's relationships with the parishioners were improved through Susanna Wesley's attention.[17]

At her death in 1742, John recognized his mother's ministry, "I cannot but farther observe that even she (as well as her father and grandfather, her husband, and her three sons) had been, in her measure and degree, a preacher of righteousness."[18] As a "preacher of righteousness," Susanna Wesley was involved in formational practices such as reading sermons, discussing faith issues, praying, and pro-

viding individual spiritual direction for her family and parishioners. As she wrote, "With those few neighbours that then came to me I discoursed more freely and affectionately."[19]

John Wesley was eight years old at the time he participated in these Sunday services and witnessed a successful religious society under his mother's leadership. The disciplines advocated by Susanna Wesley provided the means to focus on the Providence of God, to resist the sinfulness of earthly pleasures, and to practice faith as necessary for salvation. Her views were expressed later in a letter to John. "Take this rule. Whatever weakens your reason, impairs the tenderness of your conscience, obscures your sense of God, or takes off your relish of spiritual things; in short, whatever increases the strength and authority of your body over your mind; that thing is sin to you, however innocent it may be in itself."[20] Susanna Wesley's instruction would deeply affect John Wesley's understanding of personal holiness, the inner life of faith, and a person's relationship with God.

THE OXFORD DISCIPLINE

With this background, John Wesley was sent to Charterhouse School in London at ten and a half years old, where he reported losing at least some of his religion. "Outward restraints being removed, I was much more negligent than before even of outward duties, and almost continually guilty of outward sins, which I knew to be such, though they were not scandalous in the eye of the world. However, I still read the Scriptures, and said my prayers, morning and evening."[21] Then, in July 1720, John Wesley entered Christ Church in Oxford. It was at Oxford as a member of the Holy Club that John and Charles Wesley began a more serious application of Susanna Wesley's rule and developed the practices of faith learned at home into a daily discipline. In the words of John Wesley, "Our design was to read over the classics, which we had before read in private, on common nights, and on Sunday some books in divinity."[22] As we can see from the suggested reading, these meetings were not particularly focused on growth in faith. That would come in time. As the disciplined life of the Holy Club developed, "social work" and "observance of the fasts of the church" were added through the initiative of various members of the group.[23] William Morgan, for example, had involved the members of the Holy Club in prison ministry, but he

also engaged them in visiting the sick by 1730.[24] These spiritual practices developed in the Holy Club continued as the Wesleys embarked on a trip to Georgia.

Six months after Samuel Wesley's death in 1735, the two Wesley brothers, along with Mr. Delamotte and Mr. Ingham, departed for a mission in Georgia on board the *Simmons*. What follows is John Wesley's account of their daily disciplines on board the ship.

> We now began to be a little regular. Our common way of living was this: from four in the morning till five each of us used **private prayer**. From five to seven we **read the Bible** together, carefully comparing it (that we might not lean to our own understandings) with the writings of the earliest ages. At seven we breakfasted. At eight were the **public prayers**. From nine to twelve I usually learned German, and Mr. Delamotte, Greek. My brother writ **sermons**, and Mr. Ingham **instructed the children**. At twelve we **met to give an account** to one another what we had done since our last meeting, and what we designed to do before our next. About one we dined. The time from dinner to four we spent in **reading** to those of whom each of us had taken charge, or in **speaking to them severally**, as need required. At four were the **evening prayers**, when either the Second Lesson was explained (as it always was in the morning), or the **children were catechized** and instructed before the congregation. From five to six we again used **private prayer**. From six to seven I **read in our cabin to two or three of the passengers** (of whom there were about eighty English on board), and each of my brethren to a few more in theirs. At seven I joined with the Germans in their **public service**, while Mr. Ingham was **reading** between the decks to as many as desired to hear. At eight we met again, **to exhort and instruct** one another. Between nine and ten we went to bed, where neither the roaring of the sea nor the motion of the ship could take away the refreshing sleep which God gave us.[25]

In addition to these practices, Wesley and his companions, when they had opportunity, boarded other ships where "many were glad to join in prayer and hearing the Word."[26] On board ship and at stops along the route to Georgia, the Wesleys instructed a family in preparation for baptism,[27] preached and "distributed a few little books,"[28] visited the sick,[29] and served Holy Communion.[30] These activities mirrored those faith practices developed at Oxford. As the Holy Club grew in their practice of faith, they used the same practices to instruct and nurture other souls. Prayer, searching the Scripture, self-examination

in the faith, religious conversation, public worship, reading sermons or authors from the Christian tradition, exhorting, and instructing both adults and children were all practices used by these early Methodists for faith formation.

The Holy Club adopted a disciplined life in an attempt to be faithful and to hold each other accountable. It is helpful to remember that during this time John Wesley's understanding of faith was a highly rational one. His view of faithful discipleship emphasized obedience to God's will, and the disciplines practiced by the Holy Club fulfilled this aim. Later, as John Wesley's understanding of faith matured, the focus of the disciplined life would change from striving to do God's will to living a disciplined life in response to God's grace. As John Wesley wrote, "For his [or her] obedience is in proportion to [God's] love, the source from whence it flows."[31] And a disciplined life meant practicing the means of grace.

THE MEANS OF GRACE

The conflict with the Moravians in the Fetter Lane Society over the doctrine of stillness became an occasion for John Wesley to clarify his doctrinal understanding of the means of grace. The English Moravian Philip Molther taught that Christ is the only means of grace, so Christians should be "still" before God to wait for their salvation. As a result, the Moravians in the Fetter Lane Society would not participate in the Lord's Supper or other means of grace until they were saved. John Wesley argued for "Scriptural stillness" or waiting for assurance of salvation through Jesus Christ by practicing the means of grace. He was able to make this argument based on church tradition. "I understand outward signs, words, or actions ordained of God, and appointed for this end—to be the *ordinary* channels whereby [God] might convey to [humanity] preventing, justifying, or sanctifying grace."[32] Wesley later developed this doctrine more fully in his sermon on "The Means of Grace," dated sometime between 1741 and 1746 since the doctrine of stillness continued to be found in the Methodist movement during this period. As Albert Outler observed, "a sizeable group of Methodists in 1746 still continued to regard all 'outward observances' as superfluous, or even harmful, in their spiritual life."[33] The intent of this sermon was to convince these Methodists of the "validity, and even the necessity, of 'the means of grace' as taught and administered in the Church of England."[34]

151

John Wesley believed the power of the Holy Spirit is active in us through the means of grace. But he was quick to warn that participating in the means of grace does not earn our salvation. In Wesley's understanding, salvation is God's work and God gives us the means of grace as a way to salvation. In no way do we merit these gifts, but we do have a role in our own salvation by making ourselves available to the work of the Holy Spirit with the help of God's grace. There is neither *"power"* nor *"merit"* in using the means of grace[35] because "Christ is the only source of grace, but he has appointed meeting places where we may receive his grace."[36]

But there were those who abused the means of grace because, as Wesley wrote, they "began to mistake the *means* for the *end*, and to place religion rather in doing those outward works than in a heart renewed after the image of God."[37] Wesley wanted the Methodists to remember that God is the source of grace. God "can convey [God's] grace, either in or out of any of the means which [God] hath appointed."[38] Because of our human disposition toward sinfulness, these means of grace or "meeting places" provide a disciplined life that frees us from our worldly attachments so we can love God and our neighbor more fully.

We have already learned that John Wesley came to define the relationship between faith in God's active grace and human response through a long personal pilgrimage toward a mature understanding of faith. Salvation comes through faith alone, but salvation, as well as the desire for salvation, is a gift from God. The means of grace were vehicles through which God acted in the lives of women and men for their growth in faith. But the means of grace also became a way of teaching the faith. Early Methodists learned what it meant to be faithful by participating in the means of grace. We will use John Wesley's own words from his sermon on "The Means of Grace" to help us discover the meaning of these practices of faith: "I use this expression, 'means of grace,' because I know none better, and because it has been generally used in the Christian church for many ages: in particular by our own church, which directs us to bless God both for the 'means of grace and hope of glory'; and teaches us that a sacrament is 'an outward sign of inward *grace*, and a *means* whereby we receive the same.' "[39] Wesley broadened this understanding to other practices of faith that resulted in changed lives and a new dedication to love of

neighbor. This transformation is the work of God's grace experienced through the means of grace. Therefore it is imperative that Christians participate in the instituted and prudential means of grace whether they are already saved or on the way to salvation, because the means of grace open their hearts to God's work in them.

The Instituted Means of Grace

For John Wesley, the instituted means of grace are those means specifically instituted by Christ and are often referred to as "works of piety"—those practices that serve to deepen our relationship with God. "The Chief of these means are **prayer**, whether in secret or with the great congregation; **searching the Scriptures** (which implies reading, hearing, and meditating thereon) and receiving the **Lord's Supper**, eating bread and drinking wine in remembrance of him; and these we believe to be ordained of God as the ordinary channels of conveying [God's] grace to the souls of [humanity]."[40] The Holy Spirit works through these instituted means of grace to transform lives as persons grow in communion with God and neighbor.

Prayer. John Wesley based his understanding of prayer as an instituted means of grace in a reflection on the Sermon on the Mount: " 'Ask, and it shall be given you; seek, and ye shall find; knock, and it shall be opened unto you.' . . . Here we are in the plainest manner directed to ask in order to, or as a *means* of, receiving; to seek in order to find the grace of God."[41] Prayer is not an option for those who are seeking salvation because it is the door to our relationship with God. We have seen Susanna Wesley's concern for continuing prayer services during Samuel Wesley's absences. In the Wesleys' view, Christians must practice public, as well as private, prayer. We have already seen Wesley's admonition for the "constant use of family prayer."[42] In fact, Wesley wrote that one of the marks of a Methodist is that "he [she] 'prays without ceasing'. . . . Whether he [she] lie down or rise up, 'God is in all his [her] thoughts'; he [she] 'walks with God' continually, having the loving eye of his [her] mind still fixed upon [God]."[43]

The shipboard account of daily activities recorded by John Wesley noted two occasions of private prayer, public prayer in the morning and evening, and an evening worship service with the Moravians. On April 1, 1738, Wesley wrote that he was no longer confined to partic-

ular forms of prayers common to the Anglican tradition. "Being at Mr. Fox's society, my heart was so full that I could not confine myself to the forms of prayer, which we were accustomed to use there. Neither do I purpose to be confined to them any more, but to pray indifferently, with a form or without, as I may find suitable to particular occasions."[44] Whatever the form of the prayers, they shared some common elements in the Wesleys' practice. Colin Williams wrote that these elements included "the expression of our awareness of sin (deprecation), the longing for the fulfillment of God's promises within us (petition), requests for the needs of others (intercession), and our gratitude for all God's goodness and lovingkindness (thanksgiving)."[45]

Searching the Scripture. Prayer is closely connected with God's self-revelation in Scripture. John Wesley found "our Lord's direction" in John 5:39 when Jesus said, " 'Search the Scriptures.' . . . And for this very end did he direct them to search the Scriptures, that they might *believe in him*."[46] Through reading, hearing, discussing and meditating on Scripture, we discover God's will and direction for us. As Wesley wrote, "all who desire the grace of God are to wait for it in 'searching the Scriptures.' "[47] Wesley's shipboard account demonstrated his method of searching the Scriptures and comparing the message with writings from early church tradition. "From five to seven we **read the Bible** together, carefully comparing it (that we might not lean to our own understandings) with the writings of the earliest ages."[48] And in his *Journal*, Wesley reflected on the personal renewal that came from reading Scripture when he led public prayers in South Carolina. "I was much refreshed with those glorious promises contained both in the seventy-second Psalm and in the First Lesson, the fortieth chapter of Isaiah. Yea, 'they that wait upon the Lord shall renew their strength, and mount up with wings as eagles; they shall run and not be weary; they shall walk, and not faint!' "[49]

It is evident that Wesley intended for Methodists to do more than recreational reading of Scripture; they were to **search** the Scriptures. John Wesley drew on the experience of religious conversation with his mother about the meaning of Scripture and its implications for a way of life. As Williams explained it, a "knowledge of the whole of revelation" is needed, so Wesley believed Christians should read Scripture every day and carefully apply Scripture to life, "immediately practising what you learn there."[50] Susanna Wesley's teaching

about practical divinity is evident in this instruction—to practice what you know. As we saw in John Wesley's interpretation of the Beatitudes in chapter 3, Scripture provides Christians with all they need to know to follow the Way of Salvation.

The Lord's Supper. Instructions for the Lord's Supper are clearly articulated in the New Testament as John Wesley noted:

> Here then the direction first given by our Lord is expressly repeated by the Apostle: "Let him eat," "let him drink" . . . words not implying a bare permission only, but a clear explicit command; a command to all those either who already are filled with peace and joy in believing, or who can truly say, "The remembrance of our sins is grievous unto us; the burden of them is intolerable."[51]

We can see in this statement that the Lord's Supper was not limited to those who had experienced salvation. Wesley clearly believed that persons' lives could be transformed by God's grace through participation in the Lord's Supper. In light of this belief, it is no surprise that this was the means of grace most often advocated by the Wesleys; Christ has promised to meet us at Holy Communion so that our lives might be transformed. "Is not the eating of that bread, and the drinking of that cup, the outward, visible means whereby God conveys into our souls all that spiritual grace, that righteousness, and peace, and joy in the Holy Ghost, which were purchased by the body of Christ once broken and the blood of Christ once shed for us? Let all, therefore, who truly desire the grace of God, eat of that bread and drink of that cup."[52] We find a record of regular participation in this means of grace during the trip to Georgia, when Holy Communion was celebrated on Sundays and special days. According to John Wesley's account, on December 21, 1735, "we had fifteen communicants, which was our usual number on Sundays. On Christmas Day we had nineteen; but on New Year's Day, fifteen only."[53] Wesley also indicated that "one who was big with child, in a high fever, and almost wasted away with a violent cough, desired to receive the Holy Communion before she died."[54] But, according to Wesley's account, the woman began to recover as soon as she received the Lord's Supper. This sacrament was so important as a means of grace because it confirmed those who had been saved, it could convert those seeking salvation, and it brought healing to those who were physically and spiritually ill.

Fasting. In addition to prayer, searching the Scriptures, and partaking in the Lord's Supper, which John Wesley discussed in his sermon, he later included fasting and Christian conference as instituted means of grace. Rack reported that through the influence of new adherents like John Clayton, the Holy Club began to observe the fasts of the Anglican Church.[55] Williams indicated that "the purpose of fasting is to wean the soul from its natural attachment to earthly things and to keep before us our spiritual destiny."[56] John Wesley knew how easy it was to lose one's focus on God through the distractions of the world. He often experimented with diet to see what the body needed to sustain the practices of holy living.[57] On board the *Simmons* there was some evidence of fasting in Wesley's account. Prior to the ship's embarking, Wesley and his companions decided to live on a limited diet. "Believing the denying ourselves, even in the smallest instances, might by the blessing of God be helpful to us, we wholly left off the use of flesh and wine, and confined ourselves to vegetable food, chiefly rice and biscuit."[58] And at sea, Wesley reported the group had "agreed to leave off suppers; from doing which we have hitherto found no inconvenience."[59] For the Wesleys and their friends, fasting was a means of renewing their intention and energy for a Christian life.

Christian Conference. John Wesley had inherited the tradition of religious conversation from his parents and believed "that if one is to grow in the Christian life, [one] must see [one's] conversation as a divine trust given for the purpose of witnessing to [one's] faith."[60] This kind of examination of faith must be done in company with other faithful Christians. In our example of the daily activities on the trip to Georgia, we find occasions of Christian conferencing. One example is the three hours of reading and religious conversation scheduled each day. "The time from dinner to four we spent in reading to those of whom each of us had taken charge, or in speaking to them severally, as need required."[61] Another example of Christian conference is the meeting of the Oxford group for accountability and support in their ministry. "At twelve we met to give an account to one another what we had done since our last meeting, and what we designed to do before our next."[62] Gathering in small groups to share one another's burdens not only served as an occasion for accountability but also provided nurture and support for ongoing practice of the faith. During their third storm at sea, Wesley's group found com-

fort in Christian conference. "We spent two or three hours after prayers in conversing suitably to the occasion, confirming one another in a calm submission to the wise, holy, gracious will of God. And now a storm did not appear so terrible as before. Blessed be the God of all consolation!"[63]

Participation in the means of grace instituted by Christ is essential for faith formation in the Wesleyan tradition. These appointed meeting places are the places where those who are seeking to escape their sin may meet Christ and receive God's grace. The Wesleys believed that the instituted means of grace are for those already established in the faith, but they are also for persons who are seeking strength for repentance and saving faith.[64] Those who participate in the instituted means of grace were also exhorted to participate in the prudential means of grace by practicing a holy life.

The Prudential Means of Grace

The prudential means of grace provide the shape or structure of a faithful life, the discipline created by faithful Christians in response to God's mercy and grace. A variety of practices of faith could be included in the prudential means of grace. In the early Methodist movement, those who sought salvation participated in a society and the small-group system. The Rules for the societies, classes, and bands were prudential means of grace because they included works of piety and works of mercy—places where God could meet persons on the Way of Salvation. As John Wesley wrote:

> It is generally supposed that "the means of grace" and "the ordinances of God" are equivalent terms. We usually mean by that expression [the ordinances of God] those that are usually termed "works of piety," namely, hearing and reading the Scripture, receiving the Lord's Supper, public and private prayer, and fasting. And it is certain these are the ordinary channels which convey the grace of God to the souls of [humanity]. But are they the only means of grace? . . . Surely there are works of mercy, as well as works of piety, which are real means of grace. They are more especially such to those that perform them with a single eye.[65]

Christians who keep the "eye of their mind" focused on God while participating in acts of mercy will receive the blessing of God's grace. Several examples of Methodist involvement in loving their neighbors

157

are given here to illustrate how participation in these activities may become a means of grace.

First, the practice of visiting the sick began with the Holy Club and continued throughout the ministry of the Wesleys. As John Wesley wrote, "By the sick I do not mean only those that keep their bed, or that are sick in the strictest sense. Rather I would include all such as are in a state of affliction, whether of mind or body; and that whether they are good or bad, whether they fear God or not."[66] Wesley had a deep conviction about the connection between the mind and the body and believed that physical illness often came from conflicted minds and hearts. His *Journal* reported numerous instances of visiting the sick, sometimes naming the physical disease such as smallpox, violent pain, and spotted fever.[67] Both John and Charles Wesley dedicated much of their time to visiting the sick because they believed in the healing power of faith.

Visiting the sick in person was important because it was a means of grace. Just as we may feel that more comes to us through our good works than we have given, so it was with the early Methodists and their works of mercy. As John Wesley wrote,

> But these things you must do in your own person; you see, they cannot be done by proxy. Or suppose you could give the same relief to the sick by another, you could not reap the same advantage to yourself. You could not gain that increase in lowliness, in patience, in tenderness of spirit, in sympathy with the afflicted, which you might have gained if you had assisted them in person.[68]

Before entering into this work of mercy, John Wesley admonished Methodists that "you have neither sufficient grace, nor sufficient understanding, to perform it in the most excellent manner."[69] As a result, those who visit the sick must petition God for the strength and the wisdom to do this work. Once the visitors have attended to the "outward condition" of those who are ill and help meet their physical needs, they are to turn to spiritual care.[70] As Wesley wrote, "Having shown that you have a regard for their bodies you may proceed to inquire concerning their souls."[71] And the inquiry often turned into exhortation and instruction. In his sermon "On Visiting the Sick," John Wesley emphasized that anyone could do this work, including the rich, the poor, the young, and women.[72] Eventually, John Wesley

˙designated specific persons to serve as visitors of the sick. "I chose six and forty of them, whom I judged to be of the most tender, loving spirit, divided the town into twenty-three parts, and desired two of them to visit the sick in each division."[73] This work of mercy became part of the structure for holy living in the Methodist movement.

A second prudential means of grace that provided practice in holy living was the Wesleys' work with the poor. One work of mercy was collecting and distributing clothing. In 1740, John Wesley wrote, "We distributed, as everyone had need, among the numerous poor of our society, the clothes of several kinds which many who could spare them had brought for that purpose."[74] Another work of mercy provided houses for widows "who, although not sick, were not able to provide for themselves, and had none who took care to provide for them."[75] Collections from the bands helped to finance this project. Another work of mercy helped find employment for the poor and was also described by Wesley: "We took twelve of the poorest and a teacher into the society room, where they were employed for four months, till spring came on, in carding and spinning of cotton. And the design answered: they were employed and maintained with very little more than the produce of their own labour."[76] In each of these works of mercy both the poor and those who cared for the souls of the poor received the benefits of God's grace.

Other works of mercy included activities such as distributing free medicine to the sick poor,[77] establishing a lending fund for the poor,[78] and taking collections for the poor.[79] Each of these works of mercy involved members of the Methodist societies, classes, and bands through the donation of goods and money, or through participating in person in the love of neighbor. By God's grace, Methodists were given the strength to address these social issues and provide for the needs of their neighbors.

PRACTICING A HOLY LIFE

Practicing a holy life through the means of grace is central to a Wesleyan ecology of faith formation. Participation in the means of grace is a reflection of the Scriptural and theological grounding of the Wesleys' teaching and contributes to growing in communion with God and neighbor. The Wesleys guided persons in their practice of the means of grace by making expectations clear in the Rules and

providing support and accountability through individual counsel and Christian conference. Figure 5 records some of the practices we have seen in this chapter and throughout this text. They are grouped as instituted means of grace, also known as works of piety, and prudential means of grace that include the Rules for the Methodist groups and works of mercy. Some examples of additional practices addressed here or in other parts of this text are also listed.

FIGURE 5
A WESLEYAN ECOLOGY OF FAITH FORMATION
"HOW TO TEACH?"
(PRACTICES AND DISCIPLINE)

INVITATION TO COMMUNION	DEEPENING COMMUNION	FULL COMMUNION
Preventing and Justifying Grace "The God of grace, who all invites."[80]	Sanctifying Grace "Still let us in thy Spirit live.	Glorification "Till to a perfect man we rise."
How to Teach? **Practices and Discipline:** Instituted means of grace: Works of piety Prayer—private and public Searching the Scriptures Lord's Supper Fasting Christian Conference	**How to Teach?** **Practices and Discipline:** Instituted means of grace: Works of piety Prayer—private and public Searching the Scriptures Lord's Supper Fasting Christian Conference	**How to Teach?** **Practices and Discipline:** Instituted means of grace: Works of piety Prayer—private and public Searching the Scriptures Lord's Supper Fasting Christian Conference
Prudential means of grace Rules Works of mercy	Prudential means of grace Rules Works of mercy	Prudential means of grace Rules Works of mercy
Other Practices Plain truth Sermons Sing hymns Read Scripture, Christian writings, and letters of faith Individual counsel Supervision	Other Practices Plain truth Sermons Sing hymns Read Scripture, Christian writings, and letters of faith Dialogue Supervision	Other Practices Plain truth Sermons Sing hymns Read Scripture, Christian writings, and letters of faith Reflection on practice Mutual supervision

If we were to assess these practices in light of contemporary educational theory, we would commend the Wesleys for employing a most effective means of teaching so students learn through practicing a Christian life. And the learning was transformative because God's grace was at work as people participated in works of piety and mercy and then had opportunity to reflect on their experiences through self-examination in a small-group process.[81] Practicing holy living and reflecting on that practice in terms of a Wesleyan understanding of faith accompanied the work of the Holy Spirit to help people grow in communion with God and neighbor on the Way of Salvation.

Whatever means of grace we experience in our own faith journeys, we need to remember John Wesley's admonitions for practicing the faith from his sermon "The Means of Grace." First, he admonished that Methodists "retain a lively sense that God is above all means."[82] In other words, God is unlimited and acts in the ways God chooses. We should be careful not to limit God by our assumptions about the way God's benevolent care is expressed in the world.

A second word of admonition from John Wesley reminds us that the spiritual practice does not carry power in itself: "*before* you use any means let it be deeply impressed on your soul: There is no *power* in this. It is in itself a poor, dead, empty thing: separate from God, it is a dry leaf, a shadow. Neither is there any *merit* in my using this, nothing intrinsically pleasing to God, nothing whereby I deserve any favour at [God's] hands."[83] Wesley did not want us ever to forget that we cannot earn God's grace by our own faithful devotion. Our practices of faith open us to the working of the Holy Spirit, but that work of grace is always a gift.

Finally, John Wesley reminds us of the sole purpose for any means of grace: "in using all means, seek God alone."[84] We can abuse the means of grace by practicing them for other reasons, such as demonstrating what good Christians we are or using them to judge others' faithfulness. In Wesley's words, "Remember also to use all means as *means*; as ordained, not for their own sake, but in order to the renewal of your soul in righteousness and true holiness."[85] The goal of a faithful life is to seek God's grace for renewal of our lives of faith.

Wesley's focus on religious experience through participation in the means of grace led him to what Stephen Gunter described as "an adaptation of formal ecclesiology into a 'practical ecclesiology' that

met the need of the specific situation occasioned by the revival."[86] The practices that were encouraged and the structures for Christian faith formation that emerged were those that nurtured growth in holiness of heart and life. Through their work of faith formation, the Wesleys challenge the church today to involve ourselves in the vocation of saving souls, to provide foundational knowledge of the faith in creative ways, to model the practice of ministry for our time, and to be open to the grace of God in the intertwining of critical learning and practical divinity.

Part III

FAITH FORMATION FOR A NEW COMMUNION

Throughout this reflection, we have explored several elements of faith formation for holiness of heart and life in the Wesleyan tradition. In part 3 of this text we construct a complete picture of all that we have discussed. Then we turn to consider Christian faith formation in our day and the church's ministry of faith formation.

Chapter 8	explores the question of what this study of a Wesleyan ecology of formation for holiness of heart and life teaches us about the church's role in Christian faith formation today.
For Your Reflection:	How would you describe your vision for making disciples?

Chapter 8

MAKING DISCIPLES FOR A NEW DAY

We began our reflection by asking two questions: "How do we come to know ourselves as Christian?" and "How do we pass on a living faith so that the ministry and mission of the church will continue?" Our primary concern was the need for greater intentionality about faith formation in light of the complex personal, communal, and global issues faced by those who live on the doorstep of a new century. In his sermon "The Means of Grace," John Wesley quoted Psalm 89:1 from *The Book of Common Prayer*: "My song shall be always of the loving-kindness of the Lord: With my mouth will I ever be telling of thy truth, from one generation to another!"[1] But how do we tell the truth to the next generations? In light of this concern, it is even more important to assume that the venue for forming Christian identity and Christian vocation is participation in the life of a faith community so that together we might explore

what it means to be faithful disciples in our world. Our goal is Christian discipleship built on a living faith—a witnessing and serving faith.

As we examined the formative activities of the early Methodist movement, we discovered a complex process of faith formation for holiness of heart and life. In this chapter, we will review the larger picture of a Wesleyan ecology of formation for holiness of heart and life based on what we have learned about the eighteenth-century Methodist movement. Then we will turn to a discussion of formation for holiness of heart and life in our time. We will also reflect on renewing the Wesleyan tradition in our work as church leaders and educators in a new day and dream of creating a new Wesleyan ecology of faith in a new century.

From the beginning of this discussion, we have attempted to provide definitions and develop concepts that would help us understand each component of a Wesleyan ecology of faith formation as it developed. From the foundational elements of Scripture and theology interpreted through the lens of Christian tradition to specific faith practices, each chapter added another building block to our construction of a Wesleyan ecology of faith formation. The contribution of many witnesses, from the Wesleys and other early Methodists to modern-day interpreters, provided windows of understanding into the Wesleyan tradition and our rich inheritance from the faithful disciples who have led the way before us. Now our task is to make a critical and imaginative appropriation of the Wesleyan educational beliefs and practices, a task that will extend beyond the scope of this book.

A WESLEYAN ECOLOGY OF FAITH FORMATION

With all the elements assembled, figure 6 now offers a whole picture of my representation of a Wesleyan ecology of faith formation in the early Methodist movement. It is clear that ongoing research and reflection may contribute additional elements or reinterpret those represented here. So this construction is a work in progress and an invitation to the churches in the Wesleyan tradition to refine, reinterpret, and amend in light of their own research and reflection. And more important, perhaps, this is an invitation to consider how you might create a Wesleyan ecology of faith formation in your own local congregation so that faithful disciples are created for loving God and neighbor. For this reason, we will briefly review each element in the Wesleyan ecology of faith

formation represented here. We will then turn to a discussion of some particular insights from our reflection and their gift and challenge for our ministry of Christian faith formation.

FIGURE 6
A WHOLE PICTURE

INVITATION TO COMMNION Preventing and Justifying Grace "The God of grace, who all invites."[2]	DEEPENING COMMUNION Sanctifying Grace "Still let us in thy Spirit live."	FULL COMMUNION Glorification "Till to a perfect man we rise."
Vision: **Scriptural Foundation:** Matt. 5:3-5. Poverty of spirit, mourning, and meekness are evidence that God has removed barriers to faith so that humans might know themselves as totally dependent on God's grace and "become as little children." Love God and neighbor.	*Vision:* **Scriptural Foundation:** Matt. 5:6-7. Hunger and thirst for righteousness is filled by God so that we might love God and neighbor more fully. The merciful love their neighbors as themselves. Increase in love of God and neighbor.	*Vision:* **Scriptural Foundation:** Matt. 5:8-9. The pure in heart and the peace-makers love God with all their hearts and souls and minds and strength. God will adopt them as God's children. Fully love God and neighbor.
Theological Foundation: God as loving Parent is the giver of prevenient grace and invites us to repent of our sin. God's justifying grace overcomes barriers to communion through Christ's work in the atonement, and communion with God is restored.	**Theological Foundation:** The sanctifying grace of the perfecting work of the Holy Spirit empowers us to grow in love of God and neighbor.	**Theological Foundation:** Sanctification is participating in the Divine character and constant communion with the Three-One God.
Context: The Church Repentance of sin and anticipation of full communion with God.	*Context: The Church* Renewing work of the Spirit to build community of faith.	*Context: The Church* Life in communion with God and neighbor. Life patterned after

Life patterned after
communion of the Trinity.
Life together as
curriculum for formation.

Life patterned after
communion of the Trinity.
Nurturing progressive
growth in holiness.

communion of the Trinity.
Agent now of the coming
kingdom of God.

What to Teach?
**Gaining Christian Belief
and Practice:** Emphasizes
an **instructional mode**
teaching what it means to
live in communion.

What to Teach?
**Clarifying Christian Belief
and Practice**: Emphasizes a
dialogical mode of conversing about the meaning of the
communion of faith.

What to Teach?
**Extending Christian
Belief and Practice:**
Emphasizes an
embodied mode of
practicing the means
of grace and living in
communion with God
and neighbor.

Formative Process:
Instructing persons in
the beliefs and practices
of the Christian life.
Nurturing the Christian
life through the means
of grace.

Formative Process:
Exploring the beliefs and
practices of the Christian
life. Nurturing the Christian
life through the means
of grace.

Formative Process:
Embodying the beliefs
and practices of the
Christian life. Nurturing
the Christian life through
the means of grace.

Who Shall Teach?
Qualities:

Who Shall Teach?
Qualities:

Who Shall Teach?
Qualities:

1. **True dedication to
   God and to the care
   of souls.**
2. **Knowledge of
   Methodist doctrine
   and practice.**
3. Commitment to
   Christian disciplines
   of practicing the
   means of grace and
   dedication to
   teaching others.
4. Ability to work with
   a diverse group of
   people. "Plain talk
   for plain people."
5. Life pattern of
   personal and social

1. True dedication to
   God and to the care
   of souls.
2. Knowledge of
   Methodist doctrine
   and practice.
3. **Commitment to
   Christian disciplines
   of practicing the
   means of grace and
   dedication to
   teaching others.**
4. **Ability to work with
   a diverse group of
   people. "Plain talk
   for plain people."**
5. Life pattern of
   personal and social

1. True dedication to
   God and to the care
   of souls.
2. Knowledge of
   Methodist doctrine
   and practice.
3. Commitment to
   Christian disciplines
   of practicing the
   means of grace and
   dedication to
   teaching others.
4. Ability to work with
   a diverse group of
   people. "Plain talk
   for plain people."
5. **Life pattern of
   personal and social**

holiness—a model of living faith, seeking nothing on earth, and glorifying God with body and spirit. 6. Evidence of continued growth in love of God and neighbor.	holiness—a model of living faith, seeking nothing on earth, and glorifying God with body and spirit. 6. Evidence of continued growth in love of God and neighbor.	**holiness—a model of living faith, seeking nothing on earth, and glorifying God with body and spirit.** **6. Evidence of continued growth in love of God and neighbor.**
Teaching Relationships: Instructional relationships. Life pattern. Parent-child. Christian family.	**Teaching Relationships:** Dialogical relationships. Life pattern. Teacher-student. Christian family.	**Teaching Relationships:** Mutually accountable relationships. Life pattern. Mutual participation in teaching and learning. Christian family.
How to Teach? **Structures:** Society: Instruction in the Christian life Class: behavioral change Penitents: rehabilitation Rules for these three groups: Do no harm Do all the good you can Attend to God's ordinances Accountability: Mandatory attendance Examination in faith	***How to Teach?*** **Structures:** Society: Reflection on the Christian life Class: behavioral change Rules: Do no harm Do all the good you can Attend to God's ordinances Accountability: Mandatory attendance Examination in faith Band: deeper faith experience Rules: Answer five questions Accountability: Speak freely about state of one's soul and one's faults Examination in faith	***How to Teach?*** **Structures:** Society: Exhortation to the Christian life Band: deeper faith experience Rules: Answer five questions each week Accountability: Speak freely about state of one's soul and one's faults Select Society: leaders sharing Rules: Confidentiality Obey minister Contribute to charitable fund Accountability: Mutual examination in faith
Structures for vital piety Structures for holy living	Structures for vital piety Structures for holy living	Structures for vital piety Structures for holy living
Critical / Practical **Learning Divinity**	**Critical - Practical** **Learning Divinity**	**Critical \ Practical** **Learning Divinity**

Practices and Discipline:	Practices and Discipline:	Practices and Discipline:
Instituted means of grace:	Instituted means of grace:	Instituted means of grace:
Works of piety	Works of piety	Works of piety
Prayer—private and public	Prayer—private and public	Prayer—private and public
Searching the Scriptures	Searching the Scriptures	Searching the Scriptures
Lord's Supper	Lord's Supper	Lord's Supper
Fasting	Fasting	Fasting
Christian Conference	Christian Conference	Christian Conference
Prudential means of grace	Prudential means of grace	Prudential means of grace
Rules	Rules	Rules
Works of mercy	Works of mercy	Works of mercy
Other Practices	Other Practices	Other Practices
Plain truth	Plain truth	Plain truth
Sermons	Sermons	Sermons
Sing hymns	Sing hymns	Sing hymns
Read Scripture, Christian writings, and letters of faith	Read Scripture, Christian writings, and letters of faith	Read Scripture, Christian writings, and letters of faith
Individual counsel	Dialogue	Reflection on practice
Supervision	Supervision	Mutual supervision
Christian / Christian **Identity Vocation**	**Christian - Christian** **Identity Vocation**	**Christian \ Christian** **Identity Vocation**

The **aim** of a Wesleyan ecology of faith formation is to make disciples—to shape Christian identity and Christian vocation so that persons respond to God's prevenient grace and find new meaning for their lives in faithful discipleship. Formation for holiness of heart and life helps persons grow in relationship to God and neighbor. This growth was evident in John Wesley's own struggle to understand the nature of faith and salvation. He moved from his first emphasis on what we must do to obey God's will, to what God alone does for us in Jesus Christ, and then to a more balanced focus on what God does for us through Jesus Christ and our response to God's abundant grace. Wesley concluded that there are "degrees of faith" and that the Way of Salvation is marked by God's transforming power, which continues in a process of growth over time. As a result, the primary aim of Christian faith formation for the Wesleys was to awaken per-

170

sons to the availability of God's grace so that they might surrender their wills to God and be transformed for a holy life. A second aim of faith formation was to develop the church's role in nurturing and supporting human response to the prompting of the Holy Spirit, including holding a person accountable for the practice of a holy life.

The **vision** of a Wesleyan ecology of faith formation comes from the Wesleys' conviction that Scripture provides us all we need to know to be saved. By drawing on "The Sermon on the Mount," John Wesley proclaimed that our progress along on the Way of Salvation is described and guided by Scripture. The Beatitudes teach us how to live and reveal God's promises to us. By responding to God's grace in our lives and following the guidance of the Beatitudes, the work of the Holy Spirit will help us grow in communion with God and our neighbor. Theologically, the Wesleys taught that God's grace is free for all. The Three-One God provides the Way of Salvation through preventing, justifying, and sanctifying grace, inviting us to share in the communion of the Trinity. Our part in our salvation is to respond to God's invitation to communion by repenting of our sin and loving God and our neighbor. While we wait for assurance of our salvation, we are to practice a holy life, loving God and neighbor. Through the work of the Holy Spirit, we continue to grow in deepening communion with God and our neighbor until in full communion we are adopted as God's children and live in peace with one another.

The **context** for a Wesleyan ecology of faith formation is the community of the church that is called to pattern its life after the communion of the Trinity. Formation for holiness of heart and life occurs through participation in the shared life of the faith community. In his discussion of the Way of Salvation, John Wesley described the church as a community that is growing in communion with God along with its individual members. John Wesley's primary metaphor for the Christian community was the "Christian family," signifying a small group of people who knew each other well, who could bear one another's burdens, and who would hold each other accountable for practicing the Christian life. The early Methodists gathered in larger societies but also participated in small groups. Through this structure we begin to see the church as the whole community of Christian formation, composed of smaller communities that nurture a holy life.

The question of **what to teach** addressed the proposition that

171

shared belief and practice is the content of Christian faith formation. In this discussion, I proposed that instructing, dialoguing, and embodying modes of faith formation are needed to help members of a faith community gain, clarify, and extend Christian belief and practice so that they might grow in communion with God and neighbor. As we saw in the case of the Fetter Lane Society, the Wesleys worked toward consensus about belief and practice to fulfill their vision of living in communion with God and one another. The controversy over the doctrine of stillness illustrated the fact that differing beliefs about how God works to change human lives carry implications for spiritual practices. The Wesleys believed that participating in the means of grace was necessary for a holy life.

The question of what to teach also impacts the question of **who shall teach**. This component of a Wesleyan ecology of faith formation highlighted the role of educators in the whole Christian family. The Wesleys' emphasis on teaching relationships in the home, in the schools, and in the Methodist movement relied on small groups with an appointed teacher or leader charged with care of souls. It was clear that **leaders are educators** in the Wesleys' view. John Wesley provided instruction and guidance for parents, schoolteachers, and church leaders, specifically addressing preachers, lay leaders, and women about their responsibilities for Christian education. From these examples, we determined that the qualities that were particularly important for teachers in the early Methodist movement included their dedication to God and to the care of souls; their knowledge of doctrine, discipline, and practice; and their continued growth in faith. And, more important, teachers were to be life patterns of a living faith, providing a model of a holy life.

The question of **how to teach** first led us to structures and practices for formation of holiness of heart and life that provided an opportunity for critical learning and practical divinity through participation in the life of the faith community. The Wesleys' commitment to a combination of instructing in the faith and nurturing the practice of faith led to the structures and practices that emerged in the early Methodist movement. The small-group structures in the Methodist movement were patterned after the Wesleys' image of Christian family—groups that fostered intimate relationships in which honest examination of one's faith could occur. The Christian family not only

provided guidance and support for formation for holiness of heart and life but also was a source of accountability as persons learned to practice a holy life. Practicing a holy life was nourished through sermons, hymns, exhortation, searching the Scripture, and Christian conferencing. Structures for vital piety and holy living, particularly the rules for the small groups, gave early Methodists an opportunity to participate in practices necessary for growth in faith, such as the instituted and prudential means of grace. Works of piety and works of mercy were practices through which God worked to deepen their love of God and neighbor. Not only did this Wesleyan ecology of faith formation serve to renew the church in the eighteenth century, but it also holds important insights for the renewal of faith formation in the church today.

FORMATION FOR HOLINESS OF HEART AND LIFE

The focus of the Wesleys' ministry on the salvation of souls, an aim undoubtedly influenced by Susanna Wesley's expressed desire to contribute to the salvation of her children's souls, calls the church to renew its commitment to making disciples through Christian faith formation. When the aim of individual salvation and the care of souls is united with the Wesleys' belief that grace is available to all and free for all, it is not difficult to see how John Wesley came to claim the whole world as his parish. "I look upon *all the world as my parish*; thus far I mean, that in whatever part of it I am, I judge it meet, right, and my bounden duty to declare unto all that are willing to hear the glad tidings of salvation."[3] In the Wesleyan tradition, we proclaim the good news by loving God and neighbor. As leaders in the church, our mandate is to make disciples who love God and neighbor through a process of Christian faith formation in the Christian community. As we move into a new century, the churches in the Wesleyan tradition must imaginatively create a vision for a new communion grounded in God's redeeming grace, a communion that fosters formation for holiness of heart and life.

Grounded in Faith

John Wesley proclaimed that there will be "an uninterrupted union with God; a constant communion with the Father and his Son Jesus

Christ, through the Spirit; a continual enjoyment of the Three-One God, and of all the creatures in [God]!"[4] Out of this heritage comes our shared vision of God's intention for the world—living in peace as children of God in full communion. How this vision is embodied in our shared life together has been and is being created as members of the faith community come together to grow in their knowledge and love of God and neighbor. The vision becomes a guide for forming lives of faith, engaging us to create a Wesleyan ecology of faith formation that helps people grow toward full communion with God through the perfecting work of the Holy Spirit.

At the heart of formation for holiness of heart and life is the belief that God's grace is free for all and is already at work in all persons. We have seen that the message of the unlimited nature of God's grace was a powerful word in the faith formation of early Methodists. This word of grace is also a word of justice, because **all persons** have equal access to God's preventing, justifying, and sanctifying grace. With the faith that God's grace was available to all and denied to no one, many persons in eighteenth-century England were transformed for faithful discipleship. That same grace is available to us now for the transformation of those who seek a new life in Christ. Transformation means that lives are radically changed. For Wesley, evidence of transformation was found in the ways persons loved God and their neighbors. Robert Evans of Plowshares Institute noted that transformation by God's grace affects all of life: "Transformation calls for nothing less than a *metanoia* or conversion that encompasses the whole person and society. The conversion affects relationships among God's children—the whole of creation."[5] Through this profound transformation, priorities change and lifestyles reflect a new relationship with God and neighbor.

In formation for holiness of heart and life, a new relationship with God and its resulting lifestyle changes are formed and nurtured in a community of faithful Christians who participate together in the means of grace. Through worship, instruction, service, and fellowship, God is at work so persons may come to know themselves as Christian. We have already heard that Susanna Wesley admonished her son "to shun the company of profane wits as [he] would the plague,"[6] and to keep company with those who are faithful. As members of a local congregation, we are the company of the faithful who

provide witness to God's transforming power through our words and actions. Our role in Christian faith formation is to build community by valuing each person who comes into our midst, regardless of how different they are from us. One of the churches in the Wesleyan tradition stated it this way: "Primary for us is the gospel understanding that all persons are important—because they are human beings created by God and loved through and by Jesus Christ and not because they have merited significance. We therefore support social climates in which human communities are maintained and strengthened for the sake of all persons and their growth."[7] This statement reflects a shared commitment to carry on the Wesleyan tradition through the care of souls by nurturing communities that form in the intersections of life. A recent discussion about the role of community in formation proposed a "new commons"—"a place where the diverse parts of a community could come together and hold a conversation within a shared sense of participation and responsibility."[8] This proposal provides one way to name the role of the faith community in faith formation.

In creating a Wesleyan ecology of faith formation in the new century, the faith community needs to provide opportunities for dialogue about our Wesleyan heritage with an openness to the theological diversity that meets us in the intersection of faith and life. John Wesley believed we could be united in the midst of theological diversity through our shared belief in Jesus Christ: "But as to all opinions which do not strike at the root of Christianity, we 'think and let think.' "[9] Yet the Wesleys were quite clear about doctrinal claims that were non-negotiable and therefore formed the boundaries of what was theologically acceptable in the Methodist movement. It is important to note, however, that dismissal from a Methodist group was more often due to a combination of lack of desire to escape one's sins and lack of commitment to a Christian life than to theological diversity. Our concern in creating an ecology of formation for holiness of heart and life in our time needs to be focused on invitation to new life in Christ as well as instruction and nurture to grow and sustain lives of faith. It is in the intersections of the shared life of a community that persons find a new identity in communion as they are formed for holiness of heart and life.

175

A New Identity in Communion

Formation for holiness of heart and life invites persons to keep their eyes on God, leaving individualism behind and taking on a new identity in the communion of community. They become part of the Christian family. A new Wesleyan ecology of faith formation needs to help persons make sense of their lives through eyes of faith as they tell their own stories of faith and hear the faith stories of others in light of our shared vision of a new communion. Christian belief and practice are shaped by the Christian tradition, the Wesleyan heritage, and shared faith experience through this interaction. Thinking together about the implications of love of God and love of neighbor leads to action as Christians answer the question "What does it mean to be Christian in our time?"

The Wesleys' understanding of the nature of the church as communion provides an important context for faith formation for new generations that seek authentic and meaningful relationships in their lives.[10] Just as God relates to us in different ways through the persons of the Trinity and invites us into fellowship, so we are to invite others into fellowship with us through God's grace. Living in communion with one another helps us overcome our individualism and binds us together as we find our Christian identity through our relationship to God and God's people. Our Christian vocation as a community of faith is to make disciples through our shared life, to pass on a living faith to each new generation. The aim of Christian faith formation is that souls might be saved and the work of God might continue through hearts, hands, feet, and minds dedicated to new life in Christ.

The Wesleys challenge us with the metaphor of "Christian family" to denote the intimacy of communion in the faith community. In an age of on-line relationships, video consultations, and constant cell-phone chatter, what does "Christian family" mean? What do we do with the Wesleys' notion that face-to-face relationships are critical for formation for holiness of heart and life? While some of us may have experienced one or more of the small groups within the life of our congregation that have served to provide this more intimate fellowship and mutual sharing of the faith journey, others are finding more meaningful relationships outside the church. The Wesleys have taught us that a Wesleyan ecology of faith formation must be atten-

tive to the needs of people in the places where they live. While not giving up on the importance of face-to-face relationships, a new Wesleyan ecology of faith formation will need to be creative in its use of technology to build a community of disciples. And the goal of this new community is still to focus our eyes on God in order to grow in love of God and neighbor.

If formation for holiness of heart and life is to occur within the life of the faith community, we need to be clear about our vision for Christian formation. As we establish small-group ministries, whether in person or on-line, we need to be intentional about their connection to the whole process of faith formation. We need to be able to articulate the biblical sources and theological understandings that provide grounding for these groups. We need to assess how they fit into an appropriate balance between critical learning and practical divinity. And we need to find ways to be in ministry to those who do not participate in any small groups within the faith community.

The process of constructing a Wesleyan ecology of faith formation also raises the question of accountability in community. What are our expectations for those who would be Wesleyan and Christian? We have already seen that in order to be part of the Methodist movement, one had to attend a class meeting every week and practice the means of grace. What is it that we require for continuing participation in the life of our congregations? In some of our churches, new members are asked, "Will you faithfully participate in [the church's] ministries by your prayers, your presence, your gifts, and your service?"[11] How do we hold persons accountable for these vows? What is our role as the faith community in educating and supporting our members as they strive to uphold these commitments? We have numerous examples of ministries within our congregations that make high demand and receive enthusiastic participation, such as Disciple Bible Study and Volunteers in Mission. The enthusiasm for these ministries calls us to reevaluate what we as leaders have often assumed about the lack of motivation and commitment of our laity to growth in love of God and neighbor.

As we create a new Wesleyan ecology of faith formation in our own congregations, our focus must be on building community where persons hear God's invitation to communion through us. We need to provide hospitable places where people can meet to share their sto-

ries. We need to tell more of the story about who we are and how we came to be. Just as we learn who we are in relationship to our family tradition by hearing the stories of our parents and grandparents, we also learn who we are as Christians and Wesleyans by hearing the story of the Wesleys and the early Methodists. As individual stories come into contact with the story of God's invitation to communion, the community as well as the individual is enriched and transformed. By sharing stories about the theology and vision of the Wesleys, we contribute to the formation of Christian identity and vocation. In general conferences, in districts and annual conferences, or in other regional meetings, lay gatherings, or clergy conferences, we need to celebrate the faith and heritage we hold in common, dialogue about the differences in emphasis and interpretation, and renew our commitment to holy living.

Holy Living—Growing in Discipleship

In our observation of the work of the Wesleys and the lives of the early Methodists, the belief that the Way of Salvation begins and ends with holy living provides an important clue to constructing a new Wesleyan ecology of faith formation. Holy living includes works of piety and works of mercy—loving God, the source of grace, and loving neighbor in response to God's grace. With the involvement of so many early Methodists in works of mercy, participating in the shared life of service or mission became a primary means for faith formation. Through serving others, persons grew in their Christian identity and vocation as faithful disciples called to love God and their neighbors, even those they did not know. If our life together in service is the curriculum of faith formation, then practicing the faith becomes the occasion for reflecting on faith.

The early Methodists challenge us to be more diligent in providing opportunities for theological exploration as we construct a new Wesleyan ecology of faith formation. Doctrinal instruction as persons work together to interpret the faith meaning of their experiences would help them grow in knowledge and in faith. Through dialogue and exploration of faith, persons could learn to hear different theological perspectives as attempts to be faithful. By putting more effort into building community and nurturing the life of community, the church could cultivate openness to the richness of diversity while

celebrating our shared identity. Our parents in the faith invite us to reflect on our own lives together in light of God's invitation to communion.

The model of offering instruction in Christian belief and practice while nurturing a Christian lifestyle was a powerful formative influence in the Methodist movement. The key was providing opportunities to reflect on issues of living in light of one's faith. Guidelines for a Christian life can be found in the Rules and in Wesley's sermons, so the early Methodists knew what it meant to be faithful. The Wesleys also challenge us to be more attentive to evaluation of our efforts and to learn from our experiences in light of our vision. The Wesleys evaluated all aspects of the early Methodist movement by their adherence to loving God and neighbor. Were lives changed? Was increasing love of God and neighbor evident through works of piety and works of mercy? The Wesleys' aim was not growth in congregational size, but increase in the number of souls saved to love God and neighbor.

As members of the communion of the faithful today, we are called to make disciples who love their neighbors. Formation for holiness of heart and life prepares persons to see, hear, and minister to those who might be invisible to others, those who indeed live and work in our midst. Parker Palmer wrote that community is a gift from God. In fact, as Palmer notes, "In a true community we will not choose our companions, for our choices are so often limited by self-serving motives. Instead, our companions will be given to us by grace. Often they will be persons who will upset our settled view of self and world. In fact, we might define true community as that place where the person you least want to live with always lives!"[12] Being part of the Christian family does not mean that all of us look alike or share the same background. We may not even come together with much shared experience. Yet the image of full communion with God and adoption as God's children provides a vision for our life together.

As members of a diverse faith community growing in communion, we need to create new forms of shared experience. One example of a shared experience that holds great possibility for critical learning in the midst of practical divinity in our time is Volunteers in Mission. As Volunteers in Mission meet their neighbors at home or in other neighborhoods or countries, new communities are formed. And in

179

these meetings, participants come to know themselves and God more deeply. Reflection on experience is part of group life, but what would it be like for each group to be accompanied by someone who has knowledge of Wesleyan history and doctrine and could serve as a resource for theological exploration in the midst of the work they share? This type of reflection could be planned for any group of church people who serve meals to the homeless, build houses for Habitat for Humanity, or tutor inner-city children in an after-school program. Christian faith formation takes place as disciples move into the world to serve and then gather together to reflect in faith on their experience. Including instruction, exploration, and embodiment of Christian belief and practice in mission ministry would contribute to faith formation for holiness of heart and life.

A MINISTRY OF FAITH FORMATION

For John Wesley, the whole economy of the people called Methodists meant having a clear sense of relationships, structures, and practices of faith formation, including the rationale for each practice and an evaluation of its effectiveness. Wesley's growing awareness and articulation of a ministry of faith formation brings the gift of insight to us as we attempt to construct a new Wesleyan ecology of faith formation. As we have learned, Wesley's economy was not planned far in advance but evolved through trial and error as shared Christian belief and practice were more clearly articulated and as human need was observed. Close ties between physical and spiritual well-being were recognized in developing practices for loving one's neighbor. The Wesleys' emphasis on self-examination and openness to learning led to the incorporation of grassroots ministries that bore fruit. Tradition or convention was sometimes reluctantly set aside if other means were more fruitful for saving souls. The relationships, structures, and practices of the Wesleys' economy were grounded in their theological interpretation of the central message of Scripture: All persons are invited by God's prevenient grace to communion with God; they will be saved from sin through the work of Jesus Christ; and they will continue to grow in communion with God and neighbor through the work of the Holy Spirit.

In this text, I have claimed that the ministry of Christian education

addresses the tasks of shaping Christian identity and vocation through faith formation by helping us grow in our relationship with God. Our aim is to make disciples who respond to God's grace by loving God and their neighbors. All of the ministries of the church are needed to create a new Wesleyan ecology of faith formation, but the discipline of Christian education has the expertise to guide the construction of the formational system. If the shared life of the faith community is the curriculum of faith formation, and if an effective means of making disciples is instruction in the midst of holy living, then leaders of the church should be about creating and exploring intersections in the world. They may be intersections between individuals and groups within the local congregation, intersections between the church and the world, or intersections with other churches in the Wesleyan tradition. A new Wesleyan ecology of faith formation would be based in contextual formation for holiness of heart and life in these intersections by combining practical divinity and critical learning through works of piety and works of mercy in love of God and neighbor.

We have used the word "ecology" to mean an interconnected, interrelated, and interactive system of relationships, structures, and practices. In a Wesleyan ecology of faith formation, all of the parts work together: proclaiming, inviting, teaching, caring, and serving. We have seen this type of ecology come alive in the work of the Wesleys as they proclaimed the gospel, then invited persons to come together to form a society and participate in Methodist classes. Through this system, Methodists were taught about Christian belief and Christian lifestyle. They also were engaged in caring for each other's souls and serving their neighbors. All of these elements composed their life together and became the curriculum for ongoing faith formation.

A new Wesleyan ecology of faith formation needs to include proclamation and witness to the good news of God's grace, invitation to respond to God's grace, ongoing instruction and nurture in faith, caring support for persons on their pilgrimages of faith, opportunities for service on behalf of one's neighbors, and fellowship with other Christians. A ministry of faith formation in the Wesleyan tradition requires that we share the vision, see the need, then reflect and act. We have explored the Wesleys' message that we are invited into

181

communion with the Three-One God. We have seen John Wesley's awareness of the needs of people of his time, sometimes through the innovations of others. And we have watched the Wesleys weigh their options for ministry in Christian conference, beginning with the Holy Club and then creating ministries in which Methodists participated in caring for the souls of others.

It is not enough that we only cultivate personal piety or spirituality in a Wesleyan ecology of faith formation. In John Wesley's understanding, personal holiness must be accompanied by social holiness. This social responsibility is a stand persons take on behalf of others in response to God's gift of grace in their own lives. Formation for holiness of heart and life must include opportunities for social witness. We use the word "vocation" to describe this response to God's grace. In the words of James Fowler, a professor at Candler School of Theology, "Vocation is the response a person makes with his or her total self to the address of God and to the calling to partnership."[13] In other words, we love God by participating in God's new communion as agents of the coming reign of God now. The role of educators in a ministry of faith formation is to help the church become God's hands and feet, heart and mind—Christ's body in the world in which we live. When persons live in the intersections of life **as if** the reign of God is now, they become vehicles of God's grace.

If our aim is for persons to grow in communion with God and our neighbor, then formation for holiness of heart and life must address the injustice and oppression in the world. One of the realities of living in a world of instant communication is that we are inundated with the demands a global society places on us as individuals and as communities. How do we celebrate the diversity that surrounds us while sharing our commitment to a denominational tradition in the Christian community? If we are honest with ourselves, we might find that theological diversity is not the most difficult issue for us. Questions of race, class, and sexual orientation are waiting to be addressed by those who profess faith in God's new creation. And these are not new issues for the Wesleyan tradition. John Wesley addressed matters of slavery, poverty, and even sexual orientation when he helped a man imprisoned for his homosexuality.[14] These issues do raise a critical question for us—Who is our neighbor? What

does it mean to make disciples who love God and neighbor? How do we love the neighbor in our midst? If effective faith formation occurs through a contextual education of critical learning in the midst of practical divinity, we do not have to travel far from our homes to find settings for faith formation. As faithful Christians in the Wesleyan tradition, we must make disciples who seek out and combat injustice in the institutions of business, government, education, health care, and criminal justice, as well as in the church. Through Scripture and tradition, as well as through our own religious experiences, we hear God calling to us. Through the needs of our neighbors, God calls to us. The free gift of God's grace calls to us. We are called to share the vision, to see the need, to think and act. We are called to make disciples through formation for holiness of heart and life.

NOTES

INTRODUCTION

1. Richard P. Heitzenrater, *Mirror and Memory: Reflections on Early Methodism* (Nashville: Kingswood Books, 1989), 206.

2. Ibid.

3. Randy Maddox, *Responsible Grace: John Wesley's Practical Theology* (Nashville: Kingswood Books, 1994), 259.

4. Written by Susanna Wesley on 7/24/1732 and recorded in John Wesley's *Journal* in August 1742, *Works,* vol. 19, "Journal and Diaries II: 1738–1743," ed. W. Reginald Ward and Richard P. Heitzenrater (Nashville: Abingdon, 1990), 291.

5. Heitzenrater, *Mirror and Memory,* 206.

CHAPTER 1. MAKING DISCIPLES: FORMATION FOR HOLINESS OF HEART AND LIFE

1. This understanding of faith as a dynamic process of an interpretive act and a responsive act was first proposed in Sondra Higgins Matthaei, *Faith Matters: Faith-Mentoring in the Faith Community* (Valley Forge, Pa.: Trinity Press International, 1996), 15.

2. *Webster's Third New International Dictionary* (Springfield, Mass.: Merriam, 1981), 893.

3. Robert T. O'Gorman, "The Faith Community," in *Mapping Christian Education: Approaches to Congregational Learning,* ed. Jack L. Seymour (Nashville: Abingdon, 1997), 45.

4. Thomas Edward Frank, *Polity, Practice, and the Mission of the United Methodist Church* (Nashville: Abingdon, 1997), 68. Frank teaches church administration and congregational life at Candler School of Theology, Emory University.

5. Charles R. Foster, *Educating Congregations: The Future of Christian Education* (Nashville: Abingdon, 1994), 13.

6. Randy Maddox developed the interpretation of "responsible grace" that is offered by God to all, but to which no one is forced to respond. This view unites God's initiative and human responsibility. Randy L. Maddox, *Responsible Grace: John Wesley's Practical Theology* (Nashville: Kingswood Books, 1994), 86.

7. Letter of January 25, 1725, from Samuel Wesley Sr. to John Wesley, *Works,* vol. 25, "Letters I: 1721–1739," ed. Frank Baker (Oxford: Clarendon Press, 1980), 157.

8. Susanna Wesley, Morning Meditation 76, "Let our good works be seen to God's glory," in

Susanna Wesley: The Complete Writings, ed. Charles Wallace, Jr. (New York: Oxford University, 1997), 253.

9. John H. Westerhoff III discussed four "styles of faith": "experienced faith," "affiliative faith," "searching faith," and "owned faith" in *Will Our Children Have Faith?* (New York: Seabury, 1976), 89.

10. These questions were addressed at the first conference for Methodist preachers in 1744. See Henry D. Rack, *Reasonable Enthusiast: John Wesley and the Rise of Methodism*, 2nd ed. (Nashville: Abingdon, 1993), 243.

11. Maddox, *Responsible Grace*, 152.

12. Letter of December 6, 1738, from Susanna Wesley to Charles Wesley, *Susanna Wesley*, 176.

13. John Wesley, Sermon #18, "The Marks of the New Birth" (1748), *Works*, vol. 1, "Sermons I: 1-33," ed. Albert C. Outler (Nashville: Abingdon, 1984), 421-27.

14. Letter of September 8, 1773, from John Wesley to Philothea Briggs, *Letters* (Telford), vol. 6, 39.

15. John Wesley, Sermon #2, "The Almost Christian" (1741), *Works*, vol. 1, 137.

16. Charles Yrigoyen, Jr., *John Wesley: Holiness of Heart and Life* (Nashville: Abingdon, 1999), 37.

17. John Wesley, Sermon #2, "The Almost Christian" (1741), *Works*, vol. 1, 137-38.

18. Yrigoyen, *John Wesley*, 37.

19. John Wesley, "The Character of a Methodist" (1742), *Works*, vol. 9, "The Methodist Societies: History, Nature, and Design," ed. Rupert E. Davies (Nashville: Abingdon, 1989), 35.

20. This is a summary of fruits John Wesley discussed in "The Character of a Methodist" (1742), *Works*, vol. 9, 35-41.

21. John Wesley (12/16/1739), *Works*, vol. 19, "Journal and Diaries II: 1738–1743," ed. W. Reginald Ward and Richard P. Heitzenrater (Nashville: Abingdon, 1990), 28.

22. In 1785, John Wesley recounted some principle formative events of his life to correct mis-information appearing in "Some Remarks on Article X of Mr. Maty's *New Review* for December 1784," *Works*, vol. 9, 526.

23. Letter of February 6, 1712, *Susanna Wesley*, 79.

24. Letter of February 6, 1712, from Susanna Wesley to Samuel Wesley Sr., *Susanna Wesley*, 80. And these were not lighthearted casual conversations. A sample from Susanna Wesley's " 'little manual' of divinity" written in 1711/12 is found in *Susanna Wesley*, 425-61. This document presents a discussion with Emilia Wesley about theological matters of the eighteenth century.

25. John Newton, cited by Charles Wallace Jr., in *Susanna Wesley*, 10.

26. Letter of February 6, 1712, from Susanna Wesley to Samuel Wesley Sr., *Susanna Wesley*, 79.

27. Written by Susanna Wesley on 7/24/1732 and recorded in John Wesley's *Journal* in August 1742, *Works*, vol. 19, 287.

28. Letter of July 24, 1732, from Susanna Wesley to John Wesley, *Susanna Wesley*, 370.

29. Many of these letters can be found in the John Rylands Collection in Manchester, England, according to Stephen Gunter's response to this chapter, June 1999.

30. John Wesley (11/29/1747), *Works*, vol. 20, "Journal and Diaries III: 1743–1754," ed. W. Reginald Ward and Richard P. Heitzenrater (Nashville: Abingdon, 1991), 198.

31. Charles Wallace, Jr., ed., *Susanna Wesley: The Complete Writings* (New York: Oxford Press, 1997).

32. Resources written by David Lowes Watson include *Accountable Discipleship* (Nashville: Discipleship Resources, 1984); *The Early Methodist Class Meeting* (Nashville: Discipleship Resources, 1985); *Covenant Discipleship* (Nashville: Discipleship Resources, 1991); and *Forming Christian Disciples* (Nashville: Discipleship Resources, 1989).

33. Yrigoyen, *John Wesley: Holiness of Heart and Life* (Nashville: Abingdon, 1999).

34. Ibid., 23.

35. Stephen A. Seamands, *Holiness of Heart and Life* (Nashville: Abingdon, 1990).

36. Gayle Carlton Felton, "John Wesley and the Teaching Ministry: Ramifications for Education in the Church Today," *Religious Education* 92, no. 1 (winter 1997): 92-106.

37. Gayle Carlton Felton, *This Gift of Water: The Practice and Theology of Baptism Among Methodists in America* (Nashville: Abingdon, 1992) and *By Water and the Spirit: Making Connections for Identity and Ministry* (Nashville: Discipleship Resources, 1997).

38. Mariellen Sawada, *John Wesley: Holiness of Heart and Life*: Youth Study (New York: Women's Division, General Board of Global Ministries, The United Methodist Church, 1996).

39. David Michael Henderson, "John Wesley's Instructional Groups" (Ph.D. diss., Indiana University, 1980).

40. Rack, *Reasonable Enthusiast*, 243.

41. Several authors have been addressing these topics including Charles R. Foster in *Embracing Diversity: Leadership in Multicultural Congregations* (Bethesda, Md.: Alban Institute, 1997); with Theodore Brelsford in *We Are the Church Together: Cultural Diversity in Congregational Life* (Valley Forge, Pa.: Trinity Press International, 1996); Jack L. Seymour and Donald E. Miller in *Theological Approaches to Christian Education* (Nashville: Abingdon, 1990); and Linda J. Vogel in *Teaching and Learning in Communities of Faith: Empowering Adults Through Religious Education* (San Francisco: Jossey-Bass, 1991).

42. John Wesley, "A Plain Account of the People Called Methodists" (1749), *Works*, vol. 9, 254.

43. John Wesley frequently used this phrase to point to his understanding of the Trinity. "I believe this *fact* also (if I may use the expression)—that God is Three and One," Sermon #55, "On the Trinity" (1775), *Works*, vol. 2, "Sermons II: 34-70," ed. Albert C. Outler (Nashville: Abingdon, 1985), 384. An example of its use can be found in the comments on Luke 4:18, *NT Notes* (1754; reprint, London: Epworth, 1958), 216, note 18.

44. This paradigm was first proposed by Sondra H. Matthaei in "Transcripts of the Trinity: Communion and Community in Formation for Holiness of Heart and Life," a paper given at the Tenth Oxford Institute on Methodist Theological Studies in 1997 and subsequently published in an abbreviated version in *Quarterly Review* 18, no. 2 (summer 1998): 123-37.

45. James C. Logan, "The Evangelical Imperative: A Wesleyan Perspective," in *Theology and Evangelism in the Wesleyan Heritage* (Nashville: Kingswood Books, 1994), 20.

46. Precedent for this use of the word "ecology" is found in a chapter on "The Ecology for Nurturing Faith: Education, Disciplines, and Programs for Faith Development." The authors wrote "Presbyterians and evangelical Protestants of the nineteenth century were unusually successful at constructing a network of institutions and practices that together comprised an ecology for nurturing faith." Milton J. Coalter, John M. Mulder, and Louis B. Weeks, *The Re-forming Tradition: Presbyterians and Mainstream Protestantism* (Louisville: Westminster/John Knox, 1992), 193.

47. John B. Cobb, Jr., "Christian Theism and the Ecological Crisis," *Religious Education* 66, no. 1 (January-February 1971): 31-32 (emphasis added).

48. Coalter, Mulder, and Weeks, *The Re-forming Tradition*, 220.

49. Heitzenrater was describing an experiment by the Wesleys that sent preachers into the west and the north without establishing societies, in Richard P. Heitzenrater, *Wesley and the People Called Methodists* (Nashville: Abingdon, 1995), 165.

50. Thomas E. Frank, "Harmon-ic Convergences: Constituting a Church for a New Century," *Quarterly Review* 18, no. 1 (spring 1998): 22.

CHAPTER 2. WHAT IT MEANS TO BE CHRISTIAN: THE AIM OF FORMATION FOR HOLINESS OF HEART AND LIFE

1. Randy L. Maddox, *Responsible Grace: John Wesley's Practical Theology* (Nashville: Kingswood Books, 1994), 153.

2. John Wesley, "The Character of a Methodist" (1742), *Works*, vol. 9, "The Methodist Societies: History, Nature, and Design," ed. Rupert E. Davies (Nashville: Abingdon, 1989), 41.

3. Letter of November 10, 1725, from Susanna Wesley to John Wesley, *Works*, vol. 25, "Letters I: 1721–1739," ed. Frank Baker (Oxford: Clarendon, 1980), 185.

4. John Wesley (5/24/1738), *Works*, vol. 18, "Journal and Diaries I: 1735–1738," ed. W. Reginald Ward and Richard P. Heitzenrater (Nashville: Abingdon, 1988), 243.

5. Ibid.

6. Ibid.

7. Matthews' work is summarized in W. Stephen Gunter, *The Limits of 'Love Divine': John Wesley's Response to Antinomianism and Enthusiasm* (Nashville: Kingswood Books, 1989), 70, and in Randy L. Maddox, *Responsible Grace*, 127-28.

8. Letter of July 29, 1725, from John Wesley to Susanna Wesley, *Works*, vol. 25, 175.

9. Letter of August 18, 1725, from Susanna Wesley to John Wesley, *Works*, vol. 25, 179.

10. Ibid.

11. Ibid.

12. Letter of November 10, 1725, from Susanna Wesley to John Wesley, *Works*, vol. 25, 183.

13. Letter of November 22, 1725, from John Wesley to Susanna Wesley, *Works*, vol. 25, 188.

14. In a letter of February 15, 1733, John referred to a discussion he had with Susanna at Epworth, *Works*, vol. 25, 347.

15. Letter of February 14, 1734, from Susanna Wesley to John Wesley, *Works*, vol. 25, 377.

16. Letter of October 19, 1732, from John Wesley to Richard Morgan, *Works*, vol. 25, 336-37.

17. Rev. L. Tyerman. *The Life and Times of Rev. John Wesley* (London: Hodder & Stoughton, 1890), vol. 1, 83.

18. J. Brazier Green, *John Wesley and William Law* (London: Epworth, 1945), 42-43.

19. V. H. H. Green, *The Young Mr. Wesley* (New York: St. Martin's, 1961), 277, note 4 cited in *Susanna Wesley: The Complete Writings*, ed. Charles Wallace, Jr. (New York: Oxford University Press, 1999), 169, note 21.

20. *Susanna Wesley*, 161.

21. Twenty references to William Law are found in John Wesley's diaries. Eighteen of these notations dated from October 1735 to November 1739 mention Wesley's use of Law's teaching for himself and others. This relationship was discussed in more depth in "Behind the Scenes at Aldersgate: Mediating the Faith in John Wesley's Conversion," a presentation by the author to the American Academy of Religion in 1987.

22. Rex Matthews as discussed in Maddox, *Responsible Grace*, 127.

23. Richard P. Heitzenrater, *Wesley and the People Called Methodists* (Nashville: Abingdon, 1995), 58-73, and Henry D. Rack, *Reasonable Enthusiast: John Wesley and the Rise of Methodism*, 2nd ed. (Nashville: Abingdon, 1993), 107-36.

24. Letter Of October 10, 1735, from John Wesley to Dr. John Burton, Georgia Trustee, *Works*, vol. 25, 439 (emphasis added).

25. John Wesley's (1/24/1738), *Works*, vol. 18, 211; and (1/25/1738) 212, note 95, his "second memorandum on his spiritual condition."

26. John Wesley (5/24/1738), *Works*, vol. 18, 247.

27. Letter of May 14, 1738, from John Wesley to William Law, *Works*, vol. 25, 540-41.

28. Law named Thomas à Kempis, *Theologica Germanica*, and his book against the *Plain Account of the Sacraments* in *Works*, vol. 25, 543-46.

29. John Wesley, *Works*, vol. 25, 546-48.

30. Letter of May 22?, 1738, from William Law to John Wesley, *Works*, vol. 25, 549.

31. John Wesley (5/24/1738), *Works*, vol. 18, 244.

32. Letter of January 9, 1789, from John Wesley to Miss Bolton, *Works* (Jackson), vol. 12, 486.

33. John Wesley, *Journal* account of his spiritual journey, May 24, 1738, *Works*, vol. 18, 247-48. Also in a *Journal* notation on February 18, 1738, John Wesley wrote "All this time I conversed

much with Peter Böhler; but I understood him not; and least of all when he said, . . . 'My brother, my brother, that philosophy of yours must be purged away.'" *Works*, vol. 18, 226.

34. Martin Schmidt, *John Wesley: A Theological Biography*, trans. Norman P. Goldhawk (New York: Abingdon, 1963), vol. 1, 241.

35. John Wesley (4/26/1738), *Works*, vol. 18, 235.

36. John Wesley (5/10/1738), *Works*, vol. 18, 239.

37. John Wesley (5/24/1738), *Works*, vol. 18, 250.

38. Robert L. Moore, *John Wesley and Authority: A Psychological Perspective* (Missoula, Mont.: Scholars Press, 1979), 104.

39. Discussion of Rex Matthew's proposal in W. Stephen Gunter, *Limits of 'Love Divine,'* 70.

40. W. Stephen Gunter, *Limits of 'Love Divine,'* 74.

41. Randy Maddox, *Responsible Grace*, 127.

42. John Wesley, Sermon #110, "Free Grace" (1739), *Works*, vol. 3, "Sermons III: 71-114," ed. Albert C. Outler (Nashville: Abingdon, 1986), 544.

43. We talk about "experience" as one of the sources and criteria for theological reflection in The United Methodist Church along with Scripture, tradition, and reason. For Wesley, experience means religious experience and the Way of Salvation is one way of describing the whole process of our growth through religious experience. For a helpful contemporary discussion of the sources of faith, see W. Stephen Gunter, Scott J. Jones, Ted A. Campbell, Rebekah L. Miles, and Randy L. Maddox, *Wesley and the Quadrilateral: Renewing the Conversation* (Nashville: Abingdon, 1997).

44. John Wesley wrote, "All experience, as well as Scripture, shows this salvation to be both instantaneous and gradual." Sermon #85, "On Working Out Our Own Salvation" (1732), *Works*, vol. 3, 204.

45. Maddox, *Responsible Grace*, 152.

46. John Wesley, Sermon #85, "On Working Out Our Own Salvation" (1732), *Works*, vol. 3, 199-209.

47. John Wesley, "The Principles of a Methodist" (1742), *Works*, vol. 9, 51.

48. Maddox, *Responsible Grace*, 55.

49. Philip S. Watson, *The Message of the Wesleys* (Grand Rapids: Zondervan, 1984), 29.

50. John Wesley, Sermon #85, "On Working Out Our Own Salvation" (1732), *Works*, vol. 3, 202.

51. Watson, *The Message of the Wesleys*, 41.

52. John Wesley, Sermon #85, "On Working Out Our Own Salvation" (1732), *Works*, vol. 3, 203.

53. Ibid., 205-6.

54. John Wesley (3/4/1738), *Works*, vol. 18, 228.

55. John Wesley, Sermon #85, "On Working Out Our Own Salvation" (1732), *Works*, vol. 3, 204.

56. Rupert E. Davies, "Justification, Sanctification, and the Liberation of the Person" in *Sanctification and Liberation: Liberation Theologies in Light of the Wesleyan Tradition*, ed. Theodore Runyon (Nashville: Abingdon, 1981), 69.

57. Ibid.

58. John Wesley, "The Principles of a Methodist" (1742), *Works*, vol. 9, 53.

59. John Wesley, Sermon #85, "On Working Out Our Own Salvation" (1732), *Works*, vol. 3, 204.

60. Davies, "Justification, Sanctification, and the Liberation of the Person," 68.

CHAPTER 3. COMMUNITY AND COMMUNION: VISION AND CONTEXT OF FORMATION FOR HOLINESS OF HEART AND LIFE

1. Portions of this material were previously published in Sondra Matthaei, "Transcripts of the Trinity: Communion and Community in Formation for Holiness of Heart and Life," *Quarterly Review* 18, no. 2 (summer 1998): 123-37.

2. Geoffrey Wainwright, *Doxology: The Praise of God in Worship, Doctrine, and Life* (New York: Oxford University Press, 1980), 200.

3. Charles Wesley, Hymn #501, Part I: "The Communion of Saints" (1740), from "For the Society, Praying," *Works*, vol. 7: "A Collection of Hymns for the Use of the People Called Methodists," ed. Franz Hildebrandt and Oliver A. Beckerlegge with the assistance of James Dale (Nashville: Abingdon, 1983), 690 (emphasis added).

4. John D. Zizioulas, *Being as Communion* (Crestwood, N.Y.: St. Vladimir's Seminary Press, 1993), 105.

5. Randy Maddox, *Responsible Grace: John Wesley's Practical Theology* (Nashville: Kingswood Books, 1994), 138.

6. John Wesley, Comments on 1 John 5:8, *NT Notes* (London: Epworth, 1958), 917-18.

7. *Webster's Third New International Dictionary* (Springfield, Mass.: Merriam, 1981), 460.

8. Zizioulas, *Being as Communion*, 212.

9. Robert O'Gorman, "The Faith Community," in *Mapping Christian Education: Approaches to Congregational Learning*, ed. Jack L. Seymour (Nashville: Abingdon, 1997), 52.

10. Zizioulas, *Being as Communion*, 134.

11. John Wesley, Sermon #23, "Upon Our Lord's Sermon on the Mount," Part III (1725ff.), *Works*, vol. 1, "Sermons I: 1-33," ed. Albert C. Outler (Nashville: Abingdon, 1984), 517.

12. John Wesley, Sermon #55, "On the Trinity" (1775), *Works*, vol. 2, "Sermons II: 34-70," ed. Albert C. Outler (Nashville: Abingdon, 1985), 384.

13. Charles Wesley, Hymn #255 (1767) from "For Believers Rejoicing," *Works*, vol. 7, 397.

14. Letter of April 17, 1776, from John Wesley to Mary Bishop, *Letters* (Telford), vol. 6, 213.

15. John Wesley, Comments on Mark 12:29, *NT Notes*, 181.

16. Maddox, *Responsible Grace*, 140.

17. Geoffrey Wainwright, "Why Wesley Was a Trinitarian," *The Drew Gateway*, 59, no. 2, (spring 1990): 35 (emphasis added).

18. Maddox discussed these roles in some depth in *Responsible Grace*, 58-63 (emphasis added).

19. Maddox noted that Wesley is known for the way he interrelates the four roles, but gave evidence that Wesley favored Physician and Provider. In *Responsible Grace*, 63.

20. Maddox argued that Wesley could have called God "Parent" since there is "biblical warrant to do so . . . [but] Wesley remained a man of his context." In *Responsible Grace*, 64.

21. Maddox, *Responsible Grace*, 109.

22. John Wesley, Sermon # 5, "Justification by Faith" (1738-1742), *Works*, vol. 1, 187.

23. Maddox, *Responsible Grace*, 120-21.

24. John Wesley, Sermon # 5, "Justification by Faith" (1738-1742), *Works*, vol. 1, 187.

25. John Wesley, Sermon #127, "On the Wedding Garment" (1791), *Works*, vol. 4, "Sermons IV: 115-151," ed. Albert C. Outler (Nashville: Abingdon, 1987), 148. Or as Maddox observed, "Wesley understood grace . . . to be resistible or co-operant. Put in my suggested terms, he understood grace to be responsible—it empowers our response, but does not coerce that response." In *Responsible Grace*, 86.

26. A transcript is defined as "a copy, reproduction, or rendering . . . set forth or expressed usually in an art form." In *Webster's Third New International Dictionary* (Springfield, Mass.: Merriam, 1981), 2426.

27. Charles Wesley, Hymn #7 (1742), from "Exhorting, and beseeching to return to God," *Works*, vol. 7, 88 (emphasis added).

28. Charles Wesley, Hymn #253 (1767), from "For Believers Rejoicing," *Works*, vol. 7, 394-95 (emphasis added).

29. Maddox wrote, "The process of straining and rupturing our relationship with God's restored empowering Presence is as gradual as the process of commencing and nurturing this relationship." In *Responsible Grace*, 153.

30. Letter of April 26, 1777, from John Wesley to Miss March, *Letters* (Telford), vol. 6, 263.

31. Maddox, *Responsible Grace*, 151.

32. Randy Maddox found that Wesley had named "three dimensions of salvation" in various ways: "pardon—salvation begun, holiness—salvation continued, and heaven—salvation finished. Some other common threefold formulations were justification, sanctification, and consummation; or pardon, grace, and glory." In *Responsible Grace*, 143.

33. Henry D. Rack, *Reasonable Enthusiast: John Wesley and the Rise of Methodism*, 2nd ed. (Nashville: Abingdon, 1993), 205.

34. This particular formulation is my own interpretation and was first presented in a paper on "Transcripts of the Trinity: Communion and Community in Formation for Holiness of Heart and Life" at the Tenth Oxford Institute of Methodist Theological Studies, August 1997.

35. John Wesley, Sermon #21, "Upon Our Lord's Sermon on the Mount," Part I (1725ff.), *Works*, vol. 1, 470 (emphasis added).

36. John Wesley, Comments on Matt. 5:2, *NT Notes*, 28 (emphasis added).

37. The following discussion of blessing was first published in Sondra Higgins Matthaei, *The God We Worship* (Nashville: Abingdon, 1993), 29-30.

38. Walter Brueggemann, *Genesis*, Interpretation: A Biblical Commentary for Teaching and Preaching (Atlanta: John Knox, 1982), 227.

39. John Wesley, Sermon #22, "Upon Our Lord's Sermon on the Mount," Part II (1725ff.), *Works*, vol. 1, 495.

40. John Wesley, Sermon #21, "Upon Our Lord's Sermon on the Mount," Part I (1725ff.), *Works*, vol. 1, 475.

41. Ibid., 476.

42. Ibid., 481. In his comments on Matt. 5:3, Wesley talked about both "the present inward kingdom: righteousness, and peace, and joy in the Holy Ghost," and "the eternal kingdom, if they endure to the end." *NT Notes*, 28.

43. John Wesley, Comments on Matt. 5:4, *NT Notes*, 29.

44. John Wesley, Sermon #21, "Upon Our Lord's Sermon on the Mount," Part I (1725ff.), *Works*, vol. 1, 484.

45. John Wesley, Comments on Matt. 5:4, *NT Notes*, 29.

46. John Wesley, Sermon #21, "Upon Our Lord's Sermon on the Mount," Part I (1725ff), *Works*, vol. 1, 485.

47. John Wesley, Sermon #22, "Upon Our Lord's Sermon on the Mount," Part II (1725ff), *Works*, vol. 1, 489-90.

48. Ibid., 494.

49. John Wesley, Comments on Matt. 5:5, *NT Notes*, 29.

50. Commenting on Matt. 18.3, John Wesley wrote, "The first step toward entering into the kingdom of grace, is to *become as little children*: lowly in heart, knowing yourselves utterly ignorant and helpless, and hanging wholly on your Father who is in heaven, for a supply of all your wants." In *NT Notes*, 87-88.

51. John Wesley, Sermon #22, "Upon Our Lord's Sermon on the Mount," Part II (1725ff.), *Works*, vol. 1, 496.

52. Ibid., 497 (emphasis added).

53. Ibid.

54. John Wesley, Comments on Luke 2:52, *NT Notes*, 211.

55. John Wesley, Sermon #22, "Upon Our Lord's Sermon on the Mount," Part II (1725ff.), *Works*, vol. 1, 499 (emphasis added). Wesley's sermon continues with a detailed discussion of this kind of "brotherly love," 499-507.

56. Ibid., 507.

57. John Wesley, Sermon #23, "Upon Our Lord's Sermon on the Mount," Part III (1725ff.), *Works*, vol. 1, 510.

58. Ibid., 510-11.

59. Ibid., 513, 514 (emphasis added).

60. Ibid., 517, 518.

61. Ibid., 520.

62. Ibid., 528-29.

63. John Wesley, Sermon #64, "The New Creation" (1785), *Works*, vol. 2, 510 (emphasis added).

64. John Wesley, "The Character of a Methodist" (1742), *Works*, vol. 9, "The Methodist Societies: History, Nature, and Design," ed. Rupert E. Davies (Nashville: Abingdon, 1989), 42.

65. John Wesley, Sermon #23, "Upon Our Lord's Sermon on the Mount," Part III (1725ff.), *Works*, vol. 1, 530 (emphasis added).

66. Charles Wesley, Hymn #477 (1767), from "For the Society, giving Thanks," *Works*, vol. 7, 662 (emphasis added).

67. John Wesley, Comments on Matt. 4:17, *NT Notes*, 27.

68. Albert C. Outler, qtd. in Howard A. Snyder, *The Radical Wesley and Patterns for Church Renewal* (Downers Grove, Ill.: Inter-Varsity, 1980, 76.

69. John Wesley, Sermon #74, "Of the Church" (1785), *Works*, vol. 3, "Sermons III: 71-114," ed. Albert C. Outler (Nashville: Abingdon, 1986), 53-55.

70. Howard A. Snyder, *The Radical Wesley*, 83.

71. Maddox indicated that this view of the church is consistent with the notion of responsible grace in *Responsible Grace*, 242.

72. Snyder, *The Radical Wesley*, 89.

73. Snyder says, "The new birth began a process that reached into eternity." In *The Radical Wesley*, 87.

74. These elements of a Wesleyan ecology of faith formation will be addressed in the remaining chapters of this book.

75. Maddox, *Responsible Grace*, 96. Maddox claimed that Wesley's understanding of the Trinity is a pattern for formation: "proper worship helps structure the formation of Christian character, while openness to the Spirit's witness provides access to the empowerment for this formation." In *Responsible Grace*, 140.

76. John Wesley, "The Character of a Methodist" (1742), *Works*, vol. 9, 41.

77. From Charles Wesley, Hymn #477 (1767), from "For the Society, giving Thanks," *Works*, vol. 7, 662.

78. Maria Harris defined curriculum as "an activity, a *practice* of a people." In *Fashion Me a People: Curriculum in the Church* (Louisville, Ky.: Westminster/John Knox, 1989), 8.

79. In a time of doubt, John Wesley asked Peter Böhler if he should stop preaching. And Böhler replied, "Preach faith *till* you have it, and then, *because* you have it, you *will* preach faith." John Wesley (3/4/1738), *Works*, vol. 18, "Journal and Diaries I: 1735–1738," ed. W. Reginald Ward and Richard P. Heitzenrater (Nashville: Abingdon, 1988), 228.

80. Susanna Wesley is known to have encouraged her son in the matter of practical divinity, best defined in a letter to her daughter: "But, Sukey, it is not learning these things by heart, nor your saying a few prayers morning and night, that will bring you to heaven; you must understand what you say, and you must practice what you know." Letter of 13 January 1709/1710 in Adam Clarke, *Memoirs of the Wesley Family* (1848; reprint, New York: Lane and Tippett, 1976), 347-48.

81. Charles Wesley, Hymn #504, "The Communion of Saints," Part IV (1740), from "For the Society, Praying," *Works*, vol. 7, 693-94.

82. Maddox noted that this is "[John] Wesley's characteristic informal definition of the church." In *Responsible Grace*, 242.

83. Ibid., 132. Maddox indicated that Wesley "appreciated the sense in which habituated affections bring 'freedom' for human actions—the freedom that comes from disciplined practice." In *Responsible Grace*, 69.

84. Charles Wesley, Hymn #188 (1739) from "For Believers Rejoicing," *Works*, vol. 7, 317-18.

CHAPTER 4. "WHAT TO TEACH?"

1. Gayle Carlton Felton, "John Wesley and the Teaching Ministry: Ramifications for Education in the Church Today," *Religious Education* 92, no. 1 (winter 1997): 92.

2. Sara Little. *To Set One's Heart: Belief and Teaching in the Church* (Atlanta: John Knox, 1983), 9-10.

3. Horace Bushnell. *Christian Nurture* (1861; reprint, Grand Rapids: Baker Book House, 1983), 10.

4. Mary Elizabeth Moore, *Education for Continuity and Change: A New Model for Christian Religious Education* (Nashville: Abingdon, 1983), 113.

5. Henry Rack noted that John and Charles Wesley invited four other clergy and four lay preachers to this first conference in *Reasonable Enthusiast: John Wesley and the Rise of Methodism*, 2nd ed. (Nashville: Abingdon, 1993), 242-43.

6. Ibid., 243.

7. Ibid.

8. Thomas A. Langford, *God Made Known* (Nashville: Abingdon, 1992), 40.

9. "They resolved to hold fast to the Church of England . . ." (6/25/1744), *Works*, vol. 20, "Journal and Diaries III: 1743–1754)," ed. W. Reginald Ward and Richard P. Heitzenrater (Nashville: Abingdon, 1991), 34, note 71.

10. Martin Schmidt, *John Wesley: A Theological Biography*, trans. Norman P. Goldhawk, vol. 1 (New York: Abingdon, 1963), 63.

11. Richard P. Heitzenrater, *Wesley and the People Called Methodists* (Nashville: Abingdon, 1995), 129.

12. W. Stephen Gunter, *The Limits of 'Love Divine': John Wesley's Response to Antinomianism and Enthusiasm* (Nashville: Kingswood Books, 1989), 23.

13. John Wesley, Sermon #11, "The Witness of the Spirit, II" (1767), *Works*, vol. 1, "Sermons I: 1-33," ed. Albert C. Outler (Nashville: Abingdon, 1984), 297.

14. The author is indebted to Wesley scholars such as Frank Baker, *John Wesley and the Church of England* (Nashville: Abingdon, 1970); W. Stephen Gunter, *The Limits of "Love Divine": John Wesley's Response to Antinomianism and Enthusiasm* (Nashville: Kingswood Books, 1989); Richard P. Heitzenrater, *The Elusive Mr. Wesley*, vol. 2, *John Wesley as Seen by Contemporaries and Biographers* (Nashville: Abingdon, 1984), *Mirror and Memory: Reflections on Early Methodism* (Nashville: Kingswood Books, 1989), *Wesley and the People Called Methodists* (Nashville: Abingdon, 1995); Randy Maddox, *Aldersgate Reconsidered*, ed. (Nashville: Kingswood Books, 1990), and *Responsible Grace: John Wesley's Practical Theology* (Nashville: Kingswood Books, 1994); Manfred Marquardt, *John Wesley's Social Ethics: Praxis and Principles* (Nashville: Abingdon, 1991); Henry D. Rack, *Reasonable Enthusiast: John Wesley and the Rise of Methodism* (Nashville: Abingdon, 1993); and others for their in-depth research and discussion of these important historical issues.

15. Heitzenrater, *Wesley and the People Called Methodists*, 97.

16. Gunter indicated that the "spontaneity" of this openness about religious experience was most irritating in *The Limits of 'Love Divine,'* 22.

17. Ibid., 15.

18. Gunter is quick to point out that Wesley himself did not want to abandon the tradition of the church in *The Limits of 'Love Divine,'* 23.

19. Ibid., 35-40.

20. Rack, *Reasonable Enthusiast*, 205.

21. Charles Wesley recorded a meeting on October 21, 1738, with the Bishop of London to answer complaints about their doctrine of assurance and a discussion on November 14, 1738, with the same Bishop about re-baptism of a Dissenter. In *Journal CW*, ed. Thomas Jackson, 1849 (Grand Rapids: Baker Book House, 1980), vol. 1, 133, 135.

22. Charles Wesley (12/26/1739), *Journal CW*, vol. 1, 139.

23. Charles Wesley (1/17/1739), *Journal CW*, vol. 1, 140.

24. Charles Wesley (5/16/1739), *Journal CW*, vol. 1, 149.

25. Rack, *Reasonable Enthusiast*, 200.

26. Heitzenrater, *Wesley and the People Called Methodists*, 107.

27. Ibid.

28. Ibid.

29. Rack, *Reasonable Enthusiast*, 200.

30. Heitzenrater, *Wesley and the People Called Methodists*, 107.

31. Rack, *Reasonable Enthusiast*, 205.

32. Letter of December 6, 1738, from Susanna Wesley to Charles Wesley, *Susanna Wesley: The Complete Writings*, ed. Charles Wallace Jr. (Oxford: Oxford University, 1997), 176.

33. Heitzenrater, *Wesley and the People Called Methodists*, 106.

34. Gunter, *The Limits of 'Love Divine,'* 91.

35. Charles Wesley (6/18/1740), *Journal CW*, vol. 1, 241-42.

36. John Wesley (1/1/1740), *Works*, vol. 19, "Journal and Diaries II: 1738–1743," ed. W. Reginald Ward and Richard P. Heitzenrater (Nashville: Abingdon, 1990), 134.

37. Ibid., 133.

38. John Wesley (6/27/1740), *Works*, vol. 19, 158.

39. John Wesley, "The Nature, Design, and General Rules of the United Societies" (1743), *Works*, vol. 9, "The Methodist Societies: History, Nature, and Design," ed. Rupert E. Davies (Nashville: Abingdon, 1989), 70-73.

40. Gunter observed that these components were in place before Wesley went to Georgia and that later criticism would cause Wesley to clarify his theology in *The Limits of 'Love Divine,'* 54-55.

41. Rack indicated that this view led to Wesley's "two-stage view of salvation in which faith would bring first justification, then entire sanctification" in *Reasonable Enthusiast*, 206.

42. The author recognizes that the account of the conflicts of this society are mainly given and heard from Wesley's perspective. Even with this bias, the Fetter Lane Society provides an illustration of the claim of this chapter and a window into Wesley's formational approach.

43. Heitzenrater, *Wesley and the People Called Methodists*, 76.

44. Letter of January 3, 1738, from James Hutton to John Wesley, *Works*, vol. 25, "Letters I: 1721–1739," ed. Frank Baker (Oxford: Clarendon, 1980), 526.

45. This was a typical pattern for general meetings of societies and bands noted in a letter of November 24, 1738, from John Wesley to James Hutton and Mr. Fox, *Works*, vol. 25, 588.

46. Wesley's letter included a bureau key so Hutton could have access to Wesley's papers. Letter of March 26, 1738, from John Wesley to James Hutton, *Works*, vol. 25, 535-36.

47. Letter of November 16, 1738, from John Wesley to James Hutton, *Works*, vol. 25, 580.

48. Heitzenrater, *Wesley and the People Called Methodists*, 79.

49. John Wesley (5/1/1738), *Works*, vol. 18, "Journal and Diaries I: 1735–1738," ed. W. Reginald Ward and Richard P. Heitzenrater (Nashville: Abingdon, 1988), 236.

50. Letter of May 8, 1739, from John Wesley to James Hutton, *Works*, vol. 25, 644. This letter concluded with a request for Hutton to send Wesley's sermons on faith.

51. In addition, Wesley noted that many had stopped practicing the means of grace. John Wesley (11/7/1739), *Works*, vol. 19, 120.

52. John Wesley (12/19/1739), *Works*, vol. 19, 130.

53. John Wesley recorded what he heard Molther saying and then compared their views point by point (12/31/1739), *Works*, vol. 19, 131-34.

54. John Wesley (1/1/1740–1/2/1740), *Works*, vol. 19, 134.

55. Heitzenrater, *Wesley and the People Called Methodists*, 110-11.

56. Letter of March 4, 1740, from James Hutton to John Wesley, *Works*, vol. 26, "Letters II: 1740–1755," ed. Frank Baker (Oxford: Clarendon, 1982), 7 (emphasis added). When Fetter Lane split, James Hutton became a leader in the Moravian Church (Heitzenrater, *Wesley and the People Called Methodists*, 142).

57. Letter of April 12, 1740, from John Wesley to James Hutton, *Works*, vol. 26, 12.

58. John Wesley (4/25/1740), *Works*, vol. 19:147.

59. Charles Wesley (4/25/1740), *Journal CW*, vol. 1, 222-23.

60. Heitzenrater, *Wesley and the People Called Methodists*, 112.

61. John Wesley (6/11/1740), *Works*, vol. 19, 151.

62. John Wesley (11/20/1740), *Works*, vol. 19, 162.

63. Heitzenrater reported that by the next week 25 men and 48 women from Fetter Lane had followed Wesley to the United Society in *Wesley and the People Called Methodists*, 112.

64. John Wesley (5/6/1741), *Works*, vol. 19, 193.

65. Heitzenrater, *Wesley and the People Called Methodists*, 142.

66. John Wesley, Sermon #23, "Upon Our Lord's Sermon on the Mount," Part III (1725ff.), *Works*, vol. 1, 517-18.

67. It is helpful to note that each of these phases of faith formation also provided impetus and opportunity for Wesley to clarify his own theological positions.

68. Letter of November 23, 1738, from James Hutton to John Wesley, *Works*, vol. 25, 585-86.

69. Letter of November 24, 1738, from John Wesley to James Hutton and Mr. Fox, *Works*, vol. 25, 588.

70. James Hutton first proposed the use of monitors "whose business will be to tell everyone what faults are observed in him [the president of the band], concealing his informer." Letter of November 23, 1738, from James Hutton to John Wesley, *Works*, vol. 25, 586.

71. Wesley continued by indicating the dangers inherent in having assigned monitors. Letter of November 26, 1738, from John Wesley to James Hutton, *Works*, vol. 25, 591.

72. Laurent A. Parks Daloz, Cheryl H. Keen, James P. Keen, and Sharon Daloz Parks, *Common Fire: Leading Lives of Commitment in a Complex World* (Boston: Beacon, 1996), 109.

73. Ibid., 110.

74. Letter of December 1, 1738, from John Wesley to James Hutton, *Works*, vol. 25, 595.

75. John Wesley (6/16/1739), *Works*, vol. 19, 70-71.

76. John Wesley (4/25/1740), *Works*, vol. 19, 147.

77. John Wesley (6/5/1739), *Works*, vol. 19, 65.

78. John Wesley (6/13/1739), *Works*, vol. 19, 69.

79. Letter to John Wesley, recorded in the *Journal* December 13, 1739, *Works*, vol. 19, 129-30.

80. John Wesley (6/22/1740), *Works*, vol. 19, 153. See note 75: "On this and the following days of this week, JW devoted his early morning Bible expositions to expounding the basic Christian teaching as he understood it, in opposition to the quietist practices which seemed to be infecting many of those at Fetter Lane, chiefly under the influence of the Moravians." Pages 153-59 are the beginning preamble to Wesley's disciplined response to the Moravian point of view.

81. *Works*, vol. 19, 153, note 75.

82. John Wesley, Sermon #16, "The Means of Grace" (1741–1746?), *Works*, vol. 1, 376-97.

83. Ibid., 378.

84. Ibid. This point indicates that Wesley continued to address conflicts on both sides.

85. From Charles Wesley, Hymn #477 (1767), from "For the Society, giving Thanks," *Works*, vol. 7: "A Collection of Hymns for the Use of the People Called Methodists," ed. Franz Hildebrandt and Oliver A. Beckerlegge with the assistance of James Dale (Nashville: Abingdon, 1983), 662.

86. Richard Robert Osmer, "Teaching in the Reformed Tradition: The Contribution of Luther and Calvin," in *By What Authority: A Conversation on Teaching Among United Methodists*, ed. Elizabeth Box Price and Charles R. Foster (Nashville: Abingdon, 1991), 32.

87. Ibid.

88. Mary Elizabeth Moore, "A Wrestling Church: Cultural Pluralism in the Wesleyan Tradition," a paper presented to the United Methodist Association of Professors in Christian Education, July 1990, 15.

CHAPTER 5. "WHO SHALL TEACH?"

1. John Wesley (1/25ff/1743), *Works*, vol. 19, "Journal and Diaries II: 1738–1743," ed. W. Reginald Ward and Richard P. Heitzenrater (Nashville: Abingdon, 1990), 313.

2. John Wesley (3/30/1741), *Works*, vol. 19, 189.

3. John Wesley reported that fifty to sixty persons did indeed speak to him; (1/1/1742), *Works*, vol. 19, 243.

4. William Law, quoted in John Wesley, Sermon #95, "On the Education of Children" (1783), *Works*, vol. 3, "Sermons III: 71-114," ed. Albert C. Outler (Nashville: Abingdon, 1986), 349.

5. John Wesley, Sermon #95, "On the Education of Children" (1783), *Works*, vol. 3, 348.

6. Henry D. Rack, *Reasonable Enthusiast: John Wesley and the Rise of Methodism*, 2nd ed. (Nashville: Abingdon, 1993), 360.

7. Wesley Tracy, "Christian Education in the Wesleyan Mode," *Wesleyan Theological Journal* 17, no. 1 (spring 1982): 33.

8. Letter of September 1706 from Samuel Wesley Sr. to Samuel Wesley Jr. in Maldwyn Edwards, *Family Circle: A Study of the Epworth Household in Relation to John and Charles Wesley* (London: Epworth, 1949), 49-50.

9. Letter of January 20, 1722, from Susanna Wesley to Samuel Annesley in Edwards, *Family Circle*, 51.

10. Susanna Wesley, Morning Meditation 69: "Example more important than precept in the 'reforming' of children, each one of which is a talent committed to your trust," *Susanna Wesley: The Complete Writings*, ed. Charles Wallace, Jr. (New York: Oxford University, 1997), 246.

11. Letter of November 10, 1725, from Susanna Wesley to John Wesley, *Works*, vol. 25, "Letters I: 1721–1739," ed. Frank Baker (Oxford: Clarendon, 1980), 184.

12. Letter of February 14, 1734, from Susanna Wesley to John Wesley in *Works*, vol. 25, 378.

13. *Susanna Wesley*, 11.

14. Luke Tyerman, *The Life and Times of Samuel Wesley* (London: Simpkin, Marshall & Co., 1866), 320-21.

15. Letter of October 19, 1732, from John Wesley to Richard Morgan Sr., *Works*, vol. 25, 337.

16. Ibid.

17. Letter of September 28, 1730, from Samuel Wesley Sr. to John Wesley in Adam Clarke, *Memoirs of the Wesley Family* (1848; reprint, New York: Lane & Tippett, 1976), 249-50.

18. Letter of October 19, 1732, from John Wesley to Richard Morgan Sr., *Works*, vol. 25, 335, note 1.

19. Albert C. Outler, introduction to John Wesley, Sermon #94, "On Family Religion" (1783), *Works*, vol. 3, 333.

20. John Wesley, Sermon #94, "On Family Religion" (1783), *Works*, vol. 3, 338.

21. Ibid., 339.

22. John Wesley, Sermon #2, "The Almost Christian" (1741), *Works*, vol. 1, "Sermons I: 1-33," ed. Albert C. Outler (Nashville: Abingdon, 1984), 134.

23. John Wesley, Sermon #94, "On Family Religion" (1783), *Works*, vol. 3, 340.

24. Rack, *Reasonable Enthusiast*, 354.

25. John Wesley, Sermon #94, "On Family Religion" (1783), *Works*, vol. 3, 340.

26. Ibid., 341.

27. Ibid., 341-42.

28. Ibid., 342-43 (emphasis added).

29. Ibid., 343 (emphasis added).

30. Ibid., 344-45.

31. Ibid., 345.

32. Rack, *Reasonable Enthusiast*, 353.

33. Letter of April 30, 1739, to James Hutton and the Fetter Lane Society from John Wesley, *Works*, vol. 25, 639.

34. Richard P. Heitzenrater, *Wesley and the People Called Methodists* (Nashville: Abingdon, 1995), 105.

35. Whitefield had already expressed chagrin with the Wesleys for publishing a sermon against the doctrine of predestination, a primary area of contention between Whitefield and the Wesleys. Letter of February 1, 1741, from George Whitefield aboard the *Minerva* to John and Charles Wesley, *Works*, vol. 26, "Letters II: 1740–1755," ed. Frank Baker (Oxford: Clarendon, 1982), 48.

36. Letter of April 27, 1741, from John Wesley to George Whitefield, *Works*, vol. 26, 59.

37. Letter of October 10, 1741, from George Whitefield to John Wesley, *Works*, vol. 26, 66.

38. Note 73 in *Works*, vol. 20, "Journal and Diaries III: 1743–1754," ed. W. Reginald Ward and Richard P. Heitzenrater (Nashville: Abingdon, 1991), 229-30.

39. John Wesley (6/24/1748), *Works*, vol. 20, 229.

40. Charles Wesley wrote three hymns for the 1748 opening of Kingswood School. This is Hymn #463, *Works*, vol. 7, "A Collection of Hymns for the Use of the People Called Methodists," ed. Franz Hildebrandt and Oliver A. Beckerlegge with the assistance of James Dale (Nashville: Abingdon, 1983), 645-46.

41. Rack, *Reasonable Enthusiast*, 355.

42. In 1783, Wesley wrote in despair as he compared the state of Kingswood School to his vision, "My design in building the house at Kingswood was, to have therein a Christian family; every member whereof, children excepted, should be alive to God, and a pattern of all holiness." In "Remarks on the State of Kingswood School" (1783), *Works* (Jackson), vol. 13, 301.

43. John Wesley (3/14/1749), *Works*, vol. 20, 265.

44. Rack, *Reasonable Enthusiast*, 356.

45. John Wesley, "Remarks on the State of Kingswood School" (1783), *Works* (Jackson), vol. 13, 302.

46. Rack, *Reasonable Enthusiast*, 358.

47. John Wesley, "A Plain Account of Kingswood School" (1781), *Works* (Jackson) vol. 13, 292.

48. John Wesley (7/25/1749), *Works*, vol. 20, 292.

49. In a letter of December 22, 1786, to John Valton, John Wesley wrote, "It is amazing that we cannot find in the three kingdoms a fit master for Kingswood School!" *Letters* (Telford), vol. 7, 361.

50. Rack, *Reasonable Enthusiast*, 358.

51. For Wesley, the peacemakers are those who "utterly detest and abhor all strife and debate" and are adopted as God's children. See John Wesley, Sermon #23, "Upon Our Lord's Sermon on the Mount," Part III (1725ff.), *Works*, vol. 1, 517.

52. Rack, *Reasonable Enthusiast*, 358-59.
53. John Wesley (7/26/1750), *Works*, vol. 20, 353-54.
54. Michael Bishop, Director of the Wesley Centre Kingswood School.
55. Letter of December 6, 1739 from John Wesley to Thomas Price, *Works*, vol. 25, 702.
56. Mollie C. Davis, "The Countess of Huntingdon," in *Women in New Worlds: Historical Perspectives on the Wesleyan Tradition*, vol. 2, ed. Rosemary Skinner Keller, Louise L. Queen, and Hilah F. Thomas (Nashville: Abingdon, 1982), 165.
57. Ibid., 166.
58. Letter of March 25, 1742, from the Countess of Huntington to John Wesley in *Works*, vol. 26, 75.
59. Mollie C. Davis, "The Countess of Huntingdon," 167.
60. Ibid., 167-69.
61. Earl Kent Brown, "Feminist Theology and the Women of Mr. Wesley's Methodism," in *Wesleyan Theology Today: A Bicentennial Consultation*, ed. Theodore Runyon (Nashville: Kingswood Books, 1985), 146.
62. Earl Kent Brown, *Women of Mr. Wesley's Methodism* (New York: Mellen, 1983), 65.
63. Ibid.
64. Ibid., 139.
65. Ibid., 53, 58.
66. Ibid., 63-64.
67. Ibid., 66.
68. Ibid., 105.
69. Heitzenrater, *Wesley and the People Called Methodists*, 102.
70. Rack, *Reasonable Enthusiast*, 208.
71. Ibid., 209.
72. Ibid., 209-11. Rack summarizes the development of Wesley's thinking about this issue and the conflict that ensued, particularly at the emergence of lay preaching.
73. Letter from John Wesley of unknown date and recipient recorded in the *Journal* on June 11, 1739, in *Works*, vol. 19, 67.
74. John Wesley, "Minutes of Several Conversations" (1744–1789), *Works* (Jackson), vol. 8, 305.
75. Rack, *Reasonable Enthusiast*, 355.
76. John Wesley, "Minutes of Several Conversations," *Works* (Jackson), vol. 8, 305-6.
77. Ibid., 306.
78. Ibid., 315.
79. W. Stephen Gunter, *The Limits of 'Love Divine': John Wesley's Response to Antinomianism and Enthusiasm* (Nashville: Kingswood Books, 1989), 14, 26. Gunter indicated that society members and lay preachers alike expressed anti-clerical attitudes and openly opposed established clergy.
80. Rack, *Reasonable Enthusiast*, 243.
81. Ibid., 208. Rack notes that Wesley rebaptized some Dissenters, creating further controversy.
82. Gunter, *The Limits of 'Love Divine,'* 157.
83. This date is approximate, as noted in Rack, *Reasonable Enthusiast*, 210.
84. The details of this event are recorded in Maldwyn Edwards, *Family Circle*, 81.
85. Ibid., 81-82.
86. Ibid., 82.
87. Thomas R. Albin, "An Empirical Study of Early Methodist Spirituality," in *Wesleyan Theology Today*, 277.
88. Paul W. Chilcote, *She Offered Them Christ: The Legacy of Women Preachers in Early Methodism* (Nashville: Abingdon, 1993), 26.

89. Earl Kent Brown, "Women of the Word," in *Women in New Worlds: Historical Perspectives on the Wesleyan Tradition*, vol. 1, ed. Hilah F. Thomas and Rosemary Skinner Keller (Nashville: Abingdon, 1981), 69.

90. Ibid., 72.

91. Alan L. Hayes, "John Wesley and Sophy Hopkey" in *Women in New Worlds*, 31.

92. Paul Chilcote, *She Offered Them Christ*, 44.

93. John Wesley, Sermon #98, "On Visiting the Sick" (1786), *Works*, vol. 3, 395-96.

94. Portions of this section were previously published in "With Patience, Love, and Knowledge," *Circuit Rider*, May 2000.

95. John Wesley, Sermon #98, "On Visiting the Sick" (1786) *Works*, vol. 3, 396.

96. Rack, *Reasonable Enthusiast*, 244.

97. John Wesley, "A Plain Account of Kingswood School" (1781), *Works* (Jackson), vol. 13, 292.

98. Susanna Wesley, "Morning Meditation" in *Susanna Wesley*, 246.

99. John Wesley, "Minutes on Several Conversations," *Works* (Jackson), vol. 8, 315.

100. From Charles Wesley, Hymn #477 (1767), from "For the Society, giving Thanks," *Works*, vol. 7, 662.

101. Sara Little, *To Set One's Heart* (Louisville: John Knox, 1983), 30.

102. Maria Harris, *Teaching and Religious Imagination: An Essay in the Theology of Teaching* (San Francisco: Harper & Row, 1987), 41.

103. Susanna Wesley, Noon meditation from May 1711, *Susanna Wesley*, 236.

CHAPTER 6. "HOW TO TEACH?": STRUCTURES FOR TEACHING

1. Letter of November 20, 1734, from Samuel Wesley Sr. to John Wesley, *Works*, vol. 25, "Letters I: 1721–1739," ed. Frank Baker (Oxford: Clarendon, 1980), 396.

2. Letter of January 13, 1710, from Susanna Wesley to Sukey Wesley in Adam Clarke, *Memoirs of the Wesley Family* (1848; reprint, New York: Lane & Tippett, 1976), 347-48.

3. Letter of September 10, 1724, from Susanna Wesley to John Wesley, *Works*, vol. 25, 149.

4. Letter of November 1, 1724, from John Wesley to Susanna Wesley, *Works*, vol. 25, 152.

5. Letter of January 26, 1725, from Samuel Wesley Sr. to John Wesley, *Works*, vol. 25, 158.

6. Ibid.

7. Ibid.

8. Letter of February 23, 1725, from Susanna Wesley to John Wesley, *Works*, vol. 25, 160 (emphasis added).

9. Ibid.

10. Letter of March 17, 1725, from Samuel Wesley Sr. to John Wesley, *Works*, vol. 25, 160.

11. Letter of January 24, 1727, from John Wesley to Susanna Wesley, *Works*, vol. 25, 208.

12. Letter of April 22, 1727, from Susanna Wesley to John Wesley, *Works*, vol. 25, 215.

13. Luke Tyerman believed that John Wesley would have been content to stay at Epworth and Wroote if this family friend had not called him back to Oxford. *The Life and Times of the Rev. John Wesley* (New York: Harper & Brothers, 1872), vol. 1, 58.

14. Letter of February 28, 1732, from John Wesley to Susanna Wesley, *Works*, vol. 25, 328.

15. Richard P. Heitzenrater, *The Elusive Mr. Wesley*, vol. 1, *John Wesley His Own Biographer* (Nashville: Abingdon, 1984), 43.

16. Tyerman, *The Life and Times of John Wesley*, vol. 1, 96.

17. Letter of November 20, 1734, from Samuel Wesley Sr. to John Wesley, *Works*, vol. 25, 396.

18. Letter of November 15, 1734, from John Wesley to Samuel Wesley Sr., *Works*, vol. 25, 395.

19. Letter of November 20, 1734, from Samuel Wesley Sr. to John Wesley, *Works*, vol. 25, 396.

20. Letter of December 10, 1734, from John Wesley to Samuel Wesley Sr., *Works*, vol. 25, 398.

21. Ibid., 404.

22. Letter of December 25, 1734, from Samuel Wesley Jr. to John Wesley, *Works*, vol. 25, 411.

23. Letter of December 4, 1734, from Samuel Wesley Sr. to Samuel Wesley Jr., in Clarke, *Memoirs of the Wesley Family*, 273.

24. Frank Baker, *Works*, vol. 25, 422, note 1.

25. Frank Baker pointed out that these circumstances surrounding Samuel Wesley's death resulted in John Wesley's break from Oxford as Samuel had wished. *Works*, vol. 25, 422, note 1.

26. John Wesley (5/20/1753), *Works*, vol. 20, "Journal and Diaries III: 1743–1754," ed. W. Reginald Ward and Richard P. Heitzenrater (Nashville: Abingdon, 1991), 458.

27. Charles Wesley, Hymn #461, "For Children" (1763), from "For Believers Interceding for the World," *Works*, vol. 7, "A Collection of Hymns for the Use of the People Called Methodists," ed. Franz Hildebrandt and Oliver A. Beckerlegge with the assistance of James Dale (Nashville: Abingdon, 1983), 643-44 (emphasis added).

28. Richard P. Heitzenrater, *Wesley and the People Called Methodists* (Nashville: Abingdon, 1995), 85.

29. John Wesley, Sermon #16, "The Means of Grace" (1741–1746?), *Works*, vol. 1, "Sermons I: 1-33," ed. Albert C. Outler (Nashville: Abingdon, 1984), 376-97.

30. John Wesley, "A Plain Account of the People Called Methodists" (1749), *Works*, vol. 9, "The Methodist Societies: History, Nature, and Design," ed. Rupert E. Davies (Nashville: Abingdon, 1989), 254.

31. David Michael Henderson, *John Wesley's Instructional Groups* (Ph.D. diss., Indiana University, 1980), 210.

32. Ibid., 208.

33. Letter of April 26, 1777, from John Wesley to Miss March, *Letters* (Telford), vol. 6, 263.

34. Henderson, *John Wesley's Instructional Groups*, 26.

35. Henry D. Rack, *Reasonable Enthusiast: John Wesley and the Rise of Methodism*, 2nd. ed. (Nashville: Abingdon, 1993), 237.

36. John Wesley, "A Plain Account" (1749), *Works*, vol. 9, 257.

37. John Wesley, "The Nature, Design, and General Rules of the United Societies" (1743), *Works*, vol. 9, 69.

38. John Wesley (9/21/1749), *Works*, vol. 20, 299.

39. John Wesley (5/1/1738), *Works*, vol. 18, "Journal and Diaries I: 1735–1738," ed. W. Reginald Ward and Richard P. Heitzenrater (Nashville: Abingdon, 1988), 236.

40. Ibid.

41. Rupert E. Davies, introduction to *Works*, vol. 9, 12.

42. John Wesley (2/15/1742), *Works*, vol. 19, "Journal and Diaries II: 1738–1743," ed. W. Reginald Ward and Richard P. Heitzenrater (Nashville: Abingdon, 1990), 251.

43. Davies, introduction to *Works*, vol. 9, 12.

44. John Wesley, "A Plain Account," *Works*, vol. 9, 262.

45. John Wesley (5/1/1738), *Works*, vol. 18, 236.

46. Rack, *Reasonable Enthusiast*, 242.

47. Letter of February 23, 1725, from Susanna Wesley to John Wesley, *Works*, vol. 25, 160.

48. John Wesley, "General Rules of the United Societies" (1743), *Works*, vol. 9, 70-73.

49. John Wesley, "A Plain Account" (1749), *Works*, vol. 9, 261.

50. John Wesley (5/1/1738), *Works*, vol. 18, 237.

51. John Wesley (4/30/1740), *Works*, vol. 19, 148.

52. A close reading of Wesley's *Journal* reflects that he tightened this procedure following the Fetter Lane controversy.

53. John Wesley (5/13/1752), *Works*, vol. 20, 422.

54. Davies, introduction to *Works*, vol. 9, 9.

55. Ibid.
56. John Wesley, "Rules of the Band Societies" (1738), *Works*, vol. 9, 78.
57. Davies, introduction to *Works*, vol. 9, 13.
58. John Wesley, "A Plain Account" (1749), *Works*, vol. 9, 267.
59. Ibid.
60. John Wesley (5/1/1738), *Works*, vol. 18, 236.
61. John Wesley, "A Plain Account" (1749), *Works*, vol. 9, 269-70.
62. Ibid., 270.
63. Ibid.
64. Henderson, *John Wesley's Instructional Groups*, 185.
65. Davies, introduction to *Works*, vol. 9, 13.
66. Norman C. Wallwork, "Wesley's Legacy in Worship" in *John Wesley: Contemporary Perspectives*, ed. John Stacy (London: Epworth, 1988), 87.
67. Ibid., 88.
68. Ibid.
69. Ibid.
70. Ibid., 89.
71. My notes from John Walsh, Lecture on "Wesley and the Poor" at Jesus College, Oxford, July 25, 1985.
72. Ibid.
73. Ibid.
74. Ibid.
75. John Wesley (5/7/1741), *Works*, vol. 19, 193-94.
76. Rack, *Reasonable Enthusiast*, 361.
77. Henderson, *John Wesley's Instructional Groups*, 40.
78. Letter of January 13, 1710, from Susanna Wesley to Sukey Wesley in Clarke, *Memoirs of the Wesley Family*, 347.
79. Frank Baker quoting letter of December 22, 1768, from John Wesley to Joseph Benson in "Wesley's Correspondents and Correspondence," *Works*, vol. 25, 100-101.
80. John Wesley (3/4/1747), *Works*, vol. 20, 162.
81. John Wesley (2/23/1749), *Works*, vol. 20, 263.
82. John Wesley (3/11/1751), *Works*, vol. 20, 380.
83. John Wesley, "The Nature, Design, and General Rules of the United Societies" (1743), *Works*, vol. 9, 70.
84. Ibid., 72.
85. Ibid., 73.
86. Colin W. Williams, *John Wesley's Theology Today* (Nashville: Abingdon, 1960), 140.
87. From Charles Wesley, Hymn #477 (1767), from "For the Society, giving Thanks," *Works*, vol. 7, 662.

CHAPTER 7. "HOW TO TEACH?": PRACTICES AND DISCIPLINE

1. John Wesley, "A Plain Account of the People Called Methodists" (1749), *Works*, vol. 9, "The Methodist Societies: History, Nature, and Design," ed. Rupert E. Davies (Nashville: Abingdon, 1989), 263.
2. Mary Elizabeth Mullino Moore, *Teaching from the Heart: Theology and Educational Method* (Harrisburg, Pa.: Trinity Press International, 1998), 20.
3. Ibid.
4. John Wesley, "Advice to the People Called Methodists" (1745), *Works*, vol. 9, 123-24.

5. John Wesley published this account in 1778. Susanna Wesley, "Remarkable Providence," *Works* (Jackson) (Grand Rapids: Baker Book House, 1979), vol. 13, 516-18.

6. Richard P. Heitzenrater reported that this was a phrase claimed by John Wesley as early as 1737 after the story of the Epworth fire in 1709 began to focus on John's rescue and was then used "as a divine designation of some extraordinary destiny for him." *The Elusive Mr. Wesley*, vol. 1, *John Wesley His Own Biographer* (Nashville: Abingdon, 1984), 40.

7. Frank Baker indicated that "solid documentation of nine births has led to the correction of several errors in family tradition. . . . [There are] nine girls and eight boys documented, and two possible children of unknown sex. The boys were subject to greater mortality, only three of the eight surviving, while seven of the nine girls reached maturity." In "Susanna Wesley," in *Women in New Worlds: Historical Perspectives on the Wesleyan Tradition*, vol. 2, eds. Rosemary Skinner Keller, Louise L. Queen, and Hilah F. Thomas (Nashville: Abingdon, 1982), 115.

8. Letter of August 24, 1709, from Susanna Wesley to a neighboring clergyman, *Works* (Jackson), vol. 13, 517 (emphasis added).

9. Adam Clarke said Susanna "examined without restraint the whole controversy between the Established Church and the Dissenters. The issue of which was she renounced her religious fellowship with the latter, and adopted the creeds and forms of the Church of England." Adam Clarke, *Memoirs of the Wesley Family* (1848; reprint, New York: Lane & Tippett, 1976), 319.

10. Letter from Susanna Wesley to Samuel Wesley Sr., written February 6, 1712, and recorded at Susanna Wesley's death on August 1, 1742, by John Wesley, *Works*, vol. 19, "Journal and Diaries II: 1738–1743," eds. W. Reginald Ward and Richard P. Heitzenrater (Nashville: Abingdon, 1990), 284.

11. Ibid., 285.

12. Maldwyn Edwards, *Family Circle: A Study of the Epworth Household in Relation to John and Charles Wesley* (London: Epworth, 1949), 53.

13. Letter of February 6, 1712, from Susanna Wesley to Samuel Wesley Sr., *Works*, vol. 19, 284.

14. Edwards, *Family Circle*, 55.

15. Letter of February 6, 1712, from Susanna Wesley to Samuel Wesley Sr., *Works*, vol. 19, 286.

16. Ibid., 285.

17. Edwards, *Family Circle*, 56.

18. John Wesley (8/1/1742), *Works*, vol. 19, 284.

19. Letter of February 6, 1712, from Susanna Wesley to Samuel Wesley Sr., *Works*, vol. 19, 285.

20. Letter of June 8, 1725, from Susanna Wesley to John Wesley, *Works*, vol. 25, "Letters I: 1721–1738," ed. Frank Baker (Oxford: Clarendon, 1980), 166.

21. John Wesley (5/24/1738), *Works*, vol. 18, "Journal and Diaries I: 1735–1738," eds. W. Reginald Ward and Richard P. Heitzenrater (Nashville: Abingdon, 1988), 243.

22. Letter of October 19, 1732, from John Wesley to Richard Morgan Sr., *Works*, vol. 25, 337.

23. Henry D. Rack, *Reasonable Enthusiast: John Wesley and the Rise of Methodism*, 2nd ed. (Nashville: Abingdon, 1993), 84. For a full discussion of the origin and development of the Holy Club, see Rack, "A Holy Experiment," in *Reasonable Enthusiast*, 61-106.

24. Ibid., 89.

25. John Wesley (10/21/1735), *Works*, vol. 18, 138 (emphasis added).

26. John Wesley (10/24/1735), *Works*, vol. 18, 139.

27. John Wesley (11/16/1735), *Works*, vol. 18, 139.

28. John Wesley (11/20/1735), *Works*, vol. 18, 140.

29. John Wesley (11/21/1735 and 12/2/1735), *Works*, vol. 18, 140.

30. John Wesley (12/18/1735 and 12/21/1735), *Works*, vol. 18, 141.

31. John Wesley, "The Character of a Methodist" (1742), *Works*, vol. 9, 39.

32. John Wesley, Sermon #16, "The Means of Grace" (1741–1746?), *Works*, vol. 1, "Sermons I: 1-33," ed. Albert C. Outler (Nashville: Abingdon, 1984), 381.

33. Albert C. Outler, *Works*, vol. 1, 376.
34. Ibid.
35. John Wesley, Sermon #16, "The Means of Grace" (1741–1746?), *Works*, vol. 1, 396.
36. Colin W. Williams, *John Wesley's Theology Today* (Nashville: Abingdon, 1960), 132.
37. John Wesley, Sermon #16, "The Means of Grace" (1741–1746?), *Works*, vol. 1, 378.
38. Ibid., 395.
39. Ibid., 381.
40. Ibid. (emphasis added).
41. Ibid., 384.
42. John Wesley, Sermon #2, "The Almost Christian" (1741), *Works*, vol. 1, 134.
43. John Wesley, "The Character of a Methodist" (1742), *Works*, vol. 9, 37.
44. John Wesley (4/1/1738), *Works*, vol. 18, 233.
45. Williams, *John Wesley's Theology Today*, 133.
46. John Wesley, Sermon #16, "The Means of Grace" (1741–1746?), *Works*, vol. 1, 387.
47. Ibid., 386.
48. John Wesley (10/21/1735), *Works*, vol. 18, 138 (emphasis added).
49. John Wesley (12/14/1737), *Works*, vol. 18, 205-6.
50. Williams, *John Wesley's Theology Today*, 134.
51. John Wesley, Sermon #16, "The Means of Grace" (1741–1746?), *Works*, vol. 1, 389.
52. Ibid., 389-90.
53. John Wesley (12/21/1735), *Works*, vol. 18, 141.
54. John Wesley (12/18/1735), *Works*, vol. 18, 141.
55. Rack, *Reasonable Enthusiast*, 84.
56. Williams, *John Wesley's Theology Today*, 134.
57. While in Georgia, John Wesley reported that "the next day Mr. Delamotte and I began to try whether life might not be as well sustained by one sort as by a variety of food. We chose to make the experiment with bread, and were never more vigorous and healthy than while we tasted nothing else." John Wesley (3/30/1736), *Works*, vol. 18, 155.
58. John Wesley (10/20/1735), *Works*, vol. 18, 137.
59. John Wesley (12/7/1735), *Works*, vol. 18, 140.
60. Williams, *John Wesley's Theology Today*, 135.
61. John Wesley (10/21/1735), *Works*, vol. 18, 138.
62. Ibid.
63. John Wesley (1/25/1736), *Works*, vol. 18, 142.
64. For a thorough discussion of the means of grace, see Henry H. Knight, *The Presence of God in the Christian Life: John Wesley and the Means of Grace* (Metuchen, N.J.: Scarecrow, 1992).
65. A "single eye" means keeping one's focus on God. John Wesley, Sermon #98, "On Visiting the Sick" (1785), *Works*, vol. 3 "Sermons III: 71-114," ed. Albert C. Outler (Nashville: Abingdon, 1986), 385.
66. Ibid., 387.
67. These references can be found in John Wesley, *Works*, vol. 19, 149 (smallpox); vol. 19, 167 (violent pain and smallpox); and vol. 19, 172 (spotted fever).
68. John Wesley, Sermon #98, "On Visiting the Sick" (1786), *Works*, vol. 3, 389.
69. Ibid.
70. Ibid., 390.
71. Ibid., 391.
72. Ibid., 393-97.
73. John Wesley, "A Plain Account of the People Called Methodists" (1749), *Works*, vol. 9. 274.
74. John Wesley (11/3/1740), *Works*, vol. 19, 172.
75. John Wesley, "A Plain Account" (1749), *Works*, vol. 9, 277.

76. John Wesley (11/25/1740), *Works*, vol. 19, 173.

77. This project is described in some detail in John Wesley, "A Plain Account" (1749), *Works*, vol. 9, 275-76.

78. The establishment, policies, and management of the lending fund is described in John Wesley, "A Plain Account" (1749), *Works*, vol. 9, 279.

79. John Wesley (1/17/1748), *Works*, vol. 20, "Journal and Diaries III: 1743–1754," ed. W. Reginald Ward and Richard P. Heitzenrater (Nashville: Abingdon, 1991), 204.

80. From Charles Wesley, Hymn #477 (1767), from "For the Society, giving Thanks," *Works*, vol. 7: "A Collection of Hymns for the Use of the People Called Methodists," eds. Franz Hildebrandt and Oliver A. Beckerlegge with the assistance of James Dale (Nashville: Abingdon, 1983), 662.

81. Transformative learning results from critical reflection on our "habits of expectation" according to Jack Mezirow, *Transformative Dimensions of Adult Learning* (San Francisco: Jossey-Bass, 1991).

82. John Wesley, Sermon #16, "The Means of Grace" (1741–1746?), *Works*, vol. 1, 395.

83. Ibid., 396.

84. Ibid.

85. Ibid., 396-97.

86. Stephen Gunter, *The Limits of 'Love Divine': John Wesley's Response to Antinomianism and Enthusiasm* (Nashville: Kingswood Books, 1989), 157.

CHAPTER 8. MAKING DISCIPLES FOR A NEW DAY

1. John Wesley, Sermon #16, "The Means of Grace" (1741–1746), *Works*, vol. 1, "Sermons I: 1-33," ed. Albert C. Outler (Nashville: Abingdon, 1984), 397.

2. Charles Wesley, Hymn #477 (1767), from "For the Society, giving Thanks," *Works*, vol. 7, "A Collection of Hymns for the Use of the People Called Methodists," ed. Franz Hildebrandt and Oliver A. Beckerlegge with the assistance of James Dale (Nashville: Abingdon, 1983), 662.

3. Letter of March 28, 1739, from John Wesley to [the Rev. John Clayton?], *Works*, vol. 25, "Letters I: 1721–1739," ed. Frank Baker (Oxford: Clarendon, 1980), 616.

4. John Wesley, Sermon #64, "The New Creation" (1785), *Works*, vol. 2, "Sermons II: 34-70," ed. Albert C. Outler (Nashville: Abingdon, 1985), 510.

5. Robert A. Evans, "Education for Emancipation: Movement Toward Transformation," in Alice Frazer Evans, Robert A. Evans, and William Bean Kennedy, *Pedagogies for the Non-Poor* (Maryknoll, N.Y.: Orbis, 1987), 259.

6. Letter of November 10, 1725, from Susanna Wesley to John Wesley, *Works*, vol. 25, 184.

7. *The Book of Discipline of The United Methodist Church* (Nashville: United Methodist Publishing House, 1996), 87.

8. Laurent A. Parks Daloz, Cheryl H. Keen, James P. Keen, and Sharon Daloz Parks, *Common Fire: Leading Lives of Commitment in a Complex World* (Boston: Beacon, 1996), 2.

9. John Wesley, "The Character of a Methodist" (1742), *Works*, vol. 9, "The Methodist Societies: History, Nature, and Design," ed. Rupert E. Davies (Nashville: Abingdon, 1989), 34.

10. Andrés Tapia noted that the young adults in Generation X are looking for "authenticity," "community," and dialogue in "Reaching the First Post-Christian Generation," *Christianity Today*, 12 September 1994, 20.

11. *The United Methodist Book of Worship* (Nashville: United Methodist Publishing House, 1992), 93.

12. Parker Palmer, *The Promise of Paradox: A Celebration of Contradictions in the Christian Life* (Notre Dame, Ind.: Ava Maria Press, 1980), 82.

13. James Fowler, *Becoming Adult, Becoming Christian* (San Francisco: Harper, 1984), 95.

14. Henry Rack wrote that John Wesley's charity often enraged his critics. About the time Richard Morgan charged Wesley with responsibility for his son's death, he "tried to help a man called Blair who was in prison on a charge of homosexuality." Henry D. Rack, *Reasonable Enthusiast: John Wesley and the Rise of Methodism*, 2nd ed. (Nashville: Abingdon, 1993), 9.

WORKS CITED

ABBREVIATIONS

Journal CW	*The Journal of Charles Wesley, M.A.*
Letters (Telford)	*The Letters of Rev. John Wesley, A.M.*
NT Notes	*Explanatory Notes Upon the New Testament*
Works	*The Bicentennial Edition of the Works of John Wesley*
Works (Jackson)	*The Works of John Wesley*, Jackson edition
Susanna Wesley	*Susanna Wesley: The Complete Writings*

I. PRIMARY WORKS

The Bicentennial Edition of the Works of John Wesley, 35 volumes projected. Nashville: Abingdon, 1984– . (Volumes 7, 11, 25, and 26 originally appeared as the *Oxford Edition of the Works of John Wesley*. Oxford: Clarendon, 1975–1983). Abbreviation: *Works*.

Vol. 1: *Sermons I, 1-33*. Ed. Albert C. Outler, 1984.

Vol. 2: *Sermons II, 34-70*. Ed. Albert C. Outler, 1985.

Vol. 3: *Sermons III, 71-114*. Ed. Albert C. Outler, 1986.

Vol. 4: *Sermons IV, 115-151*. Ed. Albert C. Outler, 1987.

Vol. 7: *A Collection of Hymns for the Use of the People Called Methodists*. Ed. Franz Hildebrandt & Oliver A. Beckerlegge with the assistance of James Dale, 1983.

Vol. 9: *The Methodist Societies: History, Nature, and Design*. Ed. Rupert E. Davies, 1989.

Vol. 18: *Journal and Diaries I, 1735–1738*. Ed. W. Reginald Ward and Richard P. Heitzenrater, 1988.

Vol. 19: *Journal and Diaries II, 1738–1743*. Ed. W. Reginald Ward and Richard P. Heitzenrater, 1990.

Vol. 20: *Journal and Diaries III, 1743–1754*. Ed. W. Reginald Ward and Richard P. Heitzenrater, 1991.

Vol. 25: *Letters I, 1721–1739*. Ed. Frank Baker, 1980.

Vol. 26: *Letters II, 1740–1755*. Ed. Frank Baker, 1982.

John Wesley, *Explanatory Notes Upon the New Testament*. 2 vols. 1754. Reprint, London: Epworth, 1958. Abbreviation: *NT Notes*.

The Journal of Charles Wesley, M.A. 2 vols. Ed. Thomas Jackson. London: John Mason, 1849; reprint ed. Grand Rapids: Baker Book House, 1980. Abbreviation: *Journal CW*.

The Letters of the Rev. John Wesley, A.M. 8 vols. Ed. John Telford. London: Epworth Press, 1931. Abbreviation: *Letters* (Telford).

Susanna Wesley: The Complete Writings. Ed. Charles Wallace, Jr. New York: Oxford University Press, 1997. Abbreviation: *Susanna Wesley.*

The Works of John Wesley. 14 vols. 3rd ed. Ed. Thomas Jackson. London: Wesleyan Methodist Book Room, 1872; reprint ed. Grand Rapids, Mich.: Baker Book House, 1979. Abbreviation: *Works* (Jackson).

II. SECONDARY WORKS

Albin, Thomas R. "An Empirical Study of Early Methodist Spirituality." In *Wesleyan Theology Today: A Bicentennial Theological Consultation,* ed. Theodore Runyon. Nashville: Kingswood Books, 1985.

Baker, Frank. *John Wesley and the Church of England.* Nashville: Abingdon, 1970.

———. "Susanna Wesley." In *Women in New Worlds: Historical Perspectives on the Wesleyan Tradition.* Vol. 2, ed. Rosemary Skinner Keller, Louise L. Queen, and Hilah F. Thomas. Nashville: Abingdon, 1982.

The Book of Discipline of The United Methodist Church. Nashville: The United Methodist Publishing House, 1996.

Brelsford, Theodore and Charles R. Foster. *We Are the Church Together: Cultural Diversity in Congregational Life.* Valley Forge, Pa.: Trinity Press International, 1996.

Brown, Earl Kent. "Feminist Theology and the Women of Mr. Wesley's Methodism." In *Wesleyan Theology Today: A Bicentennial Theological Consultation,* ed. Theodore Runyon. Nashville: Kingswood Books, 1985.

———. *Women of Mr. Wesley's Methodism.* New York: Mellen, 1983.

———. "Women of the Word." In *Women in New Worlds: Historical Perspectives on the Wesleyan Tradition.* Vol. 1, ed. Hilah F. Thomas and Rosemary Skinner Keller. Nashville: Abingdon, 1981.

Brueggemann, Walter. *Genesis.* Interpretation: A Biblical Commentary for Teaching and Preaching. Atlanta: John Knox, 1982.

Bushnell, Horace. *Christian Nurture.* 1861. Reprint, Grand Rapids: Baker Book House, 1983.

Chilcote, Paul W. *She Offered Them Christ: The Legacy of Women Preachers in Early Methodism.* Nashville: Abingdon, 1993.

Clarke, Adam. *Memoirs of the Wesley Family.* New York: Lane & Tippett, 1848.

Coalter, Milton J., John M. Mulder, and Louis B. Weeks. *The Re-forming Tradition: Presbyterians and Mainstream Protestantism.* Louisville: Westminster/John Knox, 1992.

Cobb, John B., Jr. "Christian Theism and the Ecological Crisis." *Religious Education,* vol. 66, no. 1 (January-February 1971).

Daloz, Laurent A. Parks, Cheryl H. Keen, James P. Keen, and Sharon Daloz Parks. *Common Fire: Leading Lives of Commitment in a Complex World.* Boston: Beacon, 1996.

Davies, Rupert E. "Justification, Sanctification, and the Liberation of the Person." In *Sanctification and Liberation: Liberation Theologies in Light of the Wesleyan Tradition,* ed. Theodore Runyon. Nashville: Abingdon, 1981.

Davis, Mollie C. "The Countess of Huntingdon." In *Women in New Worlds: Historical Perspectives on the Wesleyan Tradition.* Vol. 2, ed. Rosemary Skinner Keller, Louise L. Queen, and Hilah F. Thomas. Nashville: Abingdon, 1982.

Edwards, Maldwyn. *Family Circle: A Study of the Epworth Household in Relation to John and Charles Wesley.* London: Epworth, 1949.

Evans, Robert A. "Education for Emancipation: Movement Toward Transformation." In Alice Frazer Evans, Robert A. Evans, and William Bean Kennedy. *Pedagogies for the Non-Poor.* Maryknoll, N.Y.: Orbis, 1987.

Felton, Gayle Carlton. *By Water and the Spirit: Making Connections for Identity and Ministry.* Nashville: Discipleship Resources, 1997.

———. "John Wesley and the Teaching Ministry: Ramifications for Education in the Church Today." *Religious Education* 92, no. 1 (winter 1997): 92-106.

———. *This Gift of Water: The Practice and Theology of Baptism Among Methodists in America.* Nashville: Abingdon, 1992.

Foster, Charles R. *Educating Congregations: The Future of Christian Education.* Nashville: Abingdon, 1994.

———. *Embracing Diversity: Leadership in Multicultural Congregations.* Bethesda, Md.: Alban Institute, 1997.

Fowler, James. *Becoming Adult, Becoming Christian: Adult Development and Christian Faith.* San Francisco: Harper & Row, 1984.

Frank, Thomas Edward. "Harmon-ic Convergences: Constituting a Church for a New Century." *Quarterly Review* 18, no. 1 (spring 1998): 19-36.

———. *Polity, Practice, and the Mission of The United Methodist Church.* Nashville: Abingdon, 1997.

Green, J. Brazier. *John Wesley and William Law.* London: Epworth, 1945.

Green, V. H. H. *The Young Mr. Wesley: A Study of John Wesley and Oxford.* New York: St. Martin's, 1961.

Gunter, W. Stephen. *The Limits of 'Love Divine': John Wesley's Response to Antinomianism and Enthusiasm.* Nashville: Kingswood Books, 1989.

———, Scott J. Jones, Ted A. Campbell, Rebekah L. Miles, and Randy L. Maddox. *Wesley and the Quadrilateral: Renewing the Conversation.* Nashville: Abingdon, 1997.

Harris, Maria. *Fashion Me a People: Curriculum in the Church.* Louisville: Westminster/John Knox, 1989.

———. *Teaching and Religious Imagination: An Essay in the Theology of Teaching.* San Francisco: Harper & Row, 1987.

Hayes, Alan L. "John Wesley and Sophy Hopkey" In *Women in New Worlds: Historical Perspectives on the Wesleyan Tradition.* Vol. 2, ed. Rosemary Skinner Keller, Louise L. Queen, and Hilah F. Thomas. Nashville: Abingdon, 1982.

Heitzenrater, Richard P. *The Elusive Mr. Wesley.* Vol. 1, *John Wesley His Own Biographer.* Vol. 2, *John Wesley as Seen by Contemporaries and Biographers.* Nashville: Abingdon, 1984.

———. *Mirror and Memory: Reflections on Early Methodism.* Nashville: Kingswood Books, 1989.

———. *Wesley and the People Called Methodists.* Nashville: Abingdon, 1995.

Henderson, David Michael. "John Wesley's Instructional Groups." Ph.D. diss., Indiana University, 1980.

Knight, Henry H., III. *A Future for Truth: Evangelical Theology in a Postmodern World.* Nashville: Abingdon, 1997.

———. *The Presence of God in the Christian Life: John Wesley and the Means of Grace.* Metuchen, N.J.: Scarecrow, 1992.

Langford, Thomas A. *God Made Known.* Nashville: Abingdon, 1992.

Little, Sara. *To Set One's Heart: Belief and Teaching in the Church.* Atlanta: John Knox, 1983.

Logan, James C. *Theology and Evangelism in the Wesleyan Heritage.* Nashville: Kingswood Books, 1994.

Maddox, Randy L., ed. *Aldersgate Reconsidered.* Nashville: Kingswood Books, 1990.

———. *Responsible Grace: John Wesley's Practical Theology.* Nashville: Kingswood Books, 1994.

Marquardt, Manfred. *John Wesley's Social Ethics: Praxis and Principles.* Trans. John E. Steely and W. Stephen Gunter. Nashville: Abingdon, 1992.

Matthaei, Sondra Higgins. "Behind the Scenes at Aldersgate: Mediating the Faith in John Wesley's Conversion," a paper presented to the Wesleyan Studies Group, American Academy of Religion, 1987.

———. *Faith Matters: Faith-Mentoring in the Faith Community*. Valley Forge, Pa.: Trinity Press International, 1996.

———. *The God We Worship*. Nashville: Abingdon, 1993.

———. "Transcripts of the Trinity: Communion and Community in Formation for Holiness of Heart and Life," paper given at the Tenth Oxford Institute on Methodist Theological Studies, 1997.

———. "Transcripts of the Trinity: Communion and Community in Formation for Holiness of Heart and Life," *Quarterly Review* 18, no. 2 (summer 1998): 123-37.

Mezirow, Jack. *Transformative Dimensions of Adult Learning*. San Francisco: Jossey-Bass, 1991.

Moore, Mary Elizabeth Mullino. *Education for Continuity and Change: A New Model for Christian Religious Education*. Nashville: Abingdon, 1983.

———. *Teaching from the Heart: Theology and Educational Method*. Harrisburg, Pa.: Trinity Press International, 1998.

———. "A Wrestling Church: Cultural Pluralism in the Wesleyan Tradition," a paper presented to the United Methodist Association of Professors in Christian Education, 1990.

Moore, Robert L. *John Wesley and Authority: A Psychological Perspective*. Missoula, Mont.: Scholars Press, 1979.

O'Gorman, Robert T. "The Faith Community." In *Mapping Christian Education: Approaches to Congregational Learning*, ed. Jack L. Seymour. Nashville: Abingdon, 1997.

Palmer, Parker. *The Promise of Paradox: A Celebration of Contradictions in the Christian Life*. Notre Dame, Ind.: Ava Maria Press, 1980.

Price, Elizabeth Box, and Charles R. Foster, eds. *By What Authority: A Conversation on Teaching Among United Methodists*. Nashville: Abingdon, 1991.

Rack, Henry D. *Reasonable Enthusiast: John Wesley and the Rise of Methodism*. 2nd ed. Nashville: Abingdon, 1993.

Sawada, Mariellen. *John Wesley: Holiness of Heart and Life*. New York: Women's Division, General Board of Global Ministries, The United Methodist Church, 1996.

Schmidt, Martin. *John Wesley: A Theological Biography*. Trans. Norman P. Goldhawk. 2 vols. New York: Abingdon, 1962, 1972.

Seamands, Stephen A. *Holiness of Heart and Life*. Nashville: Abingdon, 1990.

Seymour, Jack L., and Donald E. Miller, eds. *Theological Approaches to Christian Education*. Nashville: Abingdon, 1990.

Snyder, Howard A. *The Radical Wesley and Patterns for Church Renewal*. Downers Grove, Ill.: Inter-Varsity Press, 1980.

Tapia, Andrés. "Reaching the First Post-Christian Generation," *Christianity Today*, 12 September 1994, 18-23.

Tracy, Wesley. "Christian Education in the Wesleyan Mode," *Wesleyan Theological Journal*, vol. 17, no. 1 (spring 1982).

Tyerman, Rev. L. *The Life and Times of Rev. John Wesley*. 3 vols. London: Hodder & Stoughton, 1890.

———. *The Life and Times of Samuel Wesley*. London: Simpkin, Marshall & Co., 1866.

Vogel, Linda J. *Teaching and Learning in Communities of Faith: Empowering Adults Through Religious Education*. San Francisco: Jossey-Bass, 1991.

Wainwright, Geoffrey. *Doxology: The Praise of God in Worship, Doctrine and Life*. New York: Oxford University Press, 1980.

———. "Why Wesley Was a Trinitarian," *The Drew Gateway*, vol. 59, no. 2 (spring 1989).

Wallwork, Norman C. "Wesley's Legacy in Worship." In *John Wesley: Contemporary Perspectives*, ed. John Stacey. London: Epworth, 1988.

Walsh, John. "Wesley and the Poor," Lecture at Jesus College, Oxford, 1985.

Watson, David L. *Accountable Discipleship*. Nashville: Discipleship Resources, 1985.

————. *The Early Methodist Class Meeting: Its Origin and Significance.* Nashville: Discipleship Resources, 1985.

————. *Forming Christian Disciples: The Role of Covenant Discipleship and Class Leaders in the Congregation.* Nashville: Discipleship Resources, 1989.

Watson, Philip S. *The Message of the Wesleys.* Grand Rapids: Zondervan, 1984.

Westerhoff, John H., III. *Will Our Children Have Faith?* New York: Seabury, 1976.

Williams, Colin W. *John Wesley's Theology Today.* Nashville: Abingdon, 1960.

Yrigoyen, Charles, Jr. *John Wesley: Holiness of Heart and Life.* Nashville: Abingdon, 1999.

Zizioulas, John D. *Being as Communion.* Crestwood, N.Y.: St. Vladimir's Seminary Press, 1993.

INDEX

213

Wesley, Susanna (*continued*)
  infectious faith of, 146-49
  as teacher of faith, 102-7
  on teachers, 120, 122
Whitefield, George, 81-82, 108, 112
women
  and education of the poor, 111-13, 119

  leadership by, 116-18, 146-49
  as widows, 159·
"Working Out Our Own Salvation" (John
  Wesley), 47
worship, 26, 83, 119

Yrigoyen, Charles, Jr., 25, 26, 29-30

Printed in the United States
120950LV00004BA/9/A